D1154346

Opening the Doors

The Desegregation of the University of Alabama
and the Fight for Civil Rights in Tuscaloosa

Typeface: Garamond Premiere Pro

Cover photographs (clockwise from top): Autherine Lucy, February 1956 (courtesy of W. S. Hoole Special Collections Library, The University of Alabama); Reverend T. Y. Rogers, June 10, 1964 (courtesy of the William Marable II Family); Student protest on the University of Alabama campus (courtesy of the W. S. Hoole Special Collections Library, The University of Alabama); Police Chief William Marable in front of First African Baptist Church (courtesy of the William Marable II Family).
Cover design: Michele Myatt Quinn

∞

The paper on which this book is printed meets the minimum requirements of American National Standard for Information Sciences—Permanence of Paper for Printed Library Materials, ANSI Z39.48-1984.

Library of Congress Cataloging-in-Publication Data

Hollars, B. J.
Opening the doors : the desegregation of the University of Alabama and the fight for civil rights in Tuscaloosa / B. J. Hollars.
p. cm.
Includes bibliographical references and index.
ISBN 978-0-8173-1792-8 (trade cloth : alk. paper) — ISBN 978-0-8173-8669-6 (e book)
1. University of Alabama—History. 2. College integration—Alabama—History. 3. Civil rights movements—Alabama—History. I. Title.
LD73.H65 2013
378.761—dc23
2012028421

Come, my friends,
'Tis not too late to seek a newer world.

—Alfred, Lord Tennyson, "Ulysses"

(A line often quoted by Robert F. Kennedy)

Contents

Photographs follow page 130

Acknowledgments

A project of this size and scope could never have been completed without the help of an incredibly dedicated team of writers, researchers, scholars, archivists, curators, journalists, colleagues, and friends. I am indebted to so many, and while this list is sorely incomplete, allow me to offer a public thank you to Simon Wendt, E. Culpepper Clark, Anthony Blasi, Alan DeSantis, Brett Spencer, Betty Stowe, Chief Deputy Ron Abernathy, Elaine Gray, Captain Loyd Baker, Sheriff Ted Sexton, Jessica Lacher-Feldman, Laura Anderson, Steve Davis, Mary McManus, Helen Shores Lee, Laura Becherer, Jamie Vue, and in particular, to the many dedicated archivists at the W. S. Hoole Special Collections Library at the University of Alabama, the Birmingham Civil Rights Institute Archives, and the Columbia University Archives. I am also indebted to the men and women who were willing to share their stories with me: Hank Black, Harvey Burg, Theresa Burroughs, Harris Cornett, Walter Flowers III, Dr. Raymond Fowler, Joyce Lamont, Reverend Thomas (T. W.) Linton, Dick Looser, William (Bill) G. Marable, William M. Marable II, Bettye Rogers Maye, Wali Ali Meyer, Stan Murphy, Bob Penny, Don Siegal, Donald Stewart, Dr. Jim Webb, and Dr. John Worsham.

A thank you to the organizers of the University of Alabama's "Opening Doors" celebration of June 2003, whose title I have slightly altered for this book, as well as the Malone-Hood Plaza organizers, whose phrase "A New Beginning" I have employed in my epilogue.

To my spring 2011 African American literature classes at the University of Alabama.

To my colleagues both at the University of Alabama and the University of Wisconsin–Eau Claire, as well as support received from the University of Wisconsin–Eau Claire's University Research and Creative Activity Grant Program.

To the good people of Tuscaloosa past and present.

To my beautiful and understanding wife.

And most of all, to young Henry—this will always seem like ancient history to you.

Opening the Doors

Introduction

Setting the Stage for Desegregation

On the morning of June 11, 1963, two African American students—twenty-year-olds James Hood and Vivian Malone—attempted to register for classes at the University of Alabama, only to find their state's chief executive, Governor George Corley Wallace, remaining firm on his campaign pledge to stand in the schoolhouse door in an effort to block desegregation. While the governor's actions resulted in little more than a symbolic gesture—one that some initially argued propelled him to national prominence—historians later confirmed that his defiant stand against the federal government ultimately damaged his reputation rather than improved it.

While white students at the University of Alabama registered for classes with ease, for Hood and Malone, their attempt to enroll demanded the support of a newly federalized unit of the Alabama National Guard, a sweat-soaked deputy attorney general, an equally nervous attorney general, and a president so invested in the day's outcome that for a full afternoon he pushed aside Khrushchev and the Cold War to give his rapt attention to the events transpiring in a small, southern town called Tuscaloosa.

It was not the first time the city had made headlines. Seven years prior, in February of 1956, African American Autherine Lucy first attempted to desegregate the University of Alabama, an effort that culminated in unprecedented violence on a college campus, the likes of which would not be repeated until

James Meredith's desegregation of Ole Miss in October of 1962. Lucy's valiant attempt—while disastrous for the university's reputation—emboldened other African Americans to rise to the occasion, reframing the university's desegregation question from an "if" to the inevitable "when."

Running parallel to the university's desegregation battles were the battles fought by local African Americans to integrate their town. Throughout the summer of 1964, Tuscaloosa Citizens for Action Committee (TCAC) made great strides to integrate the city's courthouse, lunch counters, movie theaters, and buses—each action the result of individuals willing to risk their personal safety for the good of the collective. Local movements such as theirs often received some support from nationally recognized civil rights advocacy groups—most notably the Southern Christian Leadership Conference—though in many instances these local communities were left carrying the bulk of the burden. While national strategies were often successfully carried out by local civil rights foot soldiers, the Alabama cities that received the most attention were those most directly linked to the star power of Dr. Martin Luther King Jr., cities like Birmingham, Selma, and Montgomery. While King played but a minor role in Tuscaloosa's civil rights movement, his primary contribution was not what *he* did, but rather, whom he sent to do it in his stead.

Reverend T. Y. Rogers—of whom little is written but to whom much credit is owed—was named assistant pastor of Dexter Avenue Baptist Church in the midst of the 1955–56 Montgomery bus boycott, a time in which King's ever-expanding responsibilities demanded a capable assistant pastor to oversee the church's daily operations. Rogers accepted the post, not only to serve King throughout the early stages of his mentor's meteoric rise to fame, but also to allow himself the opportunity to observe King's tactics, awaiting the day when he, too, could put them into practice.

Rogers's opportunity presented itself in 1964, when King recommended his former assistant for a ministerial position at Tuscaloosa's First African Baptist Church, a staple within the city's African American religious community. At King's urging, Rogers—who at the time was fulfilling his pastoral duties at Galilee Baptist Church in Pennsylvania—returned home to Alabama, preparing to serve as an agent of change for a city in need of a leader.

While the University of Alabama's 1956 and 1963 desegregation attempts have been well documented (particularly in E. Culpepper Clark's all-encompassing

The Schoolhouse Door), it is my goal to look beyond the scholarly books and newspaper reports previously analyzed and instead rely heavily on the primary sources that remain in Tuscaloosa—the people, those who still recall the fervor and the fury and the smell of the quadrangle's fresh-cut grass. By exploring the personal stories behind both the 1956 and 1963 efforts to desegregate the University of Alabama, I hope to provide a contextual framework for the events leading up to the height of the city's civil rights movement in the summer of 1964.

A second though equally important goal is to offer exposure to the little-known history of a city's civil rights movement. While there was a brief window of time in which the university's desegregation attempts made front-page news, these stories have long since receded to the footnotes of history—and, in the case of Hood and Malone's efforts—a brief but memorable scene in *Forrest Gump*.

Yet perhaps far more disheartening than the relative ease with which we have dispensed with the past is our ability to leave so much unacknowledged. The efforts of Tuscaloosa's African American citizens to free themselves from the clutches of Jim Crow in the United Klans of America's stronghold receives virtually no mention beyond the city limits and rarely so within. My hope is to change that.

While much of this narrative features nationally recognized figures, Tuscaloosa's civil rights history belongs foremost to the city and its people. I lived in Tuscaloosa for four years, taught at the university for three, and almost each day had the pleasure of riding my bicycle up and down the tree-lined sidewalk opposite the quad. And yet somehow it was not until the spring of 2010 that I actually stumbled across Foster Auditorium, taking a moment to read the modest placard noting Hood and Malone's desegregation of the campus. Similarly, it took several more months before I noticed Autherine Lucy's portrait hanging in a rarely traveled hallway on the third floor of the student union. And while long overdue, after nearly one thousand days of confining myself to the university bubble, I finally found reason to cross Lurleen Wallace Boulevard—an invisible demarcation line that to this day separates blacks from whites—and began exploring an African American section of town whose restaurants and barbershops served as the headquarters of the civil rights movement fifty years before. Many of the original civil rights participants remain, though the spry twenty- and thirty-year-olds who once marched through the Tuscaloosa streets are much older now, their hair long since turned to gray.

Likewise, many of the important civil rights locales remain, and in an attempt to make good use of ambiance, portions of this book were written in the locations described. For instance, when writing of Autherine Lucy, I returned to Smith Hall, the sight of her first class, as well as to Howard and Linton's Barbershop, where hurled eggs were once washed from her hair. When writing of Governor Wallace's "stand in the schoolhouse door," I holed up with my laptop just outside of Foster Auditorium in an attempt to soak up history. I wrote of Bloody Tuesday on the steps of First African Baptist Church, and of Alabama's racial history in the ruins of the second state capitol. All of this added a unique texture to the work or, at the very least, allowed me to see and smell and feel what others had many years prior.

While it is an oversimplification to portray Tuscaloosa's civil rights movement as a result of the hard work of a few individuals, for the sake of the narrative, I have attempted to focus on those who, while representative of the others, played the most critical and enduring roles. Oftentimes, as is the case in this instance, it is the writer's burden to describe the complexities of historical figures whom he or she has never met. But as I have come to understand throughout my research, the most righteous are rarely so at all times, nor do the most reprehensible fall into such carefully constructed caricatures. Writers are forced to deal in the strange currency of gray areas, adding up the sum total of individual moments in an attempt to depict a fuller life. It is an effort that, while futile, seeks to unveil a greater understanding of those involved, offering the wide-angled view of a person rather than the close-up.

As such, there are no villains here, merely people who believed what they believed due to an amalgam of experiences, traditions, and geography. It is not my intent to judge too harshly a past in which I played no part. Rather, when possible, I encouraged this drama to be told by the participants themselves, those whose stories I gathered from personal interviews, published quotations, transcriptions, previously classified documents, and voices captured on the ancient reels of audio recordings. The result is a behind-the-scenes look at a movement told—at least in part—by those who experienced these moments firsthand.

On occasion I tiptoed into the realm of speculation; this is meant only to reflect the slipperiness of history. As I continue to find, newspaper accounts and personal accounts rarely reveal the same story. Likewise, the shortcomings of memory and reportage are equally weighty problems left for each individual writer to decipher. To this end, there are a few rare instances in which an interviewee's remembrances could not be confirmed within the published record. These remembrances should not be taken as unequivocal fact, but instead serve as anecdotal evidence to highlight the individual experiences of those who were there.

While sifting through the city's past, I was reminded of Tuscaloosa's continued importance. I write this at an interesting time in the university's history, one in which the area outside of Foster Auditorium has recently been dedicated as the Malone-Hood Plaza, upon which stands the Autherine Lucy Clock Tower—an effort to honor the first three students to break the university's color barrier so many years before. Similarly, the auditorium—which sat empty for years—was recently renovated to become the home of the women's basketball team. A happy side effect of the recent addition of the plaza (as well as the auditorium's renewed purpose) is the increased foot traffic surrounding Foster Auditorium. No longer is the auditorium a black eye for the university, but a landmark for civil rights.

In the days following Autherine Lucy's ill-fated 1956 enrollment, Emory Jackson, editor for the *Birmingham World,* foresaw this about-face in university policy, noting quite prophetically, "In more sober days when sanity has been restored, the University of Alabama's board of trustees is likely to try to make peace with history and square itself with the conscience of humanity." In the fall of 2010, the university did just that, inviting Autherine Lucy Foster, James Hood, and family members of the late Vivian Malone Jones to return to the now infamous Foster Auditorium to a standing ovation.

As we celebrate the fiftieth anniversary of the stand in the schoolhouse door, new details continue to emerge. Yet despite these details, as well as the university's recent push to commemorate the past, I have found that the general public knows startlingly little about the University of Alabama's desegregation efforts, including the students themselves. This was made clear to me in the spring of 2011, as the students in my African American literature class watched the grainy black-and-white footage from June 11, 1963, with jaws dropped and eyes widened.

"This happened *here?*" one student asked incredulously. "At *our* university?"

It is my great hope that I might extend Tuscaloosa's story for a new generation, offering a more complete picture of the people—and events—that set a southern town and its university free.

PART ONE

The Mobs

Tuscaloosa, Alabama

January–March 1956

CHAPTER 1

The Cross and the Cadillac

January 26–February 3, 1956

I don't like it, and there are plenty more of us who don't.

On the night of Thursday, January 26, 1956, a cross burned on the quadrangle of Tuscaloosa's University of Alabama. Flames leaped within view of Denny Chimes—the campus's 115-foot campanile—as shadowy figures disappeared into the trees, distancing themselves from their deed. In the nights that followed, additional crosses continued to light up the night, transforming the mostly quiet river town into a shadow of its former self.

Tuscaloosa was no stranger to racial violence. In 1934—amid a rash of murders—Alabama writer Carl Carmer described the town as "a land of quick reactions, of sudden and stunning violences." Over the next two decades, the city's racially charged reputation began to subside, only to reemerge in full force during the winter of 1956, when twenty-six-year-old Autherine Lucy attempted to desegregate The University of Alabama, causing the crosses to flicker once more.

While making his Saturday night rounds, university officer Chester L. Collins spotted a suspicious-looking vehicle parked behind the university's Gorgas Library and decided to have a look. Huddled inside were William V.

Epperson and Lee C. Beck—a pair of local citizens—alongside a gallon of oil and an eight-foot-tall cross. Their intentions couldn't have been clearer, though Officer Collins made no arrests that night. Instead, he confiscated the cross-burning materials and requested that Epperson and Beck leave the university grounds, an order to which the pair readily complied, informing the officer that they were members of an "organization which is pledged to help police officers in any way possible."

Apparently the same cooperation didn't hold true for firefighters, who remained alert as flaming crosses cast shadows across the campus.

In the week preceding Lucy's attempt to desegregate The University of Alabama, a total of eight crosses burned, four of which were lit on Tuesday, January 31, the night prior to her intended enrollment. The young African American coed never considered herself a rabble-rouser, and upon her arrival at the university, remained somewhat naive to the problems she caused by her entrance.

Born in 1929 in Alabama's rural, southwestern Marengo County, Lucy was first prompted to enroll at The University of Alabama on the advice of a close friend, Pollie Ann Myers (also known by her married name, Pollie Ann Hudson) who had applied herself, though her status as an unwed mother gave university admissions a convenient excuse to deny Myers's application. Lucy's own unblemished record gave the admissions office no such easy out, and her acceptance placed the quiet young woman in a unique position to dramatically disturb the social order. While such a disruption seemed against her nature (and horrified her parents), her acceptance into the state's flagship university was an opportunity she could hardly afford to pass up. The youngest daughter of a tenant farmer, Lucy's father armed her with the same advice he'd bestowed upon his other nine children—steer clear of whites and "give them all their respect." Instead, she found herself the source of the trouble, violating many southern customs in the process.

Lucy had previously attended Selma University and Miles College (thus, her later-in-life entrance into The University of Alabama), and with a degree already in hand, many whites began questioning the sincerity of Lucy's application.

What more did she expect to gain from the all-white institution, many wondered, except, perhaps, to further a pro-Communist, pro–civil rights agenda.

Wednesday, February 1, started out rainy and cold, the high of 50 degrees proving uncomfortably chilly for a native Alabamian like Lucy. As crosses smoldered nearby, the young coed took her first steps onto The University of Alabama campus, fully prepared to register for classes. She was flanked by her African American entourage, including Pollie Ann Myers as well as Mrs. Geneva Lee, an etiquette coach; Emory Jackson, editor for the *Birmingham World;* and Reverend Fred Shuttlesworth, a former classmate of Lucy's as well as a rising star in the Birmingham civil rights scene.

Just a few nights prior, on January 29, The University of Alabama Board of Trustees—including Governor "Big Jim" Folsom—met to formally deny Pollie Ann Myers's admission, as well as begrudgingly (and under federal court order) accept Lucy. In his rejection letter to Myers, Dean of Admissions William F. Adams informed the coed that her "conduct and marriage record" (by which he meant her born-out-of-wedlock child) disqualified her from meeting the high moral standards of the university. Lucy was shaken by her friend's rejection, and while hesitant to continue without her, Myers convinced her otherwise, reminding Lucy that she "represented not only herself but her race."

On Wednesday morning Lucy made her way to the administration building, entering dean of admissions William F. Adams's office while her supporters awaited her return in the hallway. It was a rare sight for white students to see African Americans on university grounds without brooms in hands or aprons tied tight around waists, though when Shuttlesworth was confronted by a student, it was only to ask why the NAACP didn't "send down some basketball players about 7′2,′″ to which the quick-tongued reverend replied that he would gladly send "some good football players, too."

Lucy exited the office soon after, heading toward Graves Hall to complete the enrollment process. She still had to register for classes—as did the other students—though she had hardly entered the imposing brick building before observing the long lines snaking through the hallways. In an attempt to diffuse any potential confrontations, Dean Adams encouraged registrar M. L. Roberts to allow Lucy to register in Roberts's private office, thereby bypassing the line, much to the displeasure of impatient white students who viewed the act as proof of preferential treatment.

Wholly unaware of their offense, Lucy and her advisor sat in Roberts's office and completed the necessary paperwork, while in the hallway, a growing crowd of grumbling students anxiously awaited their own chance to register. The *Tuscaloosa News* reported that while many of the students "didn't mind the Negrowoman attending school" they "didn't like to wait in line as they wait on her."

"I don't like it," one sophomore admitted, "and there are plenty more of us who don't."

Another concurred, "It's bad enough that she's here, but why can't she stand in line like the rest of us? She wants equal rights so let her stand here like everyone else."

Others chose simply to stiffen their upper lips and move beyond the inconvenience.

"I'm a died-in-the-wool Confederate," one student boasted. "I don't like her being here one bit, but I guess I'll just accept it."

This last comment best supported what the local papers described as a mood of "resignation," a feeling of helplessness that seemed to have permeated throughout campus. Yet the students' misgivings did little to deter them from witnessing what they knew to be a historic event, great swaths of young men and women milling about to catch a glimpse of Lucy as she registered behind a closed door.

Upon completing her paperwork, Lucy slipped past the perturbed students, leaving Roberts's office with a full schedule—children's literature, political science, geography, and a pair of sociology classes. As she awaited her dorm room assignment, a press release was distributed to the reporters, informing them—and simultaneously Lucy—that she had been denied room and board.

It was a bombshell, and one for which Lucy and her team had come unprepared.

"I figured all along that the University had a few tricks up the sleeve," one student remarked. "No court order will change custom overnight."

Dean of women, Sarah Healy, was tasked with explaining to Lucy that the decision was simply a matter of personal safety; that recent occurrences on campus (including the influx of cross burnings, as well as verbal threats) had made it apparent that it was not in the young woman's best interest to reside on campus overnight. Healy's warm eyes and perpetual half smile may have provided some comfort for Lucy, but the message did not sit well with Lucy's supporters, particularly a fiery Emory Jackson, who felt blindsided by the announcement.

"We don't care how many cross burnings or camp meetings or whatever they have," Jackson allegedly proclaimed. "We demand equal opportunities for her in everything."

Yet author E. Culpepper Clark recounts that even greater issues plagued Lucy throughout registration day and beyond. True enough, she was no longer guaranteed a roof over her head or food on the cafeteria table, but more troubling still were the negative perceptions of Lucy herself that had rapidly begun buzzing across campus. Many white students had a hard enough time stomaching the thought of a black student in their midst, let alone one rumored to be "impolite and obnoxious."

In the coming days, the *Montgomery Advertiser* further encouraged the rumor mill by reporting a scene in which Lucy allegedly "elbowed her way through the [class]," though later, this unflattering description was vastly amended. Nevertheless, accusations continued to swirl—that Lucy was a pawn of the NAACP, a paid participant, and as a result of her NAACP bankroll, flaunted a lavish wardrobe her white counterparts could hardly afford.

Author E. Culpepper Clark noted the many specific charges set forth in the coming days; that Lucy "arrived in a Cadillac . . . dressed to the nines" and "pushed to the head of the line where she flashed a crisp hundred dollar bill to pay tuition," bypassing not only the long registration lines at Graves Hall, but the hassle of picking up her class cards at Foster Auditorium as well.

"By simply being there, she affronted them," Clark explained, "and 'they' were offended."

Yet Clark immediately dismissed these claims, noting "every action had its explanation," such as the fact that Henry Nathaniel Guinn resorted to driving Lucy in his Cadillac on Monday morning only *after* the more modest Chevrolet refused to start. Likewise, Lucy's selection of an orange dress for her Friday ensemble was simply her attempt at professionalism in a new environment. Further, reported Clark, the hundred-dollar bill Lucy used to pay her school fees on Wednesday afternoon was simply the surest way to assure that payment would be accepted.

As to the charge of Lucy's preferential treatment, it was, in fact, a reality. Lucy *had* bypassed the chore of picking up her class card at Foster Auditorium, as well as avoiding the registration lines in Graves Hall. But these precautions were hardly a reflection of the university's attempt at rolling out the red carpet. Rather, administrators were attempting to guarantee her personal safety, rightfully assuming that thrusting the first African American student in university history amid a crowd of anxious whites might fail to provide the hoped-for first impression.

"Every gesture made that day was calculated by the NAACP to avoid giving offense," Clark explained. "But the facts also remain. A Cadillac was used, a one hundred dollar bill was tendered, Lucy was spared the drudgery of registration, and white people did not like it."

Writer Anthony Blasi concurred, admitting that these rumors haunted Lucy well into the following week. By Monday morning, it was alleged that Lucy arrived to campus by way of a limousine overflowing with NAACP ministers—a far cry from the Cadillac.

"All the criticism leveled against Miss Lucy, the story of her obnoxious conduct, the objections to her dress, were the result of resentment over the fact that she was a Negro 'out of her place,'" explained Ann Mitchell, whose 1971 thesis, "Keep 'Bama White," provides an in-depth analysis of Lucy's desegregation attempt. "The story of [Lucy] elbowing her way through students was fabricated, but gained credence because it was in keeping with the concept of the conduct of an 'uppity nigger.'"

For many students, the truth about Lucy was hardly as important as the stigma they had already attached to her.

Following her mostly successful registration, Lucy left campus, though her presence lingered. As a result of her being there, three additional crosses were burned on Wednesday night—one near the university baseball stadium, one in a nearby park, and a third in a pasture a few miles outside of town.

Meanwhile, a few hours to the southeast in Montgomery, far more deadly events had already transpired. At around 9:30 P.M., a bomb was hurled into the home of former Alabama NAACP president E. D. Nixon, while his wife and a neighbor girl chatted inside. The deafening blast toppled a gatepost, though both wife and neighbor remained unharmed. Soon after, and just miles away, a second bomb exploded at Reverend Martin Luther King Jr.'s parsonage home, decimating his porch. The night's sharp uptick in violence had nothing to do with Lucy but was likely in response to a recently filed lawsuit aimed at ending "segregated travel in Alabama." Both Nixon and King played key roles in Montgomery's bus boycott, though King's role, in particular, had spurred his rapid ascension into the national spotlight—making him a target.

While the dust settled in Montgomery, the day's top news story remained in Tuscaloosa, where it stayed for nearly a week. "No single racial clash in the South had attracted so many reporters," wrote authors Gene Roberts and Hank Klibanoff. "The bus boycott was droning on in Montgomery with extraordinary cult-like precision. But the press found the more compelling story to be about the shy, quiet woman who smiled as she walked into the lair of the segregationist lion."

This fascination proved particularly true for veteran journalist Bill Gibb, who remained hard at work reporting the day's events for the *Tuscaloosa News*. Gibb had left Alabama for Texas, though later returned and reported on the Lucy story. Given his close ties to the state, the *Tuscaloosa News* managing editor John Hamner believed Gibb to be the perfect man for the task. After an exhaustive day of reporting, Gibb filed his piece, along with a brief note to Hamner, describing the cathartic experience he felt while reporting Lucy's saga. "It was a great day for me, writing about an event which turns against prejudice. . . . University students last night at the Student Union coffee shop buzzed with talk about the arrival of Miss Lucy. The dull world of academics came to life, I think, but I still have the uneasy feeling that the air blew neither hot nor cold."

Gibb went on to describe the thrill he felt upon watching the Wednesday afternoon edition go to press: "And when the pressman pushed the button to full, I felt my stomach roll with the plates. If nobody had watched, I think I would have cried for the sheer relief and joy of seeing the papers tumble out. I may never get a raise, win another prize, but if I can keep on writing, see it printed and feel a good handshake for a job well done, I'll be as happy as I am tonight, dog-tired, wishing I'd said it better. And thinking about tomorrow's edition."

This unabashed honesty offered by a veteran newspaperman speaks to the emotional toll of Lucy's tale. For Alabama natives and nonnatives alike, the story of one young woman's pursuit of an education against all odds had the makings of a dramatic narrative.

Yet as the city soon learned, the drama was only beginning.

On Friday, February 3—Lucy's first day of classes—the students at The University of Alabama remained on edge, attempting to prepare themselves for the impending arrival of the young black woman with aspirations of becoming a librarian—a prospect that terrified, not due to her chosen profession, but because of her audacity to affirm herself in a place she did not belong. Accompanying Lucy was Reverend R. I. Alford, pastor of Sardis Baptist Church, as well as Mrs. Geneva Lee and Reverend Shuttlesworth. It's difficult to imagine the conversations shared on the morning's drive to Tuscaloosa, as well as the apprehension Lucy felt with each passing mile. There were likely last-minute instructions, a final prepping, though all the preparations in the world would do little to prepare her for what would soon follow.

From the second floor of Gorgas Library, twenty-four-year-old librarian Joyce Lamont caught her first glimpse of Lucy as the new student walked into the adjacent Smith Hall for her introductory geography class, later commenting that it appeared "as if [Lucy] was going to church." A Tuscaloosa native and recent graduate of the university, Lamont admitted that she had "never seen another freshman dressed like that going to class."

"I was all in favor of her attending the university," Lamont added, "but whoever had chosen these clothes for her, they did it very inappropriately because they didn't make her look like a student. She looked like a faculty member or a visiting movie star."

From her place inside the library, Lamont witnessed Lucy's entrance into Smith Hall, despite dean of university libraries Dr. W. S. Hoole's threat to fire any employee who dared sneak a peek out the window.

"I was standing there sharpening a pencil," Lamont explained, "and I looked down and there came Autherine Lucy with two university policemen holding an umbrella over her head. And she was heading toward Smith Hall."

Lamont wasn't alone in witnessing the historic event; she spotted Dr. Hoole doing the same. According to the young librarian, many others shared their vantage point, including Secret Servicemen scattered throughout the library.

"[The Secret Service] stuck out like sore thumbs," Lamont remembered. "They tried to act like they were visiting professors or graduate students, but we knew better."

The young librarian peered down at the scene until Lucy disappeared from view, the new student slipping into the second-floor classroom a few minutes late, taking her place in the center of the front row. We can envision Lucy clutching her raincoat as the white students watched on in perfect silence, uncertain how to proceed. Only one student was stirred to action, and in a great show, stalked from the classroom.

"For two cents I'd drop the course," he muttered—an early display of public discontent that within hours would become far more pronounced.

CHAPTER 2

"Mule Sense" and the Mobs

February 3–5, 1956

These degrading incidents of mob violence in Alabama are a disgrace to the entire Union.

Autherine Lucy's entrance into The University of Alabama captured the attention of the state, the nation, and the world, so much so that local newspaper street sales leaped nearly 75 percent on the Thursday prior to her first day of class.

"Tuscaloosa and the University of Alabama were in the eyes of the world this week as the Capstone registered its first Negro in history," the *Tuscaloosa News* reported. It was a claim that—while repeated seven years later with Governor George Wallace's infamous stand in the schoolhouse door—remained accurate; much of the world *was* watching, and nobody dared blink.

The small, southern town with a population of just over 56,000 had been thrust into the international spotlight. Representatives from the *London Express* and the *Daily Mail* (both London-based papers) called regularly for details, offering a global perspective on an event many Tuscaloosans believed to be a local matter. Nevertheless, the *Tuscaloosa News,* and in particular, its moderate editor, Buford Boone, were more than happy to take full advantage of their rapt audience.

Born in Newnan, Georgia, in 1909, Boone began his newspaper career at the *Macon Telegraph and News* before leaving to become publisher of the *Tuscaloosa News* in 1947. Yet he took with him lessons he'd learned from his first paper, especially those taught to him by Mark Ethridge and T. W. Anderson—two men who believed, much like Martin Luther King Jr., that character was more important than color. While shying away from the term *liberal,* Boone hardly minded being called a *progressive,* nor did he mind making his viewpoints clear, regardless of personal cost—a policy that failed to make him the most popular man in Tuscaloosa. Boone once remarked that the *Tuscaloosa News* held the unique honor—at least to his knowledge—of being the only newspaper in America "boycotted simultaneously by the Ku Klux Klan and the blacks." While Boone had previously infiltrated and reported on local Klan meetings—proving a great embarrassment to the group—the entrance of Lucy was destined to become Boone's first major test in reporting civil rights.

As Autherine Lucy arrived for her 9:00 A.M. class Friday morning, the newspaper's pressroom was already hard at work churning out its afternoon edition, including an editorial penned by Boone calling for peaceful desegregation. "Let us remind ourselves, again, that we are living in a period of transition," the editorial explained. "Attitudes of calmness, of reason are far better than emotional outbursts. Cross-burners haven't the same standing as those who speak up openly and candidly. The court decisions have gone in favor of our friends and fellow citizens, the Negroes of the South. They are a fine and patient people."

Later, the editorial continued: "Never have we seen a time when an abundance of good 'mule sense' was needed worse," Boone explained. "What is 'mule sense?' It is just one notch sounder than 'horse sense.' For when a horse gets in a tight spot, he is inclined to kick and struggle, oftentimes to his great injury. A mule waits patiently to be helped out of his tight spot, and he carries fewer scars."

It was a view Boone assumed would be welcomed by the moderate southerner—a call for an adjustment period.

While the South had long argued for slower racial transitions—both in schools and society at large—it's difficult to deduce whether this "not now, but later" approach was simply the region's go-to stall tactic (a tiny carrot dangling on the end of a very long stick), or rather, a sincere pronouncement from a people struggling with change.

Nevertheless, Boone's call for an easing-in to equality was the precise answer the moderates of Tuscaloosa most needed to hear. Boone undoubtedly viewed his suggestion for "mule sense" as a compromise—an attempt to placate segregationists and integrationists alike by inserting a timetable into the equation.

Only one question remained: Who precisely was the mule?

Was Boone calling for Lucy to wait patiently to be helped out of her tight spot?

Or, far more likely, was he offering a clear directive to the town: Remain calm, do not act in haste; eventually, this too shall pass.

By 11:00 P.M. on Friday night—at the conclusion of Lucy's mostly uneventful first day—crowds began gathering near the Union Building for what was shaping up to be quite an eventful night. Rumors of a panty raid had begun to take root, though sophomore Leonard Wilson—soon to become the poster child for the university's resistance to desegregation—urged the crowd to remain focused, reminding them that a grave defilement had just occurred at their beloved school, that this was no time to be thinking of panties.

Dean of women Sarah Healy—a mere two years into her seventeen-year tenure at the university—had just finished dinner at a friend's home when she heard what she later described as "disturbances on University Avenue." She was soon made aware of a mob gathering near the Union Building, and so returned hastily to campus, parking her car behind Tutwiler Hall before joining dean of men Louis Corson to observe the crowd.

"There was a large crowd of approximately 1,500 persons made up predominantly of students," Healy wrote in her daily report, "however, there were some older men in the crowd whom I did not recognize as having any connection with the University."

The local newspaper reported a more conservative estimate between 1,200 and 1,500 protesters, all of whom worked their way toward university president O. C. Carmichael's on-campus residence, the President's Mansion, to find he wasn't home. The crowd then redirected itself downtown, advancing west toward the American Legion flagpole on the corner of Greensboro Avenue. Tuscaloosa police officers watched from a safe distance while the crowd chanted, "Keep Bama White!" "To Hell with Autherine!" and sang the chorus to "Dixie."

According to one newspaper report, upon reaching the flagpole, exuberant students "spoke until their voices gave out," one of which belonged to nineteen-year-old Leonard Wilson. Due to his vocal pro-segregation stance, Wilson soon emerged as a student leader in the fight against desegregation. E. Culpepper Clark reported that as a high schooler, Wilson distinguished himself by "calling for a measure to send Alabama's Negroes back to Africa" while serving as a delegate for the Youth Legislature. Wilson also admitted to "compiling scrapbooks on segregation," averaging an hour a day to the task. His pro-white principles made him a likely candidate to rally his fellow students, a task he was happy to carry out. Undeterred by his own failings in recent student government elections, he remained ever confident in his convictions, his slender frame and steadfast demeanor providing him with the look of a man in control.

When the crowd reached the corner of University Boulevard and Greensboro Avenue, the heart of the city's downtown district, Leonard Wilson was pushed to the base of a raised flagpole and began proselytizing to the crowd, urging them to resume its force the following night at the conclusion of the Alabama–Georgia Tech basketball game. The crowd cheered their newly anointed leader, not yet aware that their Friday night rally was little more than a dress rehearsal for the more serious business that would soon follow.

On Saturday, February 4, fans crowded into Foster Auditorium—the men's basketball gymnasium as well as the future site of Governor Wallace's infamous stand in the schoolhouse door—to witness the Alabama squad rout the Georgia Tech Yellow Jackets, 90–67. Present was Dean Healy, who sat quietly in the stands for the majority of the game, slipping out a few minutes early after growing increasingly nervous by the number of students calling upon one another to meet at Denny Chimes at the game's conclusion. Healy had recently moved into the President's Mansion, and as the game drew to its close, she returned to her third floor room directly across the street from Denny Chimes, glancing out her window to observe "a small flame at approximately 10:15 P.M." From her vantage point high above, Healy watched as students began swarming the campanile, and this time, they weren't alone.

Of the estimated two thousand people present, many were believed to be from local and surrounding communities. While it's difficult to determine what percentage of the mob was composed of Klansmen, it was a well-known fact that the organization had long maintained a strong presence in Tusca-loosa, first organizing in 1868 and holding meetings in nearby Sipsey Swamp. Thanks in part to the efforts of Ryland Randolph—a high-ranking Klans-man himself, as well as the editor of the town's newspaper, the *Independent Monitor*—Klan membership began to dramatically increase in the years fol-lowing Reconstruction. Eventually, its membership leveled off, and with the exception of the summer of 1933—which saw a clear uptick in racial violence—Tuscaloosa's experiences in the decades that followed remained rela-tively quiet; that is, until Lucy became the spark that relit the Klan's crosses, their flames sending smoke signals to segregationists throughout the state.

While staring out at the Saturday night crowd, assistant to the president Jef-ferson Bennett noticed at least one difference from the previous night's gath-ering. While he described the Friday night raucous as little more than a "beer party"—an event to entertain a restless student body—he estimated that the majority of the Saturday crowd consisted of blue-collar workers between the ages of twenty-five and forty. The change in demographic had also altered the tone, and Bennett noted that within twenty-four hours the student-led protest had devolved into "a truly vicious deadly organization."

After a brief march to the Student Union Building (during which the Sat-urday night crowd chanted "Hey, Ho, Ho, Autherine has got to go!") they turned onto University Boulevard, disrupting traffic as they headed once more to the American Legion flagpole on Greensboro Avenue. Along the way, the riled crowd took to the impromptu rocking of cars and buses, proudly waving Confederate flags toward cameramen and news reporters, offering not only the city but the world a firsthand look at their riotous behavior.

One witness compared the crowd to a "lynch mob," and while the *Tusca-loosa News* was unwilling to take its description quite so far, the local paper did report how students "jeered" as university police chief Allan O. Rayfield at-tempted to maintain order and "cheered each time a photographer snapped a flash bulb." In a great shift from the reticent students who—just days before—had hidden from the cameras during Lucy's registration, the nighttime crowd actively sought recognition for their revolt. They were proving themselves sons of the South, bearing the torch of their forefathers. However, their de-sire for recognition soon backfired, particularly for one overzealous student who was caught on film hopping atop a car belonging to an African American. Another photo depicted a crowd surrounding a car "occupied by several out-of-town Negroes," shaking the vehicle and breaking its windows until the driver eventually steered his way to safety.

Photographic evidence of racial discontent proved a powerful propaganda tool far beyond Tuscaloosa's city limits. Throughout the civil rights movement, photographs often provided the much-needed pathos-based argument that swayed many from employing more violent tactics themselves—if not on humanistic grounds, then for fear of being caught on camera. Birmingham's Kelly Ingram Park photos, which depicted snarling dogs and a flood of fire hoses, became one of the better known examples, though the future held others as well: Emmett Till's bludgeoned body, Martin Luther King Jr.'s mug shot, a burned out Freedom Riders' bus. Photos from Tuscaloosa's Saturday night riot provided a similar effect, exposing young, white, college-aged men tromping atop cars and earning themselves front-page space in the papers.

The local news coverage would have worldwide reverberations, though worst of all was its reach to the nation's capital, where President Dwight D. Eisenhower was busy fighting another battle—the Cold War—prompting many to fear that Tuscaloosa's unruly behavior would quickly be appropriated for pro-Communist propaganda, proof that America's democratic ideals extended no further than the color line.

"Come, Come, Comrade!" began one letter in the *Tuscaloosa News.* "It is generally known that the [Communist] Party's 'active cell' operates on the campus and has for a number of years. . . . Blame the party, not the students, for creating a situation in the right place, at the right time, to incite mob violence—a part of the plan."

Another added similar concern: "These degrading incidents of mob violence in Alabama are a disgrace to the entire Union. . . . Every Communist on earth must smile when he ponders the stupid outrages at the University of Alabama and he must also give silent thanks to his unsuspecting comrades at that school."

With Sunday's dawn lingering deep on the horizon, Leonard Wilson took once more to the flagpole, urging students to boycott classes that—thanks to Ms. Lucy's efforts—had recently become desegregated. Wilson reportedly "cautioned his followers against violence" while simultaneously reminding the crowd that they should take it upon themselves to stop all cars with Negroes inside and ask "if they believe in segregation."

"If they say 'no,'" Wilson added cryptically from the top of his pedestal, "make them believe in it."

Shortly after, Walter Flowers, the university's well-regarded student government president, took his turn at the flagpole. The following Tuesday he would publish a front-page letter in the university's student newspaper, the *Crimson White,* in which he argued, "Mob action can never accomplish anything; in reality it serves only to discredit those things for which I know you all stand." Yet his first attempt at articulating this message occurred on Saturday night, as he urged the angered crowd to remain reasonable, reminding them that "99 per cent of you are interested in what is best for the University of Alabama."

This percentage may have held true for the student population, though as Sarah Healy and Jefferson Bennett pointed out, the makeup of Saturday night's mob transcended far beyond students. As the crowd marched back to the President's Mansion, university president O. C. Carmichael—a soft-spoken, bald-headed Rhodes scholar—appeared on his portico in an effort to calm the dissenters, echoing a sentiment first expressed by Flowers, that they should "uphold the traditions of this great University."

His pronouncement was almost immediately drowned out by further chants of "Keep Bama White!" Speechless, the sixty-five-year-old man stared out at the hundreds who had gathered on his front lawn—a sea of white faces pressed against the dark. Their fury palatable, Carmichael found himself suddenly at a loss. He was far more effective in the comfort of his office rather than shouting through the night from his portico.

"They shouted almost throughout his attempt to talk with them and threw firecrackers and other things," Healy later recalled. "We would see that there were many in the crowd who were older than students," she added, offering further credence to her conviction that the mob consisted primarily of non-students. She also noted that when Carmichael addressed the crowd as "students of the University of Alabama," many fired back: "we are not students."

Although he'd served as an educator all his life (including a stint as president of the prestigious Carnegie Foundation for the Advancement of Teaching), Carmichael had never before experienced such fierce opposition. Helpless, the tired man whispered miserably, "I don't think they want to hear me," before shuffling back to the safety of his home.

Carmichael's call to uphold tradition on behalf of their "great University" had seemed a useful rhetorical strategy given the students' well-established school pride. Yet in the early morning hours of Sunday, February 5, the "greatness" of their university remained in question.

CHAPTER 3

Monday's Misfortunes

February 6, 1956

I asked the Lord to give me strength—if I must give my life—to give it freely.

A few minutes before her 9:00 A.M. Monday class, Autherine Lucy rode in the passenger side of African American businessman Henry Nathaniel Guinn's Cadillac, entering into an unsettlingly silent campus. The ghost town atmosphere seemed greatly at odds with the weekend's excitement, though the silence wouldn't last.

As Guinn turned the corner toward Smith Hall, he and Lucy witnessed an estimated two hundred to three hundred protesters blocking the building's entrance, though the crowd was contained by a number of local police and state patrolmen. "These precautions were taken," Healy later explained, "after several messages were received stating that the girl would be physically harmed if she attended classes on Monday." Yet Lucy remained mostly naive to the very real threats with which she was confronted, and in the morning's excitement, somehow managed to slip inside the building without notice.

"I just walked through and smiled and said, 'Excuse me, please,'" Lucy recalled years later, "and I walked in the building. I took my seat on the front row again."

Just beyond the classroom walls, calls to "Lynch the nigger" erupted throughout the crowd—a rare spectacle, particularly on a Monday morning on a university campus. Throughout the South, vigilante justice had traditionally taken place in rural areas under cover of darkness—not at 9:00 A.M. outside the state university's geology building.

As Lucy tried to stay focused on Professor Hays's lecture, President Carmichael found himself struggling to maintain focus on his own difficult task. Dean Corson, Dean Healy, and assistant to the president Jefferson Bennett conferred with Carmichael on the Lucy situation, noting that while they feared for the student's safety, they were equally fearful of removing her from campus, thereby setting a dangerous precedent of caving to the will of the mob.

As the crowd swelled, Bennett took one final look at the changing ground situation and whispered to Healy, "We are never going to be able to get her out of the front door. May we use your car?"

What followed appeared more fitting for a Hollywood drama than a Monday morning in academia. As the crowd simmered just outside of Lucy's classroom, Healy hastened up the stairs of Smith Hall, calmly informing the new student of the change of plans.

"Autherine, I think we are going to have to carry you down the back way here," Healy explained, "because the crowd out there is waiting for you."

Lucy agreed, but as Dean Healy attempted to surreptitiously escort Lucy down the stairs to her car, an onlooker foiled their escape route, shouting, "There they go, there they go."

The crowd surged forward, bursting around the corner of Smith Hall while pelting Healy, Lucy, and Bennett with a hailstorm of eggs and small pebbles. With Bennett behind the wheel and the women sitting snugly beside him, the car veered onto Hackberry Lane, dodging another vehicle that threatened to block their retreat. Fearing the mob had already positioned themselves at Graves Hall—the site of Lucy's next class—Bennett took a more circuitous route, eventually screeching to a halt near the back entrance of Graves, though few were fooled by his maneuvers.

Lucy and Healy entered the building unscathed while Bennett was left to deal with the mob.

"I managed to get in [the car] and locked the doors," he explained, but while he himself was protected, Healy's car was not. The crowd began rocking the vehicle back and forth, smashing the windows with bricks. Fearing for his life, Bennett slammed the car into drive. As he sped through the crowd, he secretly "hoped that some of them would stand still," though after his blood cooled he admitted it was best for all involved that his attackers had the good sense to move out of the way.

A glance in Bennett's rearview mirror would have revealed a crowd estimated between two to three thousand strong, all of whom had gathered outside of Graves Hall to protest Lucy's admission. Included in that crowd was a young Robert "Dynamite Bob" Chambliss, a known Klansman who, in 1963, would be responsible for the Sixteenth Street Baptist Church bombing that left four little girls dead. After viewing D. W. Griffith's *Birth of a Nation* years prior, a young Chambliss believed he had found his true calling: defending white power. After a brief time spent in the mines, Chambliss began schooling himself in explosives—a skill that would come in handy for a man who would more than earn his nickname in the years to come. Not only did Chambliss participate in Monday's mobs, he had recently written a threatening letter to Carmichael as well, defending the students who played a role in the weekend riots and promising to take action if the students were punished.

Yet in 1956 it seemed just another empty threat from one more white face in the crowd.

Another white face in the crowd belonged to Morris Dees, a law student who later cofounded the Southern Poverty Law Center—a Montgomery-based civil rights law firm that gained great notoriety for its efforts to combat hate crimes, particularly by fighting the Klan in the courtroom. Dees watched from afar as the mob gathered, later remarking that Monday, February 6, "was the first time I had ever seen Klansmen in action, the first time I had ever seen a mob."

He would not soon forget it, or the lessons accompanying the scene.

"Many of these people were good, rational folks when they didn't have to think about integration," he continued, "but once they became part of the crowd, they were swept up in the frenzy and turned into mean, dangerous aggressors."

Dean Healy and Registrar Roberts attempted to circumvent this danger by making good use of an underground tunnel system connecting Graves Hall to McLure Education Library directly next door. They hoped the move might confuse the mob, allowing Graves to serve as a decoy. Newly holed up in the library, her ears ringing from the vicious chants, a shaken Lucy prayed behind the safety of a locked door.

"I asked the Lord to give me strength—if I must give my life—to give it freely," Lucy remembered. "And if I *were* to give my life, to let someone take over where I left off. And that if it were mine to see it through, to give me the courage to go through with it."

Outside Graves Hall, throngs of people continued their chants while Lucy and her makeshift guards—the dean of women and the registrar—watched on from an upper floor of the McLure Library. The three remained barricaded in the education library while administrators attempted to devise an escape plan. Yet when no plan immediately developed, they relied instead on the serendipity of a few well-timed events to cause the necessary distraction.

The theatrics began when a truck driver accidently ran his vehicle into a line of police motorcycles, one colliding into the next until the final one crashed into Mr. Guinn—the African American businessman who had chauffeured Lucy to the university earlier that morning. All eyes turned toward the commotion, and as the mob spotted the downed black man, they began closing in. Sensing the direness of the situation, a pair of white men—local Episcopalian chaplain Reverend Emmet Gribbin and *New York Times* reporter Peter Kihss—rushed to Guinn's aid, putting themselves between the black man and the mob. Attempting to exercise the full power of the press, an adrenaline-filled Kihss called, "If anybody wants to start something, let's go," and in a statement that likely riled the crowd rather than diffused it, continued: "I'm a reporter for the *New York Times* and I have gotten a wonderful impression of the University of Alabama. Now I'll be glad to take on the whole student body, two at a time."

No one took him up on the offer.

Yet as Kihss and Gribbin helped Guinn from the ground, the crowd called after them: "Nigger! Nigger-lover!" The men soon separated, though Guinn—one of the few African Americans in sight—remained the obvious target, a stand-in for Lucy. A police officer tugged him through the crowd by his belt buckle, and as the mob focused its attention on Guinn, from his perch on an upper floor of the library, the newly arrived Jefferson Bennett glimpsed a pathway to freedom.

"Well, just like a flash of lightning had hit us, we all realized that here is the minute we've been waiting for," Bennett recounted. "So, we got Autherine, got the Sergeant, and he went out and got into his car and backed up to Graves Hall annex and I practically carried her into his car; she was so frightened."

Meanwhile, the distracted crowd headed in the direction of the President's Mansion, while Lucy, Healy, and Bennett hurried to the sergeant's patrol car parked near the rear exit. Lucy lay flat in the backseat of the car, while less than a hundred yards away the mob continued its riotous behavior.

In the hours following the escape, the newspaper patched together a far different story. "Apparently, police had used a ruse of running a Negro man the mob believed to be [lawyer] Arthur Shores through the mob," reported the *Tuscaloosa News.* "A shout went up, the mob surged toward the Negro and city police hustled him into a police car and sped away. When the crowd turned its attention back to Graves, they found Miss Lucy was gone."

She was gone, to be sure, but not because of any Arthur Shores decoy or otherwise preplanned ruse, as the paper claimed. Instead, Guinn's ability to draw attention away from Lucy was sheer happenstance—the unlikely result of a truck hitting a string of motorcycles, one of which happened to hit him. Lucy escaped with her life—not due to any carefully crafted plan by university administrators, but because Guinn had the misfortune of being the wrong color in the wrong place at the wrong time, causing the crowd to blink.

While there are conflicting reports as to what happened next, by most accounts the trooper drove Lucy the short distance to the offices of the *Alabama Citizen,* the local African American newspaper. After a brief conversation with newspaper employee Emily Barrett (with whom Lucy had shared lunch just days prior), the frightened coed was taken next door, to Howard and Linton's Barbershop, to have the egg washed from her hair.

Both the barbershop and its owner, Nathaniel Howard, were destined to play pivotal roles in the city's soon-to-emerge civil rights movement, yet on that particular February afternoon, as Howard eyed the egg-splattered young woman stepping into his shop, his focus remained solely on her safety. Howard picked up the phone and began calling on other black men to protect the University of Alabama's newest student—by force, if necessary. Many answered the call, arriving at the barbershop a short time later, well armed and ready for battle.

This was, perhaps, the first—though far from the last—time in which whites and blacks nearly resorted to all-out racial warfare on the streets of Tuscaloosa. In the decade that followed, this network of armed African American defenders would continue to meet on an as-needed basis, serving as an informal answer to the black community's run-ins with the Ku Klux Klan, as well as an alternative to the local law enforcement that—according to many African Americans—failed to offer the necessary protection. Reverend T. W. Linton, who manned the barbershop alongside Nathaniel Howard for years and continues to cut hair there to this day, recalled well the details of that Monday afternoon in 1956. Although just twenty-four at the time, the memories remain fresh.

"She was all splattered with eggs and whatnot," Linton remembered, "all messed up and scared half to death.

"I just happened to be sitting here . . . when she was coming in," he added, nodding to the barber chair beside him. "And so we had two beauticians back there . . . so they took her . . . started to clean her up and whatnot. It was a beauty shop, so we didn't get to talk to her."

Barrett and the pair of beauticians hustled Lucy to the back of the shop, sat her in a black barber's chair—one that remains there to this day—and shampooed the egg from her hair. Meanwhile, the men in the front of the shop began organizing Lucy's safe passage back to Birmingham. Their conversation was soon interrupted when the student and citizen protestors began gathering on nearby Fourteenth Street, a mob forming just around the corner from the barbershop.

"They stayed on 14th Street," Linton recalled. "And right quick, her protection gathered here. So you had a whole group of white students on 14th Street and a whole group of black people right here."

Fearing the worst, Linton marched across the street and armed himself with a shotgun from an acquaintance's truck.

"I put that shotgun right there in the corner," he said, pointing to the spot closest to the barbershop's front door.

As both sides began arming themselves for what seemed an imminent confrontation, Nathaniel Howard, T. W. Linton, and various other black community leaders began frantically calling law enforcement agencies in the hope that one might be willing to assist in escorting Lucy back to Birmingham.

"We called the police department and they said, 'We can't escort you beyond the city limits,' because of jurisdiction," Linton explained. "So we called the county sheriff's department, and they didn't want anything to do with it—they just wouldn't get involved. Then we called the state troopers, but the state troopers wouldn't get involved, either."

The crowd continued to grow as Linton and the other men waited for Lucy. When she emerged freshly cleaned, Lucy recounted her on-campus experiences to an attentive audience, though many of the men had their minds on the mounting tension just beyond the edge of the block.

Nathaniel Howard continued working the phones, and by 4:00 P.M. had arranged for a six-car caravan of armed African American men to escort Lucy to Bessemer, a distance of about forty-five miles to the northeast. While some report that Lucy was driven directly to Birmingham, Linton recalled the men driving to Bessemer, instead, where another group of armed men met the Tuscaloosa caravan and accepted their charge for the remainder of the trip.

Howard's son, Nathaniel Howard Jr., was in the first car, along with three other men, all of them armed. Autherine Lucy was placed in the second car—Mr. Howard's personal vehicle—alongside three additional armed men. The four cars that trailed were each filled with four men as well, none of them lacking weapons.

Promising to keep an eye on the barbershop and do his best to prevent a clash with the white mob, Linton watched as the cars headed north.

Tensions remained high throughout the afternoon, yet in a few hours time Nathaniel Howard had not only managed to skirt disaster, but had also organized a twenty-three-man protection squad to escort Lucy safely out of the city. While the university had far more time to prepare for Lucy's arrival, it had been incapable of adequately protecting her. Historian Dan T. Carter noted that this lack of preparation may have been a conscious choice on the part of university officials, many of whom were said to be "paralyzed" by the prospect of losing state funding as a result of publicly supporting Lucy. Regardless of motive, both the university administration and local law enforcement's alleged negligence was further highlighted by Howard's impromptu caravan.

Assistant to the president Jefferson Bennett countered the negligence claim, noting that "during the week preceding [Lucy's] actual arrival here, the president and his staff spent hour after hour anticipating her arrival and trying to plan each step in the registration procedures, the courses she had expressed preference for, even identifying the professors we thought would be most sympathetic to her situation."

The problem, of course, was not the professors in the classroom, but those outside elements who lurked just beyond the classroom doors. "I advised the president that providing visible security with the presence of students in daylight should be sufficient," Bennett later admitted. "In my judgment, no Klansman had guts enough to do anything in daylight. In my experience with them, they were cowards; they worked under darkness behind a mask; no daylight attack would be made, certainly not on a state university campus."

But Bennett had underestimated the segregationists' rabid resistance to desegregation. Not only were Klan members willing to throw off their masks for the cause, they were willing to attack a college campus in broad daylight as well.

University administrators weren't the only ones to shoulder the blame; much of it fell to the state's elected officials, particularly the governor. Rather than ensuring Lucy's safety by making use of the vast resources at his disposal, Alabama Governor "Big Jim" Folsom had chosen instead to watch from a safe distance—sunny Florida—telling reporters on Monday night that he had "no plans . . . to order National Guard troops out to put down the demonstrations."

Years later, Folsom remarked on the error of his ways, defending himself and saying that he was "leaving it up to the police to let me know if they couldn't handle it," though writer Robert Sherrill reported that Alabama's oft-drunk governor was more likely "too deep in his cups to take charge."

As a result of the mob's unanticipated bold behavior (as well as the governor's unwillingness to intervene), Lucy's safety soon became dependent on a community wedded together in common interest. By some estimates, more than one thousand African Americans had successfully enrolled in southern universities prior to Lucy's attempt, though according to author Diane McWhorter, Lucy earned the dubious honor of being "the first black student in the history of desegregation to be greeted with organized violence."

As the caravan reached the edge of town, local law enforcement's squad cars began peeling away, leaving Lucy's safety wholly in the hands of the convoy barreling north. As they drove, many of the armed men in those cars grew acutely aware of the battle the young black woman fought on their behalf. And if they could not desegregate the University of Alabama, they were only too happy to assist.

CHAPTER 4

The President's Problem

February 6, 1956

Unless we can maintain law and order on the campus, we might as well close shop.

Directly following Monday's near disastrous demonstration, an all but defeated President O. C. Carmichael addressed the faculty, informing them, "unless we can maintain law and order on the campus, we might as well close shop."

Present at the meeting was librarian Joyce Lamont, who recalled the president's calls for calm. "He told us things were dangerous and we needed to be careful. Careful about what we said to each other . . . because we didn't want any more riots or the university to be torn up in any way whatsoever."

The mob's most recent actions had shaken Carmichael to the core, making him wholly uncertain of the university's future. "The question now is whether an anarchy will prevail or law and order," paraphrased the *Tuscaloosa News*, though Carmichael himself had no answer.

Despite the president's dismal assessment, the university still had a few influential players in its corner, including the charismatic Student Government

Association president, Walter Flowers Jr., who was fully credited for his previous weekend's public efforts at maintaining peace.

"We owe a great deal to Walter Flowers Jr. for addressing the crowd and trying to persuade them to return home," Dean Corson informed the faculty. "Flowers showed a great deal of intestinal fortitude."

Yet even with the student leader's support, by Monday afternoon the university had already endured three full-fledged demonstrations, and in the estimation of Dean Corson, each had been worse than the last.

"Friday's was ugly, Saturday's three times worse, and no comparison in the one held yesterday," Corson admitted the day following Monday's assault.

The violence was attributed to outside influences, proof of which was observed by the weekend's influx of out-of-town license plates—cars coming in from Birmingham and beyond.

In an effort to preserve the university's good name, on Monday afternoon President Carmichael echoed Bennett and Healy's previous misgivings, releasing a statement in which he, too, charged the recent uptick in lawlessness to nonstudent influences. "Elements from the outside not only participated in the cross burnings on the campus," he explained, "but also in the crowds that have invaded the campus."

Carmichael's statement was his first public shot aimed at his detractors. In the course of four days he had continually amped up his rhetoric, eventually going so far as to compare the mobs to an invasion—a carefully selected word to reflect his conviction that outsiders, and not students, were to blame.

Next he rallied his base, reminding dissenters that the university's students and faculty were no longer alone in the fight but had launched a successful effort to band together with local civic leaders who promised support in restoring "law and order in the community." In slightly veiled language, Carmichael appeared to be drawing a line in the sand: If the mobs chose to continue their lawless demonstrations, they would no longer have the implicit support of the community. "With all these forces dedicated to the task," Carmichael affirmed, "I have a reasonable hope that order will shortly be restored."

On Monday night, as the crowd returned to the President's Mansion once more, they were met on the portico by Mrs. Carmichael—a short-haired, frail-looking woman, timid in her attempt to speak to the crowd on her husband's behalf.

Just minutes prior, the president's wife, along with Dean Healy and university police chief Allan O. Rayfield, had been sitting quietly inside the mansion, though Healy reported that the silence was soon interrupted by "the rattle of stones as they were being thrown at the front of the house."

Rayfield and Mrs. Carmichael stepped cautiously outside, yet when the president's wife attempted to address the crowd that, by some estimates, had grown to nearly six hundred, her voice was drowned out by their shouts. Trying a new tact, Mrs. Carmichael relayed her message through Chief Rayfield, who belted the words out to the crowd.

After much shouting, the message was finally made clear: President Carmichael was not home. In fact—and unbeknownst to the crowd—that very moment he was at a meeting in downtown's McLester Hotel, where the university's board of trustees had gathered to find a way to thread a perilously thin needle: returning the campus to order without giving the appearance that they'd acquiesced to the mob.

Mrs. Carmichael attempted to calm the crowd but was soon overpowered by jeering. As the crowd reached its fever pitch, Mrs. Carmichael motioned for one particular student—believed to be one of the leaders of the mob—to meet her at the top of the portico for a private conversation. While students loyal to the president and his wife faithfully guarded both sides of the portico, they momentarily unlocked their arms to allow the chosen student up the stairs to speak with her. After a brief conversation lost to history, the student shouted, "Let's go back to the Union Building!" though by this point, he, too, had lost hold over the unruly crowd.

Mrs. Carmichael and Chief Rayfield dodged the next barrage of eggs and rocks before heading inside to safety. Meanwhile, the crowd continued wreaking its havoc, lighting firecrackers and setting NAACP literature aflame until the Tuscaloosa police arrived and threatened tear gas to disperse the crowd. Calling their bluff, the mob continued its unruly behavior, and once the canisters were launched into the crowd the young men and women simply moved out of range, chanting, "Give us some more, give us some more."

Eventually, the crowd dissipated, with newspapers reporting that just after midnight "the area was cleared but for a pair of students and a single University police officer, all three shuffling through the debris scattered by the mob."

The scene was a far cry from the university's typical pristine facade. The freshly cut quad and meticulous landscaping had given way to smoldering fire-crackers and trampled flowers—proof of the university's disorder. Despite the police officers' eventual success in diffusing the crowd, Healy later remarked on the direness of the situation, concluding, "In my best judgment, Mrs. Carmichael was in extreme danger throughout the time she was on the porch."

Meanwhile, at the McLester Hotel, the board of trustees faced danger of a different sort and, in an effort to protect their reputation (as well as their state funding), voted unanimously to "exclude Autherine Lucy until further notice from attending the University of Alabama"—a determination that would have undoubtedly placated the mob had they been made aware of the decision.

At the vote's conclusion, when President Carmichael asked his assistant, Jefferson Bennett, what he thought of the board's decision, a beleaguered Bennett replied: "There is no other, but the point is, the mob won."

Decades later, Jefferson Bennett opened up about his experiences throughout Autherine Lucy's short-lived career at the University of Alabama, beginning with what he believed to be a common misconception on his own role: "I do not claim to have saved Autherine Lucy's life as has been reported that I did."

Yet he had driven the getaway car for transporting Lucy out of harm's way. Likewise, he had put himself at further personal risk while locked in Dean Healy's automobile outside of Graves Hall. Nevertheless, he refused to credit himself with acting beyond the call of duty and reacted with great disappointment for what he viewed as the administration's failures to adequately defend the university's reputation.

"It took this University years to recover," he explained, adding later, "It earned a reputation of, not only racism, but the suspicion that maybe it really had conspired with a mob and obstructed justice."

While Lucy remained the primary victim, Bennett believed that President O. C. Carmichael, too, became a casualty of the mob. "Dr. Carmichael left here a broken man, with a sense of failure," Bennett recounted. While he deemed Carmichael "one of the great people that this state has ever produced," Bennett also acknowledged that the president was a far different man upon his exit.

In the spring of 1953, Carmichael had returned to his alma mater to great fanfare, many believing that he alone possessed the experience and know-how to propel the university into the future. Yet the future, for Carmichael, meant confronting desegregation when the issue was forced—the result of which left him weak and ineffectual, causing the board of trustees, alumni, and faculty members to quickly lose faith in their leader. More conservative-minded board members viewed him as a southern turncoat, while a portion of the liberal-minded faculty saw him kowtowing to the old order.

Rather than welcoming the challenge of desegregation, Carmichael seemed to have taken active steps to delay it. In October of 1955 Carmichael wrote a letter to Arthur Shores—attorney to both Autherine Lucy and Pollie Ann Myers—in which he informed Shores that it was too late for Lucy and Myers to enroll "during the present semester."

His phrasing—"during the present semester"—seemed to have left open the door for the possibility of their enrollment in a later semester. While impossible to discern Carmichael's true intent, the letter seemed to fit neatly within the president's general strategy—delay when possible, confronting the matter only after the delays had run out.

Chief counsel for the NAACP Thurgood Marshall had identified Carmichael's strategy years earlier. In a May 14, 1953, letter, Marshall informed a close confidant that the NAACP expected little support from the newly appointed Alabama president.

Yet perhaps Carmichael's tentative approach to desegregation was a tactical choice for a man in his position. As president of a public university reliant on state monies, he recognized that his constituency extended far beyond the students themselves; he had an obligation to placate both state politicians and the board of trustees as well. As a result of his ever-expanding clientele, his personal views soon faded into the backdrop and were rarely (if ever) expressed publicly.

Joyce Lamont—a university librarian in 1956—remembered the president as a "nice man," though his widespread unpopularity became clear to her years later, while serving as the University of Alabama's assistant dean of libraries for special collections and preservation.

"The hate mail that came to him was unbelievable," she recalled, noting the hundreds of letters that began pouring into the university, many of which are preserved to this day.

Perhaps most revealing of all was the letter Carmichael received from the treasurer of the Mississippi Society of the Sons of the American Revolution. It proved revealing, not for its pro-segregation message, but for the signature at the end: Byron De La Beckwith, who, seven years later—on the night of Wallace's stand in the schoolhouse door—pulled the trigger of his Enfield 1917 rifle, assassinating Mississippi's NAACP field secretary, Medgar Evers.

Yet the president's problems extended well beyond the race-fueled hate mail. As further proof of Carmichael's disconnect with his university, *Time Magazine* noted that the president "refused to share the concern of some alumni over the fact that 'Bama's once great football team has won only two games in the last 23." The team's abysmal record was just one more grave offense on Carmichael's watch, and his obvious disinterest in the problem proved near blasphemous to the team's dedicated fans. The president's allies were dwindling on a number of fronts, and while his heart was in the right place, he soon found that the heart was not enough without the guts to carry out its will.

The reverberations of the university's first failed attempt at desegregation went well beyond the president; his assistant, Jefferson Bennett, was affected, too. "I suppose one of the worst things that happened to any of us was to get letters from friends who didn't believe that we had made an honest effort to keep Autherine on campus," noted Bennett. "But, even worse was to get a letter from a friend saying: 'Congratulations! You worked it out.'"

In Bennett's view, they hadn't worked anything out; they'd simply kicked the can of desegregation seven long years down the road.

CHAPTER 5

A War of Words

February 7–March 1956

The question is not what we may think of integration but what we think of law and order.

In the Tuesday, February 7, edition of the *Tuscaloosa News,* editor Buford Boone struck back against the mobs.

As the board of trustees finalized their vote to suspend Lucy from campus, Boone began outlining the editorial that would one day earn him a Pulitzer Prize. In his editorial, "What a Price for Peace," Boone recounted the horrors of Monday afternoon, including having witnessed his fellow citizens resorting to such reprehensible, vigilante tactics. While others referred to the "crowd" that had gathered around Graves Hall to protest Lucy's admission, Boone settled upon a more accurate word.

"And make no mistake," he began. "There was a mob, in the worst sense, at the University of Alabama yesterday. Every person who witnessed the events there with comparative detachment speaks of the tragic nearness with which our great University came to being associated with a murder—yes, we said murder. 'If they could have gotten their hands on her, they would have killed her.' That was the considered judgment, often expressed, of many who watched the action without participating in it."

Later, he continued: "Not a single University student has been arrested on campus, and that is no indictment against the men in uniform, but against higher levels which failed to give them clean-cut authority to go along with responsibility."

In his final berating, a disgusted Boone retorted, "Yes, there's peace on the University campus this morning. But what a price has been paid for it!"

Rather than combating the mobs, the board of trustees had chosen the path of least resistance. By excluding Lucy from campus, they were relinquishing their moral authority as well.

J. T. Sullivan, the former distributor for the *Tuscaloosa News,* remembered well his initial impressions of Boone's fiery editorial. "I was in the . . . pressroom," Sullivan recounted, "and I picked up the first copy of the paper that came off with this editorial, and I handed it to Mr. Boone and I asked him was he trying to put me out of business again, and he said, 'If necessary, yes.'"

Boone offered an encore performance in the following day's edition, and while his critique was less pointed, his message remained the same.

"The recent mob action on the University of Alabama campus was not American. It was ugly, unintelligent. If the mob had succeeded in following out the shouted ex[h]ortation of a grey-haired woman, the very causes which the members of the mob sought to support would be infinitely worse off today. For this woman, perhaps the mother of a student, kept shouting during the height of Monday's outburst: 'Kill her, kill her, kill her!'"

However, Boone also took a moment to praise the university's fraternity leadership who, in his estimation, had proved "outstandingly fine in their coolness and calmness all along."

Later, Boone praised the local police department as well. "Every act of real aggressiveness in putting down violence and in trying to control the mob was performed by Tuscaloosa police. And, as so often is the case with conscientious men in uniform who have a courage which can come only from knowing they are being backed up by their superiors, their reward has been unjust criticism."

Boone's editorials seemed to strike a near perfect pitch. While the editor continually challenged his readership's viewpoints, he also managed to pull at all the right strings—influencing future behavior by preemptively praising fraternity men and police officers to ensure that they wouldn't act otherwise.

Upon realizing they much preferred being lauded as law-abiding citizens than despicable scoundrels, both fraternity members and local law enforcement appeared more inclined to accept the charge that Boone had bestowed upon them. They were happy to be heroes. Likewise, Boone was happy to pit flattery against ridicule, pushing back against the tide of public opinion by stroking a couple of egos.

Boone's "What a Price for Peace" editorial reached far beyond the Tuscaloosa readership, even falling into the hands of Reverend Martin Luther King Jr., a man in the midst of his own battle with the Montgomery bus service.

In a letter dated May 9, 1957, King wrote directly to Boone, thanking him for his strong stance against violence and noting how much he admired the southern newspaper editor for serving as an example for other white southerners.

It was high praise, though praise Boone was reticent to accept, keeping the letter hidden for many years to avoid alienating a portion of his readership that might point to the correspondence as proof of Boone's alleged sympathies toward the civil rights movement. Boone had enough trouble trying to downplay his Pulitzer Prize without the local community thinking he was cozying up to King. As a result of his outspokenness, Boone became the target of various threats, so many, in fact, that he kept his home phone buried under a pillow in an attempt to muffle the sound. His national recognition was immediately tempered by local backlash, prompting one of Boone's friends to take it upon himself to guard the editor's home with a rifle.

Given his close proximity to Martin Luther King Jr., it is quite likely that Boone's editorial made it into the hands of another up-and-coming reverend as well, the young T. Y. Rogers, who then served as King's assistant pastor, and who, within a decade's time, would find his own name regularly gracing the front pages of Boone's newspaper.

The day after Lucy's suspension, Carmichael met with the faculty in Morgan Hall—ironically named after former Alabama Senator John Tyler Morgan, a staunch segregationist during the turn of the twentieth century. Yet the irony was likely lost on Carmichael who had more pressing issues to attend to—namely, calming his already on-edge faculty. Carmichael began the meeting by offering a blitzkrieg of information. First, Dean Corson set forth his "outsiders have invaded" theory while Bennett followed up by noting "on two occasions 'twenty seconds' separated Lucy from death." Carmichael added, "Nothing worse could happen than for a student to be murdered by a mob on the campus." These dramatic pronouncements were, perhaps, Carmichael's way of softening up his less than receptive audience, though the faculty remained stone-faced throughout, even as he attempted flattery. Carmichael called his colleagues the "most loyal, understanding and intelligent," though not even kind words eased the tension permeating throughout the auditorium.

Unbeknownst to the faculty, Carmichael was under strict orders from the board of trustees to avoid intense questioning, yet his continual sidestepping frustrated more than a few vocal faculty members. According to the February 10 edition of the *Tuscaloosa News,* when asked by the faculty if National Guard troops had been requested, Dr. Carmichael replied "non-commitally."

"The truth was that such a request had been made, from Dr. Carmichael's office, by Judge Reuben Wright of Tuscaloosa," the article defended, "but Dr. Carmichael was forced to stand before the faculty and take implied abuse for not doing what actually had been done."

Angered by Carmichael's tepid responses, Charles Farris, Autherine Lucy's former political science professor, leaped to the microphone to offer his own resolution. First, he called on the faculty to release a statement condemning the violence, noting that the current situation was untenable. Next, he demanded confirmation that in the event of further violence, "police protection, either civil or military, would be provided." Finally, he concluded by noting that if these "assurances" could not be given, the faculty should stand united and suspend classes until order had been restored.

Carmichael—who had headaches far beyond a rebellious faculty—saw the motion tabled, adjourning the meeting and hurriedly beginning his retreat.

Later that evening, Leonard Wilson spoke at the Student Government Association meeting, publicly distancing himself from the mob violence. Nevertheless, his newly revised rhetoric did little to absolve him as a primary target of his classmates, many of whom blamed Wilson for the bulk of the trouble, as well as the indelible stain that had damaged the university as a result.

"It is for the long benefit of this great institution that it remain an all-white school, lest it fall from its present standards," Wilson explained.

To which one student retorted, "What about Yale and Harvard? Negroes go to school there. Have they ceased to be great?"

When asked how he would respond if Lucy returned to campus, Wilson replied that he would "do all possible by honorable means to discourage her attendance." A fellow student countered, "Do you think leading a mob is honorable?"

SGA president Walter Flowers wasn't the only student to speak out against the mob, and following Wilson's speech, another student leader emerged: Dennis Holt—a "bespectacled stringbean of a young man"—who happened also to be the 1955 National Debate Tournament champion. The previous night, as the crowd surged onto the President's Mansion lawn armed with eggs and rocks, Holt was rumored to have physically blocked three men from attempting to climb the portico stairs toward Mrs. Carmichael, his thin frame providing resistance enough to keep them from surging further.

Yet on Tuesday night, as he stood before the SGA, he fought not with brawn but with brain. Holt opened by offering a resolution before the students' governing body, reminding his fellow students that "America has been called to greatness, and we, too, have been called. Great segments of the world are watching the student government of the University of Alabama."

He continued: "We have a chance to tell the world that this, our student government, is not run by vandals, goons or thugs," adding later, "Let us say here this evening that we live by democratic means and democratic methods and that we're opposed to mob violence and mob rule."

He concluded with an old debater's trick—changing the focus of the argument—a tactic Carmichael himself would embrace in a matter of days. "The question is not what we may think of integration but what we think of law and order."

Next, Holt admonished the board of trustees for caving to outside pressure, proclaiming, "The mob is king on the campus today . . . Let us remember that high school boys were able to sway the board of trustees of a great university." In truth, Holt's closing remarks were only half accurate. The board of trustees had been swayed not only by "high school boys" but by well-seasoned segregationists as well.

Nevertheless, Holt's resolution passed unanimously, sending a strong message to the city, state, and country that University of Alabama students not only condemned mob violence but, in part, also held their administrators and trustees responsible for it. The resolution's passage seemed to offer momentary redemption to the violence-plagued university, and no one was more impressed than national correspondent Murray Kempton, who praised Alabama's student leaders for "saving their school's honor," calling the student government representatives the "elected conscience of their college."

Lucy's removal from campus became a heavily debated topic both throughout the country and its courtrooms. In late February, Birmingham's Judge Harlan Grooms worked a deal in which Lucy was officially reinstated, though her reinstatement opened the door for the university to expel her on new grounds—alleged charges of conspiracy aimed at university officials. Throughout the ordeal Lucy remained mostly quiet, though her legal team claimed that university officials had knowingly allowed the riotous scene to develop—an observation issued on Lucy's behalf that led to her expulsion.

The desegregation debate gained further steam when Langston Hughes added his own two cents in a March 1956 article in the *Chicago Defender*. "If Miss Lucy wanted to go to bed with a white man instead of to college with one, nobody at the University of Alabama would throw stones at her, nor defy the Supreme Court," he explained. He added that his own light complexion was proof enough of sexual mixing, that he was, in fact, "living proof of integration long before the Supreme Court ruled upon the subject."

In what many whites likely considered a scathing conclusion, Hughes referenced the murder of fourteen-year-old African American Emmett Till, who had been beaten, shot, and tossed in the Tallahatchie River less than six months prior for allegedly whistling at a white woman.

"And, I expect that that alleged woman in Mississippi over whom the alleged Emmett Till was allegedly killed might really have wished Emmett had been just a little older and, instead of allegedly whistling, he had actually come a little closer to her."

In no uncertain terms, Hughes was voicing a rarely acknowledged issue on the fringes of the desegregation debate; the fear that a classroom shared between races might lead to a bedroom shared as well.

For many white southerners the trouble with Lucy's admission transcended far beyond the classroom. The young woman—by her mere presence—had planted the seed to a forbidden fruit.

While Autherine Lucy remained the obvious victim of the desegregation efforts, as Buford Boone noted, the city itself paid a price.

A 1956 write-up in the *New York Times* called Tuscaloosa a "clean, prosperous city that has long been proud of its good race relations." Yet it also noted the city's weakness: a place where rumors "fly faster and farther and with more effect than honest news."

Nevertheless, in its profile of the city, the *New York Times* reported, "In Tuscaloosa, the Negroes and whites have lived side by side in peace," adding also: "Here 'separate but equal' means just that—in education, transportation, recreation, and housing."

The article further noted that in Tuscaloosa, African Americans and whites worked together, talked together, "occasionally worship[ped] together" and "until recently, respected each other."

While the *New York Times* report remained a singular—and likely optimistic—interpretation of Tuscaloosa's race relations, if taken as fact, one can begin to see glimmers of the white southerner's distrust of Autherine Lucy.

Here was a town in which much of its white populace believed they'd struck a careful balance, one in which peace had long been preserved, leading many to believe that separate but equal was working. As proof, several professors at the University of Alabama also taught at Stillman College—the nearby African American college—in an effort to ensure equal educational opportunities. Likewise, there was a strong sense of civic engagement from both races, and local bodies of governance appeared to have little problem sharing financial resources, even if they refused to share the facilities themselves.

Confirming this financial equality, the *New York Times* reported, "Negro recreation was given a share of the city's recreation funds proportionate to the population." Further, state-of-the-art African American schools had recently been erected, and whites and blacks were rumored to have come together on picket lines, white workers picketing to "preserve the jobs of Negro employees."

The article claimed that blacks and whites received equal pay and that race relations "had been so happy that, as the Lucy affair was coming to a head, Negroes only gathered to watch and laugh when a fiery cross was burned on the edge of the Negro high school campus."

Yet the *New York Times* portrait of racial harmony came to an abrupt end upon Lucy's arrival, at which time many whites were left feeling a deep and personal sense of betrayal. Had Stillman College suddenly proved insufficient? Had the city not been fair in allocating its funds?

"I think most people honestly have the mistaken belief that the Negro is completely happy, that if he were just left alone he'd be the happiest of God's children," explained local businessman George LeMaistre. "Yet I know, and I think they know, deep down inside, that that isn't true, that the colored community is entitled to much more than it's received, and that there's bound to be a great deal of unhappiness."

Upon Lucy's arrival in 1956, many whites' feelings of betrayal shifted to anger. If the mobs had failed to make this discontent abundantly clear to the African American population, the local branch of the White Citizens Council served as a further reminder.

On February 17, newly anointed White Citizens Council Chairman Leonard Wilson and hundreds of others crammed into the Tuscaloosa courthouse to stand up and be counted. They were a united front against desegregation, and on that night they extended their purpose not only to diminish blacks, but also to point fingers at their white supporters—northern carpetbaggers most of all.

Meanwhile, across town, then-judge in the Third Judicial Circuit of Alabama George Wallace drew a far more modest crowd, speaking to the American Federation of Labor and Congress of Industrial Organizations (AFL-CIO) Committee on Political Education in a high school lunchroom. As Diane McWhorter reports, as Wallace spoke to the group—likely fully aware of the far more popular meeting at the courthouse—he "confronted the basic dilemma of every liberal southern politician": how to hold on to the union vote without "running afoul of the racist status quo."

The race question would long haunt Wallace politically, though according to McWhorter, Wallace left Tuscaloosa that night a "different man," one who chose "expediency over principle"—pushing policy based on votes.

Tuscaloosa, too, was changing, and as a result of the White Citizens Council and its widespread membership, any sense of racial equality that may have existed was soon replaced with discord. As a result, Boone's previous calls for "mule sense" were all but forgotten.

"Negroes were publically ridiculed by men with whom they had lived in peace for years," reported the *New York Times,* adding later, "everyone here is preparing for a head-on collision at the University of Alabama of two of the strongest and most fearful forces of the twentieth century."

Yet could one woman's admission to the University of Alabama truly be the source of such strife? Undoubtedly, there were a host of other factors to consider—both socioeconomic and political—however, Lucy's momentary breech of the color line had proved a personal affront to the white population for a far different reason. Not only had her presence polluted the sanctity of the all-white classroom, but she also exposed the city's carefully hidden secret (and one that the *New York Times* failed to deduce).

While the city appeared stable on its surface, quiet rumblings were growing just beneath.

In retrospect, these "racial rumblings" hardly seem a secret. In 1949, University of Alabama graduate student Claude L. Dahmer Jr. completed a thesis titled "An Analysis of Student Opinion at the University of Alabama toward Current Racial Issues." The results of his questionnaire—given to 835 of the university's 7,547 total students—revealed that the vast majority of the students had trouble accepting the possibility of desegregation on their campus. Throughout the spring of 1948, 630 men and 205 women completed the questionnaire, the results of which offered rare insight into the students' true feelings on civil rights as it applied to them.

When asked if Congress should support President Truman's proposed civil rights legislation (which focused mostly on protecting African Americans' voting rights, as well as creating a few civil rights offices within the federal government), an overwhelming 76.2 percent of students responded that they should not. However, when asked if a federal antilynching bill should be passed, 67.8 percent agreed. The student response seemed to signal what would be reiterated in years to come: while the majority of southern whites were unwilling to publicly stand up in support of civil rights, they were uncomfortable employing violence as a tactic to preserve their position.

In the most revealing question of all, when asked, "Which of the following statements best expresses your opinion concerning the admission of qualified Negroes to the undergraduate colleges of the University?" out of the array of possibilities, an overwhelming 50.4 percent of students agreed that they favored Negro admission "under no circumstances at the present time."

Twenty-five years after Dahmer's study, these opinions began to change, as did the number of African Americans in attendance at the university. From 1974 to 1981, the number of African American students at the University of Alabama nearly doubled—761 students in 1974 to 1,482 seven years later.

It was progress, though this influx of African American students didn't come without its price.

On June 11, 1963, James Hood and Vivian Malone were the ones to pay it.

PART TWO

The Stand
Tuscaloosa, Alabama
Summer 1963

CHAPTER 6

Prepping for Peace

Fall 1962–Spring 1963

This was total radical action for myself anyway, and it could have gotten us killed, quite seriously.

The University of Alabama's second attempt at desegregation began in Mississippi. On the morning of Monday, October 1, 1962—at the conclusion of a nightlong firefight that left a French journalist and a jukebox repairman dead—twenty-nine-year-old African American James Meredith marched toward the Lyceum Administration Building on the Ole Miss campus to enroll in classes.

The previous day, Sunday, September 30, Mississippi's segregationist governor, Ross Barnett, began to understand that his battle against the federal government on the issue of desegregation had already been lost and what mattered most was the publicity spurred by the terms of surrender.

In a morning phone call to Attorney General Robert Kennedy, a desperate Barnett suggested a highly elaborate plan in which he would arrange three rows of patrolmen, sheriffs, and soldiers—all unarmed—to square off against federal troops. Barnett understood that the best-case scenario was losing with a winning photograph—one in which armed federal troops pointed their weapons at unarmed Mississippians.

"I think it is silly going through this whole façade . . . of your standing there; our people drawing guns; your stepping aside," Kennedy informed him. "To me it is dangerous, and I think it has gone beyond the stage of politics."

Having grown tired of their failed negotiations, the White House forged ahead with a new approach—the sneak attack. While the city of Oxford, Mississippi, prepared for a Monday showdown, President John F. Kennedy and his advisors decided to register Meredith on Sunday instead.

When word reached the locals, segregationists began gathering near the university's Lyceum Circle, a small contingency suddenly growing in strength, bugle calls and Confederate flags further adding to the drama. Emboldened by their numbers, the crowd began shouting invectives aimed at President Kennedy and blacks alike, as well as a more menacing message: "Just wait'll dark."

As darkness approached, the mob made good on its promise. Their fury mounting, they relied on the typical tools—bricks, bottles, and rocks—all hurled indiscriminately in the marshals' direction. Tear gas remained the US marshals' primary weapon, and at 7:58 P.M., after a lead pipe cracked a marshal's helmet, Chief US Marshal J. P. McShane—who had watched his men suffer the abuses of the mob long enough—ordered tear gas into the crowd. The battle waged on throughout the night, coming to its close only upon the arrival of federal troops, who successfully cleared the circle just before dawn, allowing Meredith to walk across the smoldering battlefield and register. A reported 160 US marshals sustained injuries, including twenty-eight who suffered gunshot wounds.

Meanwhile, four hours to the east in Tuscaloosa, the local newspaper reported on the violence at Ole Miss, attempting to make sense of its ramifications for its own university. One headline, in particular, managed to capture what many Tuscaloosans feared: "The Big Question: What Next?"

Within weeks of the Ole Miss riot, University of Alabama faculty, administrators, and student leaders drove to a retreat two hours east in an attempt to answer that question. Paramount to the retreat's success was a candid discussion on the race question, and President O. C. Carmichael's successor, President Frank Rose, fully encouraged such talk, his attempt at planting desegregation's seeds early to ensure a peaceful spring and summer.

Measuring in at six feet two inches, Dr. Frank Rose was a man of great charisma, whose charm and kind eyes regularly vaulted him to become the most well-liked person in the room.

"Frank Rose was a hell of a president," agreed Donald Stewart, who not only served as 1963's Student Government Association president, but also as a US senator fifteen years later. "[Rose] was a popular fella."

Stewart's characterization of Rose was shared by faculty and students alike. The ordained minister's work ethic and likability made him a perfect candidate for the difficult job of desegregating the campus, and while his responsibilities left little time for family, throughout his tenure he remained a creature of habit—waking early each morning to share a meal with his wife and children.

"Breakfast is the only time in a 15-hour work day that I can relax with the family," he explained. "I won't take a morning paper. If I did I'd know the crises I was facing before I got to the office."

Jefferson Bennett (who had traded in his title of assistant to the president for administrative vice president) believed Rose was fully aware of his intended mission from the moment he accepted the job—acclimate the campus for peaceful desegregation. Fully cognizant that he was being asked "to do something that O. C. Carmichael couldn't," Rose remained undeterred by his predecessor's failure. On one occasion, President Rose's wife approached Bennett, confiding, "Why in the hell does Frank think he can do something that destroyed O. C. Carmichael?"

To which Bennett replied, "I don't know, but maybe he can, because it will be our second attempt."

In the months prior to the university's 1963 desegregation attempt, a small contingency of Tuscaloosa businessmen began secretly meeting in the hopes of easing in integration without disrupting the business community. The men knew all too well the crippling effect civil rights could have on an economy, particularly as a result of boycotts. Aside from the economic considerations, the university and business community's primary motivation for laying the groundwork for peaceful desegregation rested squarely in the horrific events that had transpired at Ole Miss.

"We simply could not let such a thing happen here," an unidentified businessman explained later. "We had to do something."

Five high-profile community leaders attended the first meeting, including real estate broker and insurance salesman Harry Pritchett, as well as George LeMaistre, president of a local bank. Others rumored to be in attendance were paper industry titan Jack Warner, famed Alabama football coach Paul "Bear" Bryant, and newspaper editor Buford Boone.

While Boone did not make public his own involvement with the group, his newspaper nevertheless covered it. The *Tuscaloosa News* reported that Pritchett and LeMaistre became "co-chairmen of a committee without a name— but with a singular purpose: Convince Tuscaloosa it should accept desegregation of the University peacefully." The group maintained powerful ties within the state's political, economic, and journalistic spheres, and its members began working the phones to ensure that desegregation might occur with the least possible disruption, not only for the benefit of the business community, but for the sake of the community at large.

"At the time of Autherine Lucy there was little or no preparation. Most of the people thought the Supreme Court was wrong in its decision and that the situation would resolve itself and we would have no desegregation," Pritchett noted. He believed that businessmen banding together for "token integration" was a much-needed step toward resolving the issue, though the local Klan threw a wrench in the works—vowing to boycott any business that lent support toward educational mixing.

The Klan left little room for compromise, believing that even token integration was too high a price to pay. Conversely, for Tuscaloosa's emerging civil rights leaders, "token integration" was only the beginning. By 1963, Tuscaloosa was already proving itself as a testing ground, and white business owners learned soon enough that to publicly side with desegregation was to jeopardize profit margins.

As the business community struggled to find its footing, an October issue of the university newspaper, the *Crimson White,* added further pressure to the already simmering situation, reporting that the "lone Negro application" was under review for possible admission into the university. When asked for comment, former district court judge George Wallace—who would crush his competition in the state's gubernatorial election less than two weeks later— remained silent.

A source close to Wallace added, "This is nothing new. We have been expecting it. We have already said most of what we will do in this matter. What we now have to do is work out the details."

✺

Twenty-year-old African American James Hood was no stranger to Tuscaloosa. In the weeks and months preceding his official entrance into the University of Alabama, a few student leaders had the opportunity to meet with him privately, forming a foundation of friendship that administrators hoped might ease his transition.

Mel Meyer, editor of the *Crimson White,* was one of the students unofficially assigned to the task. Born in Mississippi, the young Jewish student had made a name for himself the previous October by publishing an editorial endorsing desegregation at Ole Miss—a view that many University of Alabama students and alumni found shocking and not at all representative of the university as a whole. Future editorials would have a similar effect, so much so that the university administration allegedly instituted a brief period of censoring the newspaper's opinions and editorial page. According to Meyer, in the fall of 1962, the *Crimson White*'s Birmingham printer was urged by university officials to examine the paper prior to printing, eliminating any and all controversial pieces. Meyer claimed he was made aware of this upon picking up the papers, at which point the printer admitted his complicity in the censorship. While Meyer only recalls one article ever being censored, it was proof enough that someone was tampering with his First Amendment right.

Yet a far more serious result of Meyer's liberal views was the threats against his life—threats that Meyer never took seriously.

"The truth of the matter is, I got put into this whole thing as being a kind of lightning rod for the civil rights movement, not because I was a passionate person for the cause, but just because I agreed with it," Meyer explained decades later. "It never occurred to me to make an editorial stance in the newspaper, but it was the idea of Richard Bolden and Robbie Roberts, who I had known from the university freshman debate team, and then we ended up in the honors program together."

According to Meyer, Bolden and Roberts brought him their pro-desegregation editorial and Meyer approved.

"So I decided we'd publish it," Meyer said simply, "and then, you know, all hell broke loose."

That "hell" involved cross burnings both on his fraternity's front lawn and on the lawn of his parents' home. "It wasn't a big deal," Meyer later added, "not like a scene from a movie."

Yet it *was* a big deal to university administrators, who determined that Meyer required his own personal security detail. Meyer described the pair of detectives assigned to protect him as "comical," explaining that the duo stayed with him from the publication of the Ole Miss editorial in the fall of 1962 until Christmas break a few months later. The detectives guarded his apartment day and night as well as checked under the hood of his car for bombs.

Meyer and his friends used to toy with the detectives, the young editor once going so far as to jokingly ask one of the pair, "Ever kill anyone?" To which the straight-faced detective replied, "Well, two or three."

It was quite possibly the truth. Having served under the reign of Birmingham's notorious commissioner of public safety, Eugene "Bull" Connor, the detectives thoroughly understood violent tactics as a means to an end.

As a result of the editorial, Meyer recalled hundreds of threatening letters pouring into the *Crimson White* office, many anti-Semitic in nature. Yet they were so poorly written—littered with both spelling and grammatical errors—that Meyer typically reacted with laughter rather than fear.

His tumultuous year as editor propelled him to newspaper stardom, earning him the prestigious College Newspaper Editor of the Year award. His sudden rise to fame even prompted Roger Ebert to ask Meyer to nominate the future film critic for president of the US Student Press Association, which Meyer did.

In the page dedicated to the school newspaper, the 1963 edition of the *Corolla,* the university's yearbook, noted, "There is one adjective that could never be used to describe the 1962–63 CRIMSON WHITE, and that is 'uninteresting.'"

When reflecting on his time as a student reporter for the *Crimson White,* Harris "Buddy" Cornett had little difficulty identifying Mel Meyer as one of the young heroes of the era. According to Cornett, Meyer had been a primary player in arranging the secret meetings with James Hood and other prospective African American students, though he was unsure whether Meyer took this initiative on his own or at the university's request.

While it remains unclear precisely who organized the meetings, in the spring of 1963, a small cadre of University of Alabama students, including student reporters Harris Cornett and Hank Black, drove to nearby Stillman College—the local African American college—and met with a few prospective black students.

"I was scared to death even to go to Stillman," Hank Black admitted in a recent interview. "I grew up in town, a Presbyterian, and [Stillman was] a Presbyterian college. And their choir would come sing, but I never really associated with Negroes."

Nevertheless, as the group's go-to driver, he was often coaxed into chauffeuring the others in his Renault Dauphine.

With a little prodding from friends, Cornett, too, soon found himself thrust into history—one of the few University of Alabama students to meet James Hood prior to his official registration. "We met with him and talked about what would be happening here if he came, where he would be living and everything," Cornett explained.

After a few meetings at Stillman College, Meyer, Black, and company decided to escort Hood to Cornett's apartment on the university strip to give the prospective student a clearer depiction of university life. Journalism professor Dr. Luskin and his wife owned the building, and up until then Cornett and his roommate had proven themselves model tenants. They lived in a two-story structure, the front half of the second story partitioned as a secretarial school, while the back half was a two-bedroom apartment. Today, the building is home to the Crimson Café—a popular coffee shop just a short walk from campus—but in 1963, the bottom floor housed a drugstore, while the upper floor housed Harris Cornett.

Upon reaching the apartment's entrance, the group discovered a note taped hastily to the door: *Buddy, get out. You're in danger. Don't sleep here tonight.*

The note was from Cornett's roommate, who, as a result of receiving threatening phone calls, had exited the apartment himself. "I was sweating bullets," Black recalled. "I was up and down, pacing. This was total radical action for myself anyway, and it could have gotten us killed, quite seriously."

Months earlier, on October 30, President Rose addressed the faculty to publicly dispel rumors that the university would close its doors rather than yield to desegregation. This was just one of the many disconcerting pieces of gossip floating about, and Rose felt compelled to reassure the faculty that there was "no thought on the part of the board of trustees to close the University or in any manner compromise the intellectual integrity of this University."

He further eased faculty's fears by reaffirming his commitment to law and order, stating, "The University of Alabama cannot go through another crisis like that of 1956 or like that which happened in Mississippi a few weeks ago. The University must never be made the place for troops, mobs or national news media seeking attention."

It was a strong statement, though the faculty remained unconvinced.

A few days later, the faculty solidified its voice by passing a resolution aimed at protecting the integrity of the university. An editorial in the school newspaper commended the resolution, arguing, "in unity there is strength." To illustrate, the newspaper recounted the tale of a medicine man who snapped individual twigs with ease, though when bound together, he failed even to bend the bundle. "A unified movement of mature leadership to accept the inevitable has taken place within the state," the paper reported. The university had found its medicine man in Rose.

Forty-eight hours after Rose's reassurances to the faculty, dean of men John Blackburn set to work reassuring the students as well. Sitting in the basement of Palmer Hall—the future dorm of James Hood—Blackburn said simply, "There will not be another Oxford here. This is your University. Law and Order will be maintained."

It was early November—desegregation was over seven months away—yet already the public relations machine was in full swing.

In fact, the university as a whole seemed to be preparing for the change, administrators rightfully believing that successful desegregation was dependent upon maintaining as much time as possible to prepare. Thanks, in part, to administrative vice president Jefferson Bennett, the university had some assistance in delaying the enrollment of Vivian Malone and James Hood, thereby granting itself an extension.

"Now comes a part of this drama that has never before been publically revealed," Jefferson Bennett remarked decades later. He recounted how a friend of his on the Alabama A&M faculty served as an advisor to the University of Alabama's prospective African American student, Vivian Malone, and how he had called upon his friend to sway Malone to briefly delay her enrollment so that the university might better prepare.

"I called him and explained to him that we wanted to win this time. We wanted to get this issue behind us. That we wanted to open this campus to black citizens. I asked him to please, please encourage [Malone] to delay her enrollment until the Summer Session, which she did by letter shortly thereafter. She may never know exactly why she did, but she did," Bennett explained. "The same thing was true of Jimmy Hood. He was advised to wait until the two of them could arrive together and not to go on this lonesome road alone."

❀

The University of Alabama wasn't alone in its waffling. James Hood, too, struggled to reach a decision as to whether or not to attend. Prior to completing his application, he debated between applying to the University of Alabama or Auburn University—both premier Alabama schools within a few hours of each other. His English teacher, Christine Farris of Clark University, encouraged Hood to speak to her brother, Dr. Martin Luther King Jr., to see if he might weigh in on the matter. It was a fortuitous connection, and upon conferring with King, among other civil rights leaders, Hood decided that due to the close proximity to his home church (and to a far lesser extent, his long-shot dream of playing on the Alabama football team), the University of Alabama seemed the proper choice.

After filing his application, Hood sat down with his pastor and was reminded of an experience they shared five years prior during a trip to Tuskegee University. "We had walked around the campus and the last place that we stopped was in front of the statue of Booker T. Washington," Hood recounted. "And on the base of that statue is a quotation that says, 'Once a task is begun, never leave it till it's done. Be ye labor great or small, do it well or not at all.'"

The quote stuck with him, all the way to Tuscaloosa.

CHAPTER 7

The Law of the Land

June 5–11, 1963

I don't think we're going to have any trouble whatsoever.

On the afternoon of Wednesday, June 5, 1963, J. Hal McCall—president of the Tuscaloosa Historical Society—along with probate judge David M. Cochrane, Pastor J. H. Chitwood, and other local dignitaries, placed pictures, employment lists, and a variety of other memorabilia into a copper box to be inserted into the cornerstone of the newly constructed Tuscaloosa County Courthouse. The city hoped the time capsule would preserve a piece of its history for future generations, though the city's history that would remain most preserved had yet to occur—lingering like a storm cloud less than a week away.

The day after the time capsule was sealed into place, federal officials met with administrative vice president Jefferson Bennett and district judge Seybourn H. Lynne. Justice Department lawyer John Doar and Deputy Attorney General Nicholas Katzenbach were also present—both of whom had witnessed the horrors of Ole Miss firsthand, and who hoped to put their hard-earned knowledge to use in Alabama's desegregation efforts.

Also present were the students themselves, Vivian Malone and James Hood, who planned to register at the University of Alabama's main campus in Tuscaloosa six days later, as well as African American David M. McGlathery, who would register at the Huntsville branch soon after.

Bennett, who had endured the Lucy incident years prior, remained convinced that one of the primary failures of 1956 was Lucy's limited interactions with university administrators prior to her enrollment. "In spite of all our efforts to protect her, the only personal conversation she had with any member of our staff was with [dean of women] Sarah Healy, certainly not with me. She had no reason to assume that I, a white southern university administrator, was on her team at all."

Lucy herself reiterated this problem in a 2003 interview, noting, "the president [Carmichael] said nothing to me"—further proof of a communication breakdown.

As a result, in the days leading up to the 1963 desegregation attempt, Bennett contacted Judge Lynne in the hopes that he might assist in rectifying the problems Lucy had encountered, requesting that the judge arrange a meeting between university administrators, federal officials, and the students prior to Hood and Malone's entrance. Lynne agreed, and the group met in the judge's chambers soon after. Bennett recalled chatting with the students, and in particular, how the group of men advised Hood and Malone on how they might more easily fit in, including some critical information for any new University of Alabama student: "We talked about football."

On Thursday, June 6, the *Tuscaloosa News* printed a map that marked the streets that had been sealed off to nonstudents. President Rose, Dean Blackburn, and other University of Alabama administrators had become well versed in the failings at Ole Miss and, with the university's own tarnished reputation from seven years prior, knew that this second effort at desegregation demanded far more forethought to ensure a far less damning outcome. While Ole Miss had set up ineffective barricades that did little to keep the mobs away, the University of Alabama enacted a tight seal that offered a wide berth around all sides of the campus. The perimeter stretched down toward the Black Warrior River with checkpoints set up at all entries. Clumps of armed officers guarded the checkpoints, demanding students present identification cards in order to gain access to their school.

As a further precaution to deter the possibility of outside threats, parents were barred from participating in the traditional moving-in ceremony for their sons and daughters. Instead, parents were kept outside the barriers while drivers shuttled students and their belongings onto the campus grounds. University student and *Crimson White* reporter Harris Cornett landed one of the driving jobs, earning himself a front-row seat to history.

"Everyone was worried about a bomb," Cornett recalled. "Students couldn't come on campus until someone working for the university put them on campus. Mostly we drove vans and trucks. That's what I spent all day doing," he explained, though he hardly regretted it. "That's why I was here to see what was taking place."

Days later, when George Wallace made his infamous stand in the schoolhouse door, it was not the first time Harris Cornett found himself in close proximity to the governor. "I had dated his daughter once or twice," Cornett explained, "and she had arranged for me to interview him when he came up here for Homecoming in '62."

On that fall day eight months prior to the stand, the young reporter waited patiently as the newly elected governor finished his homecoming responsibilities before slipping back into his car to be driven to his next stop in nearby Fayette. As a personal favor to Cornett, Bobbi Jo Wallace convinced her father to allow the *Crimson White* reporter to ride alongside him in the backseat.

"George told me a lot, but much of what he told me was off the record," Cornett began. "But he said such things as, 'You know if you want to be a politician, you have to say what it takes to get elected, first of all, and then get done what you can get done. If you know you're the best person to help the people because you want the people helped, you've still got to get elected. I realized that. So I said what it took to get elected in Alabama, and I'm the governor.'"

While Wallace was likely referring to some of his more racially charged campaign promises, he was, perhaps, also admitting a concern for his most memorable promise, the one he would make clear in front of the state capitol on inauguration day a few months later—"Segregation today, segregation tomorrow, segregation forever."

Wallace spoke candidly to the student reporter, enlightening Cornett on the dark underbelly of southern politics.

"George was an interesting guy," Cornett remarked, "and I had come up [to the University of Alabama] with the intention of majoring in political science, going to law school, and being a senator from the great state of Alabama, a good conservative boy. But that conversation [with Wallace] had a lot to do with my changing my mind."

Despite Wallace's off-the-record political insight, his on-the-record portion of the interview yielded little more than the usual talking points. When asked of the possibility of the university's desegregation, Wallace replied, "If there is anyone who doesn't want another Oxford incident, [it's] President Kennedy. I believe that we will resist [desegregation] in a manner that will reflect credit on the University and the state and, at the same time, impress upon the Kennedy administration that we will stand firm in our belief in those principles which made our nation great."

Likewise, when Cornett asked if the governor was concerned with the reverberations of his campaign promise to block desegregation by standing in the schoolhouse door, the reporter received an equally scripted response: "No one looks down on people who stand up for what they believe in"; Wallace explained, "it is the persons who refuse to stand up for the principles in which they believe who are looked down upon."

The great irony was that while Wallace *claimed* to be standing up for what he believed in, it was hardly what he had believed during his first failed run for the governorship four years prior, when a more racially tempered Wallace had lost the election, in part, due to his unwillingness to publicly embrace the Ku Klux Klan as had been done by his opponent, John Patterson. Thus Wallace learned a tough lesson, one that spurred an about-face on his public views on race and earned him a far more electable reputation as a staunch defender of segregation. An unnamed Alabama college president commented quite candidly on Wallace's abrupt change of heart: "[Wallace] really doesn't believe what he says about the race question," the president observed. "He uses it only as a technique to get the vote of the nonsophisticated white man."

As the zero hour approached, local law enforcement continued to work closely with state troopers to ensure that Governor Wallace stayed true to his promise of peace.

Tuscaloosa police chief William Marable informed reporters that the city police would be on "around-the-clock call," working newly approved twelve-hour shifts to ensure order. It was a scheduling tactic that the peacekeeping police chief would employ the following summer as well—a strategy that kept the most boots on the ground amid the looming threat of racial violence.

William Marable, a former military man turned police chief, was well respected throughout his department. However, he was dealing with a rough crowd—several of his officers were ex-military themselves, and several more were rumored to have close ties to the local Klan outfit. Local businessman George LeMaistre estimated that "not more than 50 to 60 per cent" of the Tuscaloosa police force were "sympathetic toward [Marable's] aims."

Regardless of his officers' questionable allegiances, Marable was a man many in the community had come to trust. His mostly cool-headed, even-handed approach to enforcing the law would thrust him into the city's civil rights spotlight the following summer, though on June 11, 1963, the Tuscaloosa police chief's primary responsibility was to provide yet another layer of defense to further deter the possibility of violence.

Bill G. Marable, the police chief's son, remembers little of his father's work that day, though he certainly recalls where he was while witnessing the stand. "I remember going to a friend of mine's house, to his grandmother's house," he began. "She had a boarding house right on the border of campus there. . . . I parked my car in that parking lot of that bank to visit my friend at his grandmother's house, and I turned that corner one evening and there were National Guardsmen standing there with rifles on their shoulder and I thought, 'Whoa, this is serious.'"

It became even more serious when state public safety director Colonel Albert Lingo arrived in Tuscaloosa with his own brigade of Birmingham state troopers. While Marable had earned a reputation as a peaceable lawman, Lingo had earned a far different reputation, though one of which he was equally proud.

Lingo was described as having the "air of a general," and "like[d] the direct command of his men."

"I don't think we're going to have any trouble whatsoever," he assured the press with his usual swagger. "We're going to have plenty of force to cope with the situation."

When asked what might occur if federal troops and state troopers found themselves in a standoff, Lingo refused to speculate, replying simply, "The governor will make that decision."

CHAPTER 8

Boone versus Bull

June 6–10, 1963

If we have violence, it will have been brought on by George Wallace.

While Governor Wallace began offering his views on desegregation, so too did the Alabama State Legislature. In a slight departure from business as usual, on Friday, June 7, the legislature gave up any semblance of a neutral stance and instead adopted a resolution "expressing its good wishes and prayers for Gov. Wallace in his promised stand next Tuesday against desegregation of the University of Alabama." The state senate also made its allegiance clear—offering a silent prayer for its governor. "It was an unusual moment," admitted the newspapers, though in Alabama, the separation of church and state was often viewed more as a suggestion than a rule.

For most, the eventual desegregation of the university appeared to be a foregone conclusion, though not for Governor Wallace—at least not publicly. In an editorial published just days prior to the stand, Buford Boone wrote: "Governor Wallace knows that regardless of what he does, and regardless of what any one else in this state may do, Negro students will be registered at the University and will attend. That leaves only the question of whether integration will be carried out peacefully, or whether rioting will occur." His editorial continued: "We believe his 'last stand' decision to be foolish and unnecessary. But we support strongly his intention to go about the proceeding peacefully."

The newspaper editor was attempting the same trick he'd pulled off during the Lucy riots years earlier—making it clear that the press was willing to take sides, commending or vilifying as necessary.

"If we have violence," Boone added, "it will have been brought on by George Wallace."

Despite his criticism, Boone appreciated Wallace's promise to maintain order—a lofty yet reasonable goal that would serve as the litmus test for the limits of the governor's power. While the success of Wallace's plan had yet to be determined, the mere promise for peace was far more than Governor Barnett had offered the previous fall at Ole Miss. Wallace's clear stance against violence played a critical role in assuring that there was none. With his wide reach and the ears of many, the former Golden Gloves boxer had little trouble throwing his weight around in an effort to ensure a particular outcome. Still, even with his safeguards in place and the support of the people, Wallace remained aware that he, too, was taking a calculated risk. If the desegregation of the University of Alabama ended in violence, not only would it be a public relations disaster for the state and university, but a referendum on Wallace as well.

Although he had recently lost his post as Birmingham's commissioner of public safety, on Thursday, June 6, the notorious segregationist Eugene "Bull" Connor held a private meeting with Governor Wallace. While reports noted that their conversation related to the possibility of Connor receiving a new post within the state bureaucracy, it is more than likely that the impending situation at the University of Alabama monopolized much of their conversation. Connor had gained notoriety just a month prior, in May of 1963, when he resorted to police dogs and fire hoses to combat Birmingham's civil rights demonstrators. The sixty-five-year-old commissioner had a reputation for bending laws in an effort to enforce them, paying little attention to notions of police brutality or excessive force.

On Friday, June 7, just a day after Wallace's meeting with his former commissioner of public safety, Bull Connor served as the governor's mouthpiece, speaking to White Citizens Council members at Tuscaloosa's Holt High School and relaying the message he'd likely been encouraged to transmit. Echoing Wallace's plea for people to steer clear of the university, he reassured the crowd that desegregation could effectively be stopped "at the ballot box and by economic boycotts."

In a bit of skewed logic, Connor went on to claim that Attorney General Robert Kennedy would "give the world if we had trouble here," and by keeping the peace, they could "beat the Kennedys at their own game."

"You are not going to whip the integration fight with bricks, guns, or sticks, or in court—there is only one way left. That is economics." He called for his audience to "do just as King is doing" and "boycott the devil" out of stores in open support of African American causes.

Despite his rhetoric, Connor remained fully aware of the uphill battle with which he was faced, adding ominously, "This is going to get worse before it gets better."

Meanwhile, just miles away, Buford Boone continued his fight on another front—pounding out an editorial to be printed in the following day's paper. Titled "Our Danger Is Fear," Boone's editorial released a pressure valve throughout the city, exposing the many unfounded rumors that had already begun taking root. He referenced one supposed mob scene from the previous day in which "a big gathering of white men and automobiles, some with out-of-state licenses," was assumed to be up to no good.

The editorial went on to debunk the vigilante assumptions—explaining simply that these out-of-towners were not gathering for any riotous behavior but instead were simply enjoying a barbecue among friends. "Tuscaloosa is a community with much good will between white and Negro neighbors," Boone reminded. "We must keep it that way."

Yet according to at least a small portion of the *Tuscaloosa News*'s readership, Boone's editorials had become more hindrance than help. In W. P. Thaxton's letter to the editor he faulted the *Tuscaloosa News* for what he believed to be sensationalized reporting. "The state of Alabama is not obligated to encourage reporters from the entire nation to make sport of our troubles," Thaxton chided. "If less publicity were given to the matter there would be a whole lot less chance of confusion. . . . Treat the news in the same manner you print news of racial strife in other sections of the country (small headlines in the back pages of your paper with short articles)."

In a near direct response to Thaxton's call for less coverage, Boone assured his readership that the *Tuscaloosa News* would, in fact, follow a "low-key" policy to combat sensationalism, though he pointed out that downplaying reports might lead to "irresponsible rumor and to wild gossip." Despite the occasional mistake, Boone argued that the press maintained "an amazing record for accuracy."

Further, he assured Tuscaloosans that they could expect to receive their news "promptly and regularly through experienced men working honestly to distill fact from fiction, to dispel rumor by making the truth known, and to render the gossip less potent by overshadowing his savory conversational tidbits with substantial fact."

Despite the high regard with which he held his colleagues, even Buford Boone conceded that the governor's stand just days away would prove a vital test for the media.

The local media—and Buford Boone, in particular—was well aware of the tests that lay ahead. While confident he could keep a tight leash on the reporters at the *Tuscaloosa News,* Boone knew it would be far more difficult to keep hundreds of other reporters on the same leash. Believing speedy and accurate communication to be the key to avoiding confrontation, Buford Boone and other area editors met with President Rose to "develop a strategy for cooperating with visiting reporters." This strategy consisted of providing a makeshift command center for reporters, allowing them easy access to telephones and newswires. Boone and Rose agreed that the *Tuscaloosa News's* former headquarters would prove an ideal space, located just steps from the reporters' hotels and equipped with all the necessities.

Local radio stations were taking a similar approach, even going so far as to share information and broadcast simultaneously in an effort to combat the possibility of rumors. "Only factual and documented reports will be broadcast from this news system," confirmed Clyde Price, a spokesman for the shared station.

While it may have seemed an unnecessary precaution, the shared media coverage added yet another layer of support, and the university—along with both federal and state representatives aimed at preserving the peace—was likely grateful for the cooperation.

"So far as we know, this is the first time radio people have exercised such a high degree of responsibility in a sensitive situation," claimed an editorial in the *Tuscaloosa News*. The piece went on to describe the failures in Oxford, in which "announcements were made before they were checked for accuracy," some of which were "fantastically incorrect."

Buford Boone—who had witnessed rumors run amuck seven years prior during the enrollment of Autherine Lucy—was determined to do his part to deter any such repeated mistakes. Boone understood that by controlling the story, he controlled the mob as well—another valuable lesson learned from James Meredith's experiences one state over.

"The Ole Miss disaster had become legend," one source confirmed. "There had been only sixteen long-distance operators for the entire Oxford area, making reporters wait an hour just to get an open line." Tuscaloosa's newly created command center ensured that an increase in communication capabilities further eased the threat of rumors.

Local journalist and photographer Camille Maxwell Elebash spent much of her time reporting on the reporters themselves, filling a yellow, spiral-bound notebook with the names of nearly two hundred newsmen. Included on the list was Dan Rather, a young reporter for the Dallas affiliate of CBS News who would go on to anchor the nightly news decades later, as well as Relman Morin, a two-time Pulitzer Prize winner and an indispensible voice for civil rights reporting. Morin's presence, in particular, proved that national news outlets weren't simply sending hoards of green-behind-the-ears reporters; oftentimes, they were sending their best.

While the Alabama National Guard provided vital support throughout the proceedings soon to come, perhaps the most powerful weapon in Tuscaloosa's arsenal remained its dedicated press corps: men and women like Boone, Rather, Morin, and Elebash—all of whom fought to dispel the myths that often led to violence.

CHAPTER 9

Guns and a Governor

June 8–9, 1963

I see in Wallace the ability to rewrite history in Tuscaloosa.

On Saturday, June 8, Governor Wallace informed President Kennedy by telegram that he was calling in five hundred Alabama National Guardsmen in an effort to keep the peace.

"Out of an abundance of caution," wrote Wallace, "I will call approximately 500 Alabama National Guardsmen effective Sunday . . . to be used only in the event they are needed to maintain law and order, and preserve the peace at the University of Alabama and in the Tuscaloosa area."

Yet in other sections of Tuscaloosa, peace hardly seemed a priority.

While a Klan rally raged just off of US Highway 11 later that night, state troopers and local sheriffs directed their attention elsewhere—to a vehicle with six white men crowded inside. Upon closer inspection, the officers discovered "a small arsenal of pistols, clubs, knives and ammunition."

Yet this was only a small sampling of their weaponry. According to Gary Thomas Rowe—a Klansman turned FBI informant—the car was actually filled with far more dangerous arms. "As we drove off toward Tuscaloosa," Rowe remembered, "I sat in back thinking what these men could do with the stuff we were carrying."

The answer: Quite a lot.

The six Klansmen were fully capable of using the weapons to their full potential, and having been given orders to "tear the school apart," that was what they intended to do.

According to Rowe, thousands of Klansmen were rumored to be ready to assist in the university's destruction, prompting Rowe to inform his FBI handlers that "the previous year's rioting at the University of Mississippi would look mild by comparison."

Fortunately, the men never got their chance.

Rowe had secretly reported their route to FBI agents prior to setting foot in the car, and when state troopers stopped the vehicle on the edge of town, all the men became acutely aware of their troubles. The weapons were confiscated, and according to Rowe, as they were driven to a dorm room at the University of Alabama for further questioning, the newly arrested men and the troopers passed around a bottle of whiskey.

"Jesus Christ, we sure hate to bust you when you came down here to help us keep the goddamn niggers away from the school!" one of the troopers sympathized. "We had it set up so you could have really worked them over, but some bastard called the FBI and told them you had all these weapons."

The bastard was in the backseat.

After further questioning, a reluctant highway patrolman was alleged to have told the Klansmen, "We had to pick you up; they'll send five thousand troops down here tonight if we don't stop this mess."

The state troopers much preferred to handle their problems in-house, and if that meant arresting a few armed Klansmen to appease the federal government, then even a sympathetic patrolman was willing to do so.

While the Tuscaloosa County Jail dealt with their new arrivals, in a nearby field off of US 11, Grand Wizard Robert Shelton convened a Klan rally reportedly several thousand strong. Crosses crackled through the darkness as Shelton spoke to the crowd, reminding them that they supported Governor Wallace in his campaign and "we support him now, we will support him Monday, Tuesday, Wednesday—and next year."

The pronouncement was met with applause.

"But I am asking you other people who do not belong to a patriotic organization such as this one to stay away from the University." He informed the crowd that Governor Wallace would stand for them, and that they should allow their governor to do his work without interference. "I see in Wallace the ability to rewrite history in Tuscaloosa in the next three or four days," Shelton prophesized, though this work could only get done if the segregationists left Wallace to his task.

Listening on the periphery were a few curious *Crimson White* reporters who had managed to infiltrate the rally. Hank Black, the newly appointed editor, and reporters Harris Cornett and Bob Penny, among others, had all managed to filter inconspicuously into the crowd.

"We were there," Cornett recalled, "and they ranted and raved about the Jewish, Northern Yankee intellectuals of the *Crimson White*. That they'd printed all this stuff because they were outsiders. . . . Well, I was from south Alabama, and Hank was from Tuscaloosa," Cornett laughed. "These were [some of the top] offices of the *Crimson White*. And we were present at the rally."

While Cornett doubted he could retrace the rally's precise location, he did recall the burning cross in the sky, as well as Shelton's commanding presence, how when the Grand Wizard opened his mouth to speak, a hush fell over the crowd.

According to Cornett, Shelton took his place in front of the crowd and said, "I have talked to Brother George, and Brother George has asked me to tell you all that he's going to stand up for you all, and you can mess everything up that he's worked for if there's any violence at all."

"That was a surprise to me," remembered fellow student reporter Bob Penny. "That [Shelton] got up there and said, 'Let George [stand for you].' I was truly surprised."

"It was a stage show," Cornett added. "It was a well orchestrated stage show."

What Bob Penny witnessed that night would play a role in his future acting career, particularly for his part in 1988's *Mississippi Burning*—a film based on the murder of three civil rights workers in Mississippi in the summer of 1964. "I was one of the murderers," Penny explained in a recent interview. "And one of the big scenes was this Klan gathering."

As the actor watched the director and film crew assemble the shots, his mind returned to his experiences at the real-life Klan rally twenty-five years before. As the actors took their marks and the cameras rolled, Penny thought, *This was what the Klan rally was like in Tuscaloosa.*

Despite the theatrics both on and off the set, to this day, Cornett remains convinced that Shelton's call for his fellow Klansmen to steer clear of the university played a critical role in ensuring a peaceful desegregation.

"I don't think [Shelton] ever got the credit he deserved," Cornett admitted, "but I think this is the main reason there wasn't much violence."

Yet Shelton's call for peace hadn't reached everyone.

As Gary Thomas Rowe promised, police soon discovered that the "small arsenal" found in possession of the six men had expanded to include "two wooden clubs, six loaded pistols, two night sticks, a hay hook, two sabres, two bayonets and 'extensive' ammunition."

While Wallace, Connor, and Shelton all pleaded with segregationists to refrain from violence, six men in a car on a Saturday night were proof that pleas were not enough.

On June 9, 1963, an editorial in the *Tuscaloosa News* dramatized the events soon to come: "In Montgomery, a former farm boy worries in the Governor's mansion. Somewhere else three Negro students [including David M. McGlathery who would desegregate the Huntsville branch] wait as the minutes tick off before they are to meet their state's chief executive and hear from him whatever he plans to say at the University door."

The editorial noted also that previous desegregation attempts had failed, in part, due to a lack of "mental preparation." Yet since October, the University of Alabama had been laying the groundwork to ensure a peaceful transition, including mentally preparing the student body. For Alabama students, the events of June 11 were a long time in the making, and many—particularly student leaders—had been aware of the inevitability of Hood and Malone's entrance for quite some time.

Don Siegal, the Student Government Association's secretary treasurer, recalled hearing the initial whispers of the university's desegregation efforts. "The first I knew about it was during the spring of 1963," Siegal remembered.

Dean of men John Blackburn had asked Siegal over for Sunday brunch, an invitation to which Siegal readily agreed. Blackburn was a "feared man," according to Siegal, "an enforcer." When Alabama's male students failed to live up to the high standards of the university, the perpetrators were often sent to Blackburn's office.

Siegal thought the invitation strange, particularly because Blackburn "was not one to fraternize with students." Yet upon arriving at Blackburn's home he was surprised to find that fifteen to twenty additional student leaders had also been invited. The students shuffled aimlessly around the house, making small talk until Dean Blackburn finally burst into the room. In a great breach of Blackburn's typical straightlaced demeanor, the dean called out, "Who would like a Bloody Mary?"

An awestruck Siegal turned to SGA president Donald Stewart.

"We got one big problem going on," Siegal whispered, "because there is no way John Blackburn would be offering Bloody Marys to students."

The "problem," of course, was that the administration was in the early stages of preparing the university for the enrollment of two African American students, the success of which they believed hinged on student support.

"He told us at that meeting that integration was coming," Siegal recalled, "that it would happen in June of '63, during summer school session, so not when the full student body was here, and that he would need help from student leaders to be sure that the students understood the ramification of a peaceful vs. non-peaceful integration."

Siegal and other student leaders began pounding the pavement, spending much of the spring semester going from fraternity house, to sorority house, to the dorms in an effort to speak on the importance of preserving the peace. "We went to all the dorms, room to room," Siegal explained, "and also organized cadres of students going across the quads picking up rocks, bottles, anything that could be thrown so we didn't have an inadvertent problem."

"There wasn't a rock as big as the end of your thumb; there wasn't even any gravel," administrative vice president Jefferson Bennett later proudly remarked. "There wasn't a piece of wood as big as your hand."

Glass bottles, a necessary ingredient for Molotov cocktails, had proven particularly troublesome during the Ole Miss crisis, and as a result, even the University of Alabama's soda machines were specially fitted to deter violence—the bottles replaced with disposable cups.

Aside from preparing the physical campus, student leaders were also charged with winning the hearts and minds of the more skeptical students. Working diligently to set the record straight, student leaders dispelled the many myths that had overtaken the campus, including rumors of a Klan force gathering on the riverbank, as well as the prospect of special treatment and chauffer services for African American students. As had been proven years prior with Autherine Lucy's one-hundred-dollar-bill tuition payment, classism rivaled racism in infuriating a student body—another problem the university hoped to avoid.

SGA president and future US senator Donald Stewart recalled the students' behind-the-scenes work as well. "Folks like Don [Siegal] and others . . . decided they would basically stand up for the university and see what they could do to quite possibly change the approach that was taken at Ole Miss. . . . They had a pretty bad situation at Ole Miss, and we didn't want to repeat that."

He continued: "The deal that was expressed at the time to us by John Blackburn—and later by others in the administration—was that they wanted us as student leaders to do what we could to encourage people to be good to Vivian [Malone] and James Hood when they came there, and to make sure they weren't being spit on or cussed at or any of the things students did at Ole Miss. And so, [the administration] went through a series of meetings with us, and then we went through a series of meetings with people that we knew."

The grassroots communication system proved surprisingly successful, in part due to the popularity of leaders like Stewart. While the University of Alabama's Student Government Association had long been dominated by "the machine"—a secret Greek-led organization committed to anointing students into high-profile leadership positions within the school—Stewart had somehow managed to topple the establishment, becoming a hero for the independent while maintaining the respect of the Greek organizations as well. In the spring of 1963 he put his celebrity to good use, walking from dorm to dorm to explain to students the necessity of a smooth desegregation.

"I told them that this was sort of an inevitable kind of thing," he explained. "It was coming. . . . And I leaned on the fact that people loved the university."

Another strength was the people's love for their town, an attribute exploited by both SGA President Donald Stewart and Police Chief William Marable. While students and citizens may have had differing views on racial issues, they all loved Tuscaloosa and its university (and in particular, its shared football team).

The relatively small size of both the town and university also proved a critical asset for law enforcement, allowing loyalties and long-forged relationships to overpower the mobs. Not everyone agreed on racial matters, but friendships often ran deeper than politics, prompting citizens of all opinions to work closely with police.

Yet perhaps most important of all to maintaining peace was the ability of the university's administration and student leaders to stay on a shared message. "It was a unified effort," Stewart agreed, "so we just stuck together, and because of that we just had a totally different experience."

On June 8—as the Klan prepared for its Saturday night rally—dozens of reporters had already found their way into Tuscaloosa's Hotel Stafford, preparing themselves for the story that would soon make front-page news. While the media control center had been set up nearby, the university also laid down a few additional ground rules, including one that barred cameras and reporters from entering any building other than the student union. Secondly, they requested there be no live broadcast of the event, though a few cameras (including Robert Drew's documentary crew) managed to record the event all the same. Further, news vehicles would not be allowed on campus, and if the press wanted inside the barricades, they were required to present the necessary credentials and pass through the checkpoints, just like everyone else. The strict adherence to these rules served as proof of the university's attempt to control as many preshow factors as possible, prompting station operator Clyde Price to call the media's collaborative efforts "unprecedented"—a point of pride for the already on-edge administrators.

On Sunday afternoon, the reporters watched on as five hundred Alabama National Guardsmen rolled into town, though Colonel Lingo already had eight hundred state troopers under his purview, providing a tight seal around the campus.

Soon after, University of Alabama president Frank Rose—who had remained tightlipped throughout much of the public preparation—held a press conference in which he attempted to back Wallace, though his words more closely resembled an observational statement than a ringing endorsement. "It is necessary for the governor to be here with the Highway Patrol to keep the peace," he explained, adding diplomatically, "Gov. Wallace is attempting to fulfill a commitment to the people he made during his campaign for governor."

When the flurry of reporters pressed further, President Rose "declined comment on the wisdom of Wallace's avowed stand."

As the University of Alabama prepared itself for the arrival of Governor Wallace, *Time Magazine* predicted that the spring of 1963 would "long be remembered as the time when the U.S. Negroes' revolution for equality exploded on all fronts,"—an assessment with which many agreed. Integration battles were being waged at lunch counters and movie theaters throughout the country, though in the days preceding Wallace's stand in the schoolhouse door, a battle of a different sort was taking place in a Birmingham courtroom.

On Wednesday, June 5, Judge Seybourn Lynne issued an injunction against the governor, ruling that Wallace could in no way interfere with Hood and Malone's enrollment, including blocking their entrance. Lynne defended his ruling, noting, "My prayer is that all of our people, in keeping with our finest traditions, will join in the resolution that law and order will be maintained."

On the surface, Wallace seemed to agree, though he himself chose to interpret the injunction quite loosely, believing that the order in no way barred him from attending the registration or decrying the encroachment of federal power every step of the way. He could only be charged with contempt if he ordered troops to block the door or blocked it himself, thereby making it impossible for Vivian Malone or James Hood to pass. There were still loopholes available to him, though Wallace played a dangerous game by exploiting them.

After receiving word of the injunction, Wallace took to the airwaves, assuring his constituents that "the action that I am going to take involves even my personal freedom . . . but I intend to carry it out, regardless of what risk I take."

The risks were clear—a maximum sentence of ten years in prison for contempt—yet Wallace appeared undeterred in his attempt to fulfill his campaign promise. Playing the part of the martyr, Wallace informed his viewers, "What happens to George Wallace is not so important, but what happens to constitutional government is very important."

"I give you my word that I will not let you down," Wallace promised, which was all the reassurance many white segregationists needed.

In the previous months, Wallace had given his constituents plenty of reasons to believe him. While his legacy would long loom in the shadow of his stand, in the months preceding, his leadership had also resulted in an aggressive tackling of the state budget, an increase in teacher salaries, the greenlighting of various construction projects, all while simultaneously managing to attract nearly "$250 million worth of new industry to locate in Alabama."

That very year *Time Magazine* deemed Wallace a "first-rate governor," and many of his policies proved transformative for the state. However, the great irony pointed out by the *New York Times* was that while Alabama's "first-rate governor" was a vocal supporter of states' rights (spitting venom at the federal government at every turn), he nevertheless relied heavily on federal funding. Only Arkansas, South Carolina, and Mississippi had lower per capita incomes, and in 1962 alone, the federal government pumped $229 million worth of grants into his state. Wallace was trying to have it both ways: while he publicly decried the growing encroachment of the federal government, he was more than happy to accept its money.

The many contradictions of George Wallace make him a difficult man to sum up. In 1968, writer Robert Sherrill called him "the greatest disturber of the political peace in this generation," as well as a "neurotic, raving egotist," and "a skilled imitator of political gimmickry." Yet in the very same sentence, Sherrill admitted that the governor also possessed "more imagination and drive and artistry of debate than all the other contemporary Deep South politicians put together."

To some, he was an egomaniacal showman, to others, segregation's greatest defender. Yet regardless of people's personal feelings toward Wallace, most everyone agreed he was a man who kept his word.

CHAPTER 10

The Calm before the Stand

June 10, 1963

Segregation is going, whether we like it or not.

Monday, June 10, began another blistering week in the heart of Alabama, though temperatures would creep even higher the following day. In anticipation of the governor's stand, over four hundred correspondents from throughout the world descended upon Tuscaloosa, some traveling from as far away as Japan, Korea, and the Netherlands. But the reporters with the most unique perspective were Americans themselves—African Americans.

One such reporter, Samuel Adams of the *St. Petersburg Times,* offered an optimistic depiction of his own on-campus experiences among the student body. "If the treatment accorded me by the students I met is any indication of the treatment the two Negro students will receive, then there is no cause to fear trouble," he assured. Adams admitted to keeping a low profile, adding that he had no trouble eating in Tuscaloosa, either, primarily because "some of my white friends who are reporters went into hamburger stands and brought me food."

When approached by white students, Adams reported that it was only out of a "subdued curiosity."

"They wanted to know how we were getting along and they asked us to tell them what was going on," he explained. "They said they felt shut out of the developments."

After a weekend spent in New York conferring with lawyers and attending a Broadway show, James Hood and Vivian Malone returned to Alabama, where the newspapers were already reporting the newly emerging details of their arrival. One of the latest details unveiled was their on-campus accommodations, the *Tuscaloosa News* reporting that Malone would be housed in Mary Burke Hall (within sight of Foster Auditorium), while Hood would be across campus in Palmer Hall. The paper also noted where the students would take their meals—assuring that the tactic of denying board (as had been the case with Lucy) would not be repeated.

In an effort to stifle the hullabaloo already set for Tuesday, students were encouraged to register on Monday. Yet that summer the student's registration required a bit more paperwork than usual, including a "no-violence pledge" that students were required to sign, along with an acknowledgment that they would not bring weapons to campus. While students understood the need for a no-weapons policy, there was more than a little grumbling related to a newly enforced curfew that demanded students stay in their dorms from 10:00 P.M. until dawn. Similarly, students were perturbed that they could no longer park their cars on campus.

Nevertheless, as students began registering for classes, the newspapers reported an "air of calmness" pervading throughout campus. The previous weekend had proved equally quiet, so much so that one experienced police officer informed reporters that Saturday had been "one of the quietest days he has seen since he joined the force."

Despite the many distractions, Alabama students somehow managed to overlook the trailers and trucks utilized as a makeshift headquarters. Similarly, just a few miles to the east, the grounds of Castle Hill Elementary School had been converted to a landing strip for the army's helicopters, yet even the sounds of overhead choppers seemed hardly to distract the students. While the university attempted to maintain a sense of normalcy, Governor Wallace's presence was making the task quite difficult.

Despite various pleas to the contrary, Wallace arrived in Tuscaloosa on Monday afternoon, beginning his show at the Hotel Stafford where, upon spotting the hoard of newspapermen, he jokingly quipped, "Let's not have any mob violence here." The *Tuscaloosa News* reported that the governor then turned serious, informing reporters that "if they had come here expecting to see mob violence or rioting, they were going home disappointed."

For the governor, much of Monday evening was spent shaking hands and touring the university campus, as well as spending time with National Guardsmen at the nearby armory. Meanwhile, not far away, Deputy Attorney General Katzenbach concluded his own final preparations. Jefferson Bennett recalled Katzenbach's last-minute concern that due to the strictly enforced barriers surrounding campus, the deputy attorney general himself might be barred entrance unless he, too, retained the necessary school identification.

"So, we issued him a faculty card," Bennett explained.

The administrative vice president went on to describe a serendipitous run-in with Katzenbach decades later, in which he asked him if he still had his University of Alabama faculty card. "And you know, he did," Bennett reported incredulously. "He had it put in plastic and still carries it."

Yet prior to being memorialized, the memento would first be put to good use, Katzenbach sticking the card in his wallet in the off chance the guards demanded ID. It seemed an unnecessary precaution, though Katzenbach, the Kennedys, and university administrators had planned for far too long to hit a snag on a technicality.

Meanwhile, the *Crimson White* editor, Hank Black, was hitting his own snags, and in the days leading up to the stand, struggled to pen an editorial that would strike the proper tone and resonate with students.

Initially, he argued that University of Alabama students were "intelligent enough to realize that demonstrations and other overt actions will seriously endanger their educational opportunities," though he later shifted his tact, arguing on "moral grounds" instead, that since the courts had made their ruling, "we must obey."

"I had an enormous amount of angst and conflict about how to write what had to be written," Black later admitted. "But I felt like I had to write something as an editor. I ended up writing what I did. Kind of a mishmash, and not saying too much of anything, really." Nevertheless, his mishmash succeeded by not further inflaming the community's emotions—a victory on its own.

Three years earlier, Black had entered the university as a self-described Buckley/Goldwater conservative, though after associating with Mel Meyer, Bob Penny, and other liberal-leaning newspaper types, he began a gradual shift to a more progressive view. His desegregation editorial, he later explained, "represented where I was in that swing."

As he grappled with his own political leanings, Black introduced a new and surprising voice into the debate: the late William Faulkner. In the weeks prior to completing the special issue of the paper, Black acquired a never-before-published letter written by Faulkner, in which the Pulitzer Prize–winning southern author responded to a student's questions on integration. The letter was previously in the possession of Dr. O. B. Emerson, who encouraged Black to make good use of it. While Faulkner's letter was originally written in 1956—in response to the Autherine Lucy riots—Black brought the letter to light for the first time just days before the university's second attempt at desegregation.

"Segregation is going, whether we like it or not," Faulkner reasoned. "We no longer have any choice between segregation or unsegregation. The only choice we have is, how, by what means."

After acknowledging that a "confederation of older men like me would not carry more weight than a sane, sober union of students," he called upon southern students to do just that—band together to ensure peace. It was a message that, while made public nearly a year after the author's death, was an important reminder to the University of Alabama students in the dawn of their new era.

At around 10:30 P.M. on Monday, June 10—on the eve of Wallace's stand—Katzenbach led one final meeting at the Hotel Stafford, the same hotel where Wallace and dozens of reporters happened to be staying as well. With Wallace and his entourage within shouting distance, Katzenbach discussed logistics with several of his closest men, including General Creighton Abrams, as well as the University of Alabama's administrative vice president, Jefferson Bennett, who served as a primary liaison between the university and the attorney general's office. The men did what they could to confirm final preparations, though many wild cards remained. While Katzenbach, Attorney General Robert Kennedy, and President Kennedy seemed to have a clear understanding of how Wallace's stand would begin, as well as how it would likely end, the primary question was how both sides would respond during the in-between. Many of the federal government's actions remained dependent on Wallace, making it difficult for Katzenbach to plan accordingly.

According to the surviving shorthand notes from the meeting, the men appeared to have discussed a range of issues, including one insightful note on local law enforcement's trustworthiness: a single scrawl indicating that Bennett assured the others that "Mirabel, plc chief, good man." The note offered a vote of support to Tuscaloosa's police chief, William Marable, who in Bennett's estimation was a "good man," and a man the federal government could trust to do his part to preserve the peace, reassuring Katzenbach that he had an important ally on the local level. Marable's reputation as a trusted peacekeeper would serve him well, not only that summer but also the one following— when civil rights demonstrators would put him to the test.

CHAPTER 11

A Stand for Segregation

June 11, 1963

You're going to have to play it a little by ear.

On Tuesday, June 11, James Hood and Vivian Malone woke early, though the federal officials woke earlier still. By 5:30 A.M. Attorney General Robert Kennedy's Tuscaloosa team—led by Deputy Attorney General Nicholas Katzenbach—was already awake and awaiting orders. The first radio transmission between Nicholas Katzenbach and Burke Marshall in the attorney general's office occurred at 7:22 A.M., a conversation in which the federal government's plan began to fully take shape.

After several minutes of squawking radio transmissions, Katzenbach and Assistant Attorney General Burke Marshall managed to sketch out their plan— Katzenbach was to approach the governor and ask him what he intended to do. If Wallace turned him away, Katzenbach would simply escort the students to their dorms, thereby ensuring no direct interaction between the governor and the students and clearing Wallace of the possibility of a contempt charge. From that point, they could revise their strategy.

By 7:35 A.M. Attorney General Robert Kennedy OK'd the plan, though added an addendum ten minutes later. In an effort to stave off the "outsiders" stigma, if the National Guardsmen were to be called, let them be from Tuscaloosa or the surrounding area—a recommendation originally offered by Jefferson Bennett and Frank Rose that was well received by Katzenbach.

While Hood and Malone prepared for their hour-long drive from Birmingham to Tuscaloosa, eight hundred miles to the northeast, Attorney General Robert Kennedy continued to rethink the tentative plan. Since any action on the federal government's part would likely be predicated on Wallace's first move, Kennedy thought it best to keep a constant watch on the situation as the drama unfolded, calling the audibles as they became necessary. Meanwhile, President Kennedy, equally invested in the outcome, had cleared his afternoon appointments to see whether or not Alabama's stubborn governor would "heed his stern advice to stay away from the Tuscaloosa campus."

As the hour approached, Attorney General Kennedy and Katzenbach exchanged a series of calls, attempting to hash out their plan. The men's primary concern was how—and when—the Alabama National Guard would be federalized. Having witnessed firsthand the battleground that had occurred months prior on the Ole Miss campus, Katzenbach was leery of any strategy involving federal troops. His suggestion was simply to bypass the governor by walking the students through another door, or better still, avoid the confrontation altogether by enrolling the students privately and sending them off to class. His reasoning was simple: "The governor cannot block all those classes." Yet Katzenbach soon offered the rebuttal to his own argument, admitting that by "making a fool of the governor," they might unintentionally box Wallace even deeper into his corner.

Katzenbach's concern for his costar was unexpected, yet practical. The deputy attorney general was well aware that they were dealing with a political favorite on his home turf, and that the least favorable outcome of all involved provoking Wallace in such a way that he lashed out unexpectedly. Katzenbach and Boone seemed wise to the same strategy: the story was best when controlled.

Yet Katzenbach, too, was capable of being provoked, and the bald-headed former prisoner of war feared the press coverage that would soon relay his semiscripted performance to the world. While he repeatedly stressed that the desegregation of the university by Vivian Malone and James Hood was not a "show," Katzenbach appeared deeply concerned with how his performance might be received. As he debated with the attorney general's office as to where

Hood and Malone might go between the morning and afternoon attempts at enrollment, Katzenbach argued for the students to remain on campus in order to make it "perfectly obvious to all of those newspaper people that they're going to their rooms."

Meanwhile, at Foster Auditorium, the stage was set, university workers having already put the finishing touches on the podium to be placed directly in front of the main entrance. Students eager for a front-row seat to the action arrived at Foster early Tuesday morning, registering and wandering leisurely within the auditorium, awaiting the governor.

In the minutes prior to Wallace's arrival, a PA squawked overhead, informing all students—whether they had completed their registration or not—that they had to leave the premises immediately. Begrudgingly, the students did as they were told, leaving only a few necessary registrars, troopers, and a rare reporter to fill the cavernous space.

Bob Penny, a graduate student at the time, happened to be one of those registrars, earning himself a clear shot of the action. "I was in the auditorium on the ground, and you know, word spread very quickly [of Wallace's arrival]."

Penny remembered the tension permeating throughout the auditorium, a pressure relieved only when a nasally voiced English professor jokingly remarked, "I wish little George would hurry up and make his little speech."

As Penny and the professor awaited their chance to glance at the governor, on the opposite side of University Boulevard, student leaders began positioning themselves equidistant to one another parallel to the street, providing an additional layer of support. SGA treasurer Don Siegal was one of those students. His behind-the-scenes work preparing the student body for the transition gave him confidence that the day's events would proceed without incident, yet he understood that peace was no guarantee.

"It was time," Siegal recalled. "And things were going to happen."

Siegal went on to describe assigning student leaders the task of keeping an eye on the situation from afar, a long line of dependable student allies stretching the length of the quad. "I remember my station was right by Denny Chimes," Siegal began, "and sure enough, here comes George Wallace riding down the street in his convertible. Standing up, waving to the crowd. And there were the students waiting to see if there was an eruption of anger, but instead all there was was laughter. So I knew they viewed Wallace more as a comic figure than a danger, so that was good."

In a last-ditch effort to change Wallace's mind, President Kennedy wired the governor, asking him to consider "the consequences to your state and its fine university if you persist in setting an example of defiant conduct."

Undeterred, Wallace replied that his presence "guarantee[d] peace."

"This is the opinion of all here familiar with the facts," Wallace explained, "including the legislature of Alabama and the president of the University of Alabama." Yet President Rose's lukewarm support the previous Sunday was hardly the vote of confidence Wallace claimed it to be. Rose wanted peaceful desegregation more than most, and in fact, throughout the morning's proceedings would offer President Kennedy the play-by-play of Wallace's defiance while perched in Coach Bear Bryant's office. While Bryant himself was conveniently sequestered on a recruiting trip, he had kept close tabs on the proceedings. Bryant understood that it was only a matter of time before desegregation would have its effect on the football field as well, and he wanted to be ready to capitalize on the new crop of untapped athletes. A secondary reason for Bryant's attention to desegregation was his desire to watch the young attorney general in action. Bryant had come to admire the reckless abandon employed by Robert F. Kennedy in his tackling of organized crime, so much so that when Bryant had the opportunity to meet Kennedy the February prior to desegregation he left convinced that the president's brother was "one of the most impressive men I have ever met." Yet on June 11, Bryant—cloistered in a restaurant in Chicago—was a long way from witnessing the history taking place just beyond his office door.

CBS journalist Nelson Benton was much closer and would long remember the day's uncharacteristic nature. "It was so hot in Tuscaloosa, Alabama, on that June day in 1963," he began. "So hot that the sun burned your skin right through your shirt. It was not a typical day on the University of Alabama campus—no between class rush, no softball games on the quadrangle."

Instead, the pristine greens of academia were infiltrated by a media circus, and by 9:50 A.M. Benton was joined by dozens of cameramen jockeying for the perfect shot to capture the arrival of the stalwart governor. After exiting the car minutes later, Wallace spoke briefly to his audience as he awaited the arrival of Hood and Malone. Moments later, he entered Foster Auditorium and began working the inside crowds as well, exuding a degree of self-assurance only to be mustered by a seasoned politician.

"Martin Luther King likes to fight these things out in the street," he told the students. "But we're going to right it in the courts. We're going to have peace here."

Wallace prepared himself for the inevitable, straightening his suit coat and awaiting the processional of federal cars. The crowd watched on in near silence as the sun pressed down on them.

It was opening night, and it was only Tuesday morning.

While Wallace and Katzenbach prepared to face off in the blazing morning sun, Secretary of the Army Cyrus Vance, along with General Earl G. Wheeler and a cadre of officers, assessed the situation in Tuscaloosa from a far different vantage point—the War Room deep in the bowels of the Pentagon.

While most believed the governor's intention to keep the peace, there was no telling if Wallace himself was a strong enough figure to keep the segregationists away. This lack of certainty kept everyone on edge, from military brass to President Kennedy himself. As the White House had already learned from their interactions with Khrushchev, when dealing with wild cards, it was only a matter of time before someone was dealt a joker.

Robert Kennedy, too, had taken steps to stay abreast of the situation, transforming his office into a personal war room, complete with various maps of Tuscaloosa. Also at his disposal was a wide range of communications equipment, the full force of the federal government, a brother in the Oval Office, and hundreds of riot-trained federal troops awaiting their call. Yet little could prepare him for a smooth-talking governor at the height of his power.

In one of the final phone conversations prior to Wallace's stand, as Kennedy and Katzenbach struggled to come to consensus on the details of their plan, the attorney general glanced up to spot his three-year-old daughter, Kerry, stumbling across his office.

"Want to say hello to Kerry?" Kennedy asked, sidetracking the conversation.

"Yeah!" Katzenbach exclaimed.

Placing the discussion on hold, Kennedy handed the phone over to his young daughter who set to work dramatically lightening the mood.

"Hi, Nick."

"Hi, Kerry. How are you, dear?" he asked, his serious exterior melting away and revealing a far softer man beneath.

"What are you doing?" she asked. "Are you at our house?"

"What?"

"Are you at our house?"

"No, I'm not out at your house. I'm way down here in the Southland, way down South. And do you know what the temperature is down here?" he asked playfully. "The temperature down here is 98 degrees. You tell your father that. Tell him we're all going to get hardship pay."

The little girl struggled to repeat the phrase "hardship pay," though the message got through, causing Kennedy to release a slight chuckle before retrieving the phone.

The lighthearted moment soon passed, though history would long remember it—proof of humanity in a tumultuous moment.

"You're going to have to play it a little by ear," Kennedy informed Katzenbach, to which the deputy agreed.

Before hanging up, Kennedy added, "Good luck, you'll do well"—a wager neither man could afford to lose.

It remains unclear at what point—if ever—Wallace began going off script. When Katzenbach first approached the governor at around 10:50 A.M. that Tuesday morning, he began by reading a proclamation on behalf of the attorney general, at which point Wallace interrupted, "We don't need your speech." The governor's brusque chiding stopped Katzenbach long enough for Wallace to launch into his own, informing Katzenbach and the country of the federal government's "unwelcomed, unwanted, unwarranted and force-induced intrusion upon the campus of the University of Alabama."

Wallace reminded both Katzenbach and his audience that the government was created to serve the people, and while Alabama citizens were "God-fearing people," they were not "government-fearing people."

Further, he defended his action by claiming his stand "for the purpose of raising basic and fundamental constitutional questions."

This state versus federal government theme continued throughout the remainder of his speech. Not once did Wallace bother mentioning that his stand against the federal government also prevented two highly qualified African American applicants from entering a public university. His silence on this particular matter seemed to imply that he believed Hood and Malone to be little more than collateral damage in a battle that did not concern them. This was not the case, though Wallace understood that one man's steadfast opposition to the federal government played far better to the country than the reality—that he was refusing a much-deserved education to black students.

In one exchange Katzenbach reminded Wallace that their standoff was "not a show," though as the words left his mouth, his eyes glanced anxiously at the rolling cameras as if to prove otherwise. A moment of silence passed between them, and as it was made clear to Katzenbach that Wallace had no intention of standing down, Hood and Malone were escorted to their respective dorms while Wallace sealed himself inside Foster Auditorium to enjoy a ketchup-covered lunch of steak and onion rings.

Newly elected *Crimson White* editor Hank Black viewed the stalemate from a second-floor window of Foster Auditorium. "I couldn't actually see George," Black explained, noting the angle, "but I could see Katzenbach."

Desperate to keep his cool in the heat, Katzenbach was turned away, and the proceedings continued as planned. By 10:58 A.M., Vivian Malone exited the car and made the short walk to Mary Burke Hall, while moments later, James Hood was driven to Palmer Hall on the far side of campus.

By 11:10 A.M. Attorney General Robert Kennedy informed Katzenbach that unless he objected, the president was prepared to sign the proclamation to federalize the National Guard. Katzenbach welcomed the support.

While the morning interaction proved anticlimactic, it was a far better outcome than the alternative—one in which bullets and tear gas obscured the university landscape, as had been the case at Ole Miss eight months earlier.

While afternoon temperatures peaked at a sweltering 95 degrees, for Katzenbach, it likely felt much hotter. Sweat poured from his forehead as the giant man towered over the stout, five foot seven governor. All the players took the stage for the second act, though the afternoon's behind-the-scenes negotiations would prove equally interesting to the performance itself.

At 1:40 P.M., General Henry Graham's helicopter touched down in Tuscaloosa, at which point he was hustled to the Army Reserve Center to negotiate with a fellow military man, General Taylor Hardin, one of Wallace's closest advisors. Within half an hour, the two men fashioned a deal that neither the Kennedys nor Wallace had been capable of striking themselves, Graham negotiating on behalf of the federal government and sending word to Katzenbach for approval.

By 2:29 P.M., the plan had been approved: Wallace would step aside only after he was given the platform once more to make a brief statement. It wasn't ideal, but it was a far better alternative than having to remove the governor by force. A scribble on the radio log noted that both generals were "aghast" at the possibility of having to physically remove the governor, a prospect that hurried both men to the negotiating table. The log also noted that the federal government's patience would extend only forty-five seconds "for a stunt," before Wallace would need to wrap it up.

Six minutes later, Katzenbach relayed the message to the attorney general, agreeing not to remove Wallace or his podium and instead would give the governor the opportunity for a "*brief* stunt" at which point Wallace would leave by the preferred method—on his own two feet. Robert Kennedy agreed. If the governor was willing to step aside, the federal government was willing to allow him to do so gracefully. Although as time would soon tell, there hardly seemed to be any grace to Wallace's removal. Historian Dan T. Carter described the governor as a "particularly disgraceful alley cat prancing back and forth in front of a firmly chained pit bull."

What might have happened had the "pit bull" come untethered or, equally problematic, if the "alley cat" refused to back down?

"It was easy enough to stand in the schoolhouse door, but what next?" asked writer Robert Sherrill. "Wallace had been a champion Golden Gloves boxer as a boy. Should he draw on that training and sock Deputy Attorney General Katzenbach, or whoever sought to get past him? Should he grab hold of the doorjamb and hang on? Should he resist until federal troops or U.S. marshals carried him away, and should he then scream and kick?"

Wallace knew he had an image to uphold, and when asked years later why the former boxer hadn't punched Katzenbach that day (though he had privately threatened to do so), he shrugged it off, replying simply that he hadn't "hit anyone for years."

At the conclusion of the morning confrontation, Katzenbach confided a clear truth to Wallace: "From the outset, Governor, all of us have known that the final chapter of this history will be the admission of these students."

Yet Wallace refused to agree, staying in character a while longer. At 3:30 P.M. General Graham—buoyed by the support of the 31st Dixie Division of the Alabama National Guard—informed Governor Wallace that it was his "sad duty" to ask him to step aside. Hearing his cue, Wallace began his brief statement, assuring the crowd (and more importantly, the news cameras) that "Alabama is winning this fight against Federal interference," and that he would return to the state capital to continue his battle from there. After an intense moment, Wallace stepped aside, and according to the radio log, at 3:33 P.M. Katzenbach announced to the attorney general that the governor had fulfilled his part of the promise and the students had entered the building.

Despite the previous weeks' Klan rallies and the more recent calls for federal troops, the drama ended quite anticlimactically.

Wallace avoided the contempt charge by stepping aside as Malone and Hood marched their way one after the other toward Foster Auditorium. One reporter noted that Malone "drew a wolf whistle" as she started toward the doorway, though she and Hood's entrance proceeded otherwise without incident. Malone dropped no book—an interpretation made famous in *Forrest Gump*—nor did any well-meaning "box of chocolate" quoting white student retrieve it for her. Instead, she and Hood simply stepped inside the auditorium's doorway, breaking through an invisible—yet symbolic—barrier.

Only one student in the audience rivaled the star power that came with Hood and Malone. Joe Namath, the Crimson Tide's rising star quarterback, stood just twenty feet away from Wallace throughout the performance. The previous fall *he* had been the center of attention—taking the football team to a dominating 10–1 record—and as a result of the publicity, he fully recognized that the new students likely shared a pressure similar to his, though for far different reasons. While Namath biographer Mark Kriegel noted the quarterback's "distaste for any kind of conflict—personal, social, and especially political," Namath couldn't help but privately admire the students' entrance into the all-white institution.

"It was a thrill to see Vivian walk through the door," Namath later recalled. "We talked sometimes, and you couldn't understand how much pressure she was under at the time."

Malone, too, appreciated being acknowledged by such a revered university figure and returned the favor by showing support for the all-white football team.

"He was so different," Malone later said of Namath. "I really did admire him."

The two were destined to meet—Namath's girlfriend regularly lunched with Malone—though for the moment, the quarterback and the African American students remained strangers.

As the crowd began to disperse and the governor was hurried away, Hood and Malone entered the cavernous room, listening only to the echoing silence that surrounded them. The auditorium was all but empty, aside from a few hand-selected journalists and the necessary personnel. The pair walked slowly toward the registration table, awaiting the final procedural hurdle that would officially enroll them at the school.

Hank Black followed close behind, and while the young reporter had been given strict instructions not to speak to the students, he recalled catching Malone's eye. Black, Malone, and Hood had met in the weeks prior to registration and for the young coed, a kind face in an unfamiliar crowd likely proved a comfort. Yet Hank Black wasn't alone in his kindness.

"Hi, there," one of the registrars smiled as the students approached. "We've been waiting for you."

A few miles away, Reverend T. W. Linton—who had played an active role in protecting Autherine Lucy at Howard and Linton's Barbershop just seven years prior—held careful watch from behind his barber chair.

"We were sitting here watching it on the news," Linton recalled, going on to describe a jam-packed barbershop filled with patrons and community members, all their eyes fixed on the screen. When the news cameras caught a glimpse of a stoic Vivian Malone walking swiftly through the door, the barbershop erupted in cheers. It was a far different outcome than had occurred seven years prior, and Linton was proud that this time, the barbershop was no longer needed to wash egg from anyone's hair.

While Wallace's stand in the schoolhouse door has long been described as a stage show, a carefully scripted stunt, after studying the minute-by-minute radio transmissions between Katzenbach and the attorney general's office, this interpretation seems only partially accurate. While Ted Sorensen, President Kennedy's special counsel and advisor, confirmed that there had been some "advance agreement," he conceded that the Kennedy administration remained "uncertain whether Wallace would in fact step aside as agreed." Meanwhile, on the Wallace side, the governor's future press secretary, Bill Jones, countered that there was "no prior agreement," though both sides knew better than to respond with violence.

"It worked out pretty well," Jones added. "[The Kennedys] knew what we were doing—which was making a national figure out of Wallace."

Undoubtedly, Wallace and his handlers had some plan in mind, and while the federal government was complicit in providing him a platform, as President Kennedy had indicated to Katzenbach, they themselves would "play it a little by ear." Wallace, too, seemed to be taking a wait-and-see approach, prompting historian Stephan Lesher to deem the stand "an uncertain parlay at best."

For Wallace and the federal government, it was less of a stage show than an improvised theater, one in which Katzenbach played lead actor in Robert Kennedy's troupe. The world waited anxiously to see who would move first and how. Yet by late afternoon Wallace put an end to the drama, removing himself and solidifying his place in history as the man who took a stand—not the man who caused a crisis.

CHAPTER 12

New Students, New Strategy

June 11–July 1963

Whenever you go to a new place you expect to be lonesome at first.

Motivated by the success in Tuscaloosa, President Kennedy informed his aides that he planned to address the nation that very night, interrupting regularly scheduled programs to outline his proposal for civil rights legislation. While the possibility of a televised speech had floated throughout the Oval Office in the weeks prior to the stand, much of Kennedy's inner circle opposed it, believing a civil rights speech should come as a result of legislation rather than a call for it. Yet Kennedy's conviction was buoyed by Hood and Malone's registration, and his insistence that he address the nation that night sent speechwriters and advisors scurrying to hash out the wording.

Ted Sorensen and President Kennedy had watched Wallace's stand from the Oval Office, Sorensen recalling that as soon as Wallace abandoned his position the president turned to him and announced, "I think we'd better give that speech tonight."

It was already 4:30 P.M. eastern time (3:30 P.M. in Alabama), and the president's call for an 8:00 P.M. television address left precious little time for Sorensen to draft the speech.

As Sorensen continued pounding out one speech, Robert Kennedy revealed his personal feelings by crafting another. "I hope when you are Attorney General," Kennedy began in a letter to his five-year-old son, Michael, "these kind of things will not go on."

According to James Hood, following the successful desegregation efforts, he received a phone call from President Kennedy, who in the midst of his team hashing out the precise wording, read an excerpt aloud to the student. "He asked if I had any problems with what he was going to say about us or referring to us and I said I didn't," Hood recalled. "And he asked me did I think that people would understand. And I said, 'I don't know,' I had no idea."

While Hood claimed to have received a sneak peek of the speech earlier that afternoon, the timelines don't fully sync up. Kennedy may have called Hood to ask permission to publicly praise the student, though given the speech's last minute edits, it would have been all but impossible for Hood to have received the final version prior to the rest of the country.

Sorensen recalled the strenuous editing process in which he met with Robert Kennedy, Burke Marshall, and the president in the hour prior to the address. The president changed Sorensen's line, "A social revolution is at hand," to read, "A great change is at hand." Likewise, Sorensen's "But the pace is still shamefully slow" was revised to the far less damning "But the pace is very slow."

While seemingly minor changes, they served as proof of President Kennedy's mindfulness of his southern audience. By nixing the phrases "social revolution" and "shamefully slow," he managed to put out the wildfires before sparking them in the first place. Decades later, Sorensen confirmed that his speech was, in fact, "toned down, but its substance remained."

And by nightfall, millions of Americans would hear it.

At 8:00 P.M. eastern time, the country remained glued to their television sets, eagerly awaiting the message President Kennedy had long been reluctant to deliver. He began by reporting the happenings in Tuscaloosa, how the Alabama National Guardsmen had successfully carried out the court order demanding that "two clearly qualified young Alabama residents" be granted admission into the university.

"That they were admitted peacefully on the campus is due in good measure to the conduct of the students of the University of Alabama," Kennedy affirmed, "who met their responsibilities in a constructive way."

After urging citizens to consider their own lives in respect to the race question, he promised that in one week's time, he would ask Congress to "make a commitment it has not fully made in this century to the proposition that race has no place in American life or law."

He began outlining what would soon become the Civil Rights Act of 1964—sweeping social legislation that would forever alter the country's moral compass and promise a new way of life. As expected, the speech garnered a mixed response in Congress. While Senate Republican leader Everett M. Dirksen of Illinois optimistically acknowledged the likelihood of civil rights legislation and pledged his support, Democratic senator Allen J. Ellender of Louisiana predicted a far more ominous result: "If the President tries to enforce his legislative proposals I think it will mean violence."

As Kennedy concluded his speech, he was unaware that another voice would soon rush to his defense. So moved by Kennedy's words (as he had been by Boone's editorial seven years prior), Dr. Martin Luther King Jr. began drafting his own response, a personal letter to the president calling the speech "one of the most eloquent, profound and unequivocal pleas for justice and freedom of all men ever made by any president."

Despite President Kennedy's recent praise on the issue of civil rights, both John and Robert Kennedy had long been faulted for their slow speed in prompting the issue. According to David Halberstam, the Kennedy brothers had but a "nominal interest" on the subject of civil rights, and JFK biographer Robert Dallek criticized the president further, calling him a "cautious leader" in his civil rights dealings. "It took crises in Mississippi and particularly in Alabama to persuade him to put a landmark civil rights bill before Congress in June 1963," Dallek argued.

Nevertheless, Robert Kennedy remained particularly committed to successful desegregation at the University of Alabama, due in part to a personal connection he shared with the school's president.

University of Alabama President Frank Rose and Attorney General Robert Kennedy had met long before beginning preparations for the university's desegregation. As administrative vice president Jefferson Bennett explained, "they were two of the Ten Outstanding Young Men in the same year."

In January of 1955, Transylvania College's president, Dr. Frank Rose, as well as the assistant counsel of the US Senate Subcommittee on Investigations, Robert Kennedy, shared a meal alongside the other honorees, including a test pilot, a tennis player, and a football coach. The United States Junior Chamber of Commerce felt it important to honor such promising young men, and as Bennett pointed out, the elite club was "sort of like a little fraternity."

When the old friends reunited to hash out a plan allowing for the successful desegregation of the university, they had long before earned each other's trust. Further, Robert Kennedy's familial ties to the president offered clear access to the Oval Office, providing power to their punch. Taken together, the University of Alabama found itself in the unique position of proving to the state and the South that desegregation—if handled properly—could occur in a peaceful manner. Yet as history soon revealed, this peacefulness would not come without the meticulous planning between university administrators, the attorney general, and the president of the United States.

"Dr. Rose and I arranged for a series of meetings with the Attorney General and the President," Jefferson Bennett explained. "It was an astonishing process. We would fly on separate planes under assumed names. I would usually drive to Montgomery and would register as John Bingham or some such name. Then, I would fly to Atlanta on a Montgomery to Atlanta ticket, and, there, buy a ticket from Atlanta to Washington as Jack Waters or some other alias."

Upon arriving in the nation's capital the pair registered at the Mayflower Hotel (under aliases once more) and proceeded to take various precautionary measures to ensure that they were never seen together in public. Bennett believed these clandestine precautions to be wholly necessary, adding, "At that time, the cry in the deep south was that somebody was in a conspiracy against the people of Alabama, plotting against the white folks." While Rose and Bennett never viewed their actions as "plotting against the white folks," they were undoubtedly taking great strides to ensure that Vivian Malone and James Hood could enroll without the threat of violence.

"We went through a series of sessions to impress on the President and the Attorney General that George Wallace was going to carry out his campaign promise. He would stand in the schoolhouse door," Bennett explained. "We had to find some way to accommodate [Wallace] while accomplishing our mission, which was to get these kids safely enrolled at The University of Alabama."

While Rose's connection to Attorney General Robert Kennedy (and by extension, the president) proved helpful in the planning phase, equally valuable was Bennett's own personal connection with Wallace. Jefferson Bennett first met the future governor while on a shared train ride from Montgomery to Tuscaloosa in the fall of their freshman year. The pair of soon-to-be students was entering their first year at the university when a young Wallace approached Bennett and asked if he had a room yet.

"No, I don't have a room," Bennett admitted to the stranger.

"Stay with me," offered Wallace. "I know the finest rooming house near the University, right behind the campus and a nice place."

"The next thing I know, George was running for President of the Freshman Class of the Commerce School and I was campaigning for him," Bennett remarked, adding, "that's the last time I voted for George Wallace."

Despite their political disagreements, Bennett believed that Wallace had proven himself a trustworthy leader, at least in regard to his personal dealings with his former housemate.

"We often opposed each other," Bennett explained, "but we understood each other and respected each other's word or promise."

The pair's history led Bennett to believe that the governor would undoubtedly stay true to his word to physically block Hood and Malone's admission. It also encouraged Bennett to recommend to President John Kennedy and Attorney General Robert Kennedy that the Alabama National Guard (consisting of local Alabamians as well as university students) would prove the most effective force to combat Wallace. In his opinion, the governor would respond far better when faced with his own men. Likewise, it would send a clear message that Alabamians were committed to enforcing the law.

Uncertain of the allegiance of the Alabama National Guard, President Kennedy asked Rose and Bennett point-blank: "Do you really think we can trust them?"

"We know them," Rose and Bennett replied.

Their answer was good enough for the president, and ultimately, the right choice for Alabama.

❄

The morning following the stand, three men began cleaning the debris outside of Foster Auditorium. The front of the auditorium "looked like a football stadium after a homecoming game," described one report, indicating that cups and film rolls and newspapers "which had been fashioned into hats to keep off the blazing sun" were now littered about the plaza. A work truck supported the cleaning efforts, a new type of army infiltrating the campus to clean up streets that resembled a "ticker-tape parade."

The platform and loudspeakers assembled for the news media were carted away, leaving behind only one piece of symbolic memorabilia: "And standing in the doorway this morning, as if it were purposefully left there as a reminder of the proceedings only hours before," reported one newspaper, "was the speaker's stand from which Gov. George Wallace read his proclamation."

Within hours, the campus returned to its former pristine state. The efficiency of the cleanup was remarkable, seeming to serve as further proof that the city hoped to quickly forget what the country would long remember.

The first day of classes began early for both students. While a federal marshal's car awaited Malone just outside of Mary Burke Hall that Wednesday morning, Malone chose instead to walk across campus with a pair of newly befriended white coeds, chatting casually as they started their stroll to class. However, for Malone, the excitement of the first day of classes was soon tarnished by news that Mississippi's NAACP field secretary Medgar Evers—one of the men credited for supporting James Meredith in his desegregation attempt at the University of Mississippi—had been assassinated the previous night.

"I walked the campus, but I was actually flanked by two students there—two young women, because I was a little confused about where I was going and partially because I was a little bit upset by what had happened with Medgar Evers," Malone recounted decades later. She struggled to maintain her composure, though the coeds provided support and acceptance on the morning Malone was at her most vulnerable. "They are probably my angels here," Malone remembered thinking. She never saw them again.

Meanwhile, across campus, an ebullient James Hood stepped out of Palmer Hall on his way to the music and speech building. He walked swiftly in what he believed to be the direction of Comer Hall while the marshals attempted to remain inconspicuous while trailing half a block behind. Unsure of the direction of his class, Hood gambled, turning toward the Gorgas House, until a man standing in front of Comer—who apparently had some knowledge of Hood's intended destination—shouted a helpful, "Hey, Hood, over this way." Snapping his fingers, Hood redirected himself and hurried toward the right building.

While the weather report for Wednesday, June 12, called for "Little or no change" from the previous day, the forecast could not have been more diametrically opposed to the campus's emotional climate. A great change *had* occurred in the past twenty-four hours, and while white students gathered their books and started to class as they'd done since the school's founding in 1831, this time, for the first time, two African American students joined them.

As Hood prepared to enter his first class, a male student called out to him: "Hood, they got one in Jackson last night."

At the time, Hood remained wholly unaware of the Evers assassination. He later blamed his ignorance on the lack of televisions inside Palmer Hall, noting, "they didn't want us to see what was going on outside or the students to be impacted by what the national framework was." While it's unclear whom precisely the "they" were, these efforts to lessen the media's influence on Hood's dorm mates served as an added safeguard to ensure that his fellow students could draw their own conclusions on the new student. "They had to treat me like they wanted to treat me in that building without the benefit of knowing what the outside world was doing," Hood later explained.

But the world soon learned of Evers's death thanks to CBS correspondent Dan Rather, who had left Tuscaloosa the previous night and flew directly to Jackson. Within hours, Rather's words had echoed back to Tuscaloosa, reaching the ears of the young male student who called out to Hood during the new student's first walk to class.

Puzzled by the ominous call, Hood stepped into Professor Harold Nelson's Introduction to Sociology class soon to find himself in the middle of another peculiar scene. As the newspaper reported, not long after his entrance, a coed "suffered a muscle spasm, causing her some pain, and fainted."

The class was dismissed, and an ambulance was called to transport the student to the University Infirmary where, after a careful inspection, Dr. James McLester announced that he did not feel "the spasm was related to the Negro man's being present."

❀

Just twenty years old at the time of enrollment, James Hood, the son of a rubber worker, was the oldest of six—the eldest sibling of three sisters and a pair of brothers. By all accounts, the brown-eyed, 160-pound former high school halfback was articulate and good-humored. A psychology major, he also had a strong interest in preaching and was said to have preached his first sermon at thirteen, at which point he "continued to work his way through every African-American church in Gadsden [Alabama]." Having served as class president (as well as captain to both his high school basketball and track teams), Hood possessed the perfect combination of social, intellectual, athletic, and leadership skills necessary to convince an all-white university of the merits of desegregation. Likewise, he had a love for football, as well as a great respect for the team's beloved coach, Paul "Bear" Bryant. In a 2002 interview, Hood admitted, "one of the things that I also had in the back of my mind when I selected The University of Alabama, was, I wanted to play on the football team. That was my passion."

Among his favorite books Hood listed John Howard Griffin's groundbreaking *Black Like Me*—in which a white author underwent a skin-darkening procedure to better report on race issues—as well as Ernest Hemingway's war epic *For Whom the Bell Tolls*. He noted an admiration for James Baldwin "as a craftsman," though he did not believe "the writer speaks for Negroes generally."

While Hood dreamed of becoming a clinical psychologist, he also had aspirations for becoming a writer, noting, "I want to write a book someday about Negro life—my life, for example."

Hood's intellect was matched by his wit—though not all appreciated the jokester's quick tongue. In one instance, when reporters inquired if his family had any pets, Hood—not long removed from hearing the reports of the Kelly Ingram Park riots—jokingly replied, "We have a police dog, imported from Birmingham."

Vivian Malone, too, was growing in popularity. At five feet six and 124 pounds, her small frame proved contradictory to her large presence. Although described as "shy to the point of inarticulateness," her serious, no-nonsense demeanor was directly at odds with Hood's more jubilant spirit. Born in 1942 in Monroeville, Alabama, Malone was the middle child, a straight A student who—when she wasn't studying—was said to enjoy sewing and dancing. When asked by reporters if she had been studying that first Wednesday night on campus, she replied, "No, some girls came by"—proof of the big-heartedness of at least some of her dorm mates. Throughout her initial weeks at the University of Alabama, Malone appeared well aware of the complications she brought to the campus. When told of the university barricades being lifted, she said, "Yes, and the girls are so glad restrictions are off. They understand about them, but are glad to have curfews off."

Within hours of Hood and Malone's enrollment, the media began questioning students on their initial impressions of the pair. One unnamed student leader described Malone as a "well-dressed girl—composed, reserved and quiet. She says little but you always have the idea she's thinking a great deal she isn't saying." Another student added that Malone appeared "fully cognizant that her stay on the campus will not be a particularly pleasant one, that her stay might well be a lonely one."

Malone seemed to agree with the student's assessment, admitting, "Whenever you go to a new place you expect to be lonesome at first."

Dr. Raymond Fowler, assistant director at the university's psychological clinic, recalled approaching both students and offering his counseling services, though both politely declined. "I was struck by the differences between these two young people," he began, recounting their brief interaction. "Vivian was cool, very controlled, very inwardly oriented it seemed. She was going to go through this, but without a whole lot of emotions. Whatever emotions were there were buried down, and she was a woman on a mission. Jimmy, on the other hand, was a real extrovert. A fun loving kid and real enthusiastic. As I heard later, [Malone] pretty much just kept to herself in the dormitories. The girls were not hostile to her, but she didn't socialize. She sort of stayed pretty much on her own.

"[When Hood] came into the dormitory," he continued, "they were expecting this wild man who was trying to break down the established order and they found him to be just kind of a fun kid. Pretty soon he was hosting poker games in his room and becoming very popular. I joked with him that he would probably be elected student body president next time I talked to him."

But Hood's sights were set on an office much higher than could be obtained at the university. In the hours leading up to the stand, he jokingly told Malone that if asked what he wanted to do most in the world, he'd reply, "Become the governor of the state of Alabama."

❀

In a letter dated just four days after the stand, Hood and Malone's attorney, Arthur Shores, informed Jack Greenberg of the NAACP's Legal Defense and Educational Fund that the students appeared mostly content in their new surroundings, and better yet, accepted by their peers.

Yet Hood and Malone's initial assessment wouldn't last for long.

Anticipating the possibility of the new students' feeling alienated by their white counterparts, Dean Blackburn urged Student Government Association president Donald Stewart to move into Palmer Hall—the dormitory in which Hood was assigned. Stewart was asked to provide social support while simultaneously serving as the eyes and ears for the administration. Stewart agreed, spending several weeks sharing a dormitory with Hood and taking it upon himself to assist the new student during his transition. A female student was asked to fulfill a similar role for Malone.

After receiving word that Hood had been eating alone in the dining hall, Stewart made a public show of joining him. "I went over and sat down," Stewart explained matter-of-factly, "and that's what broke the ice, me and him in that setting.

"At that time it made a hell of an impression on him," Stewart continued, "but for me it was just a friendly thing. . . . I knew a lot of the people in there, so it wasn't a big deal for me to walk over and sit down with James. But to James it meant an awful lot. It gave him the feeling—which he commented on later in life that, you know—[that] he thought it was a fairly significant and courageous act. To me, it was not," Stewart concluded modestly. "To me it was something that I did."

Yet Stewart's efforts made a lasting impression on the new student. "My first couple of days [were] kind of isolated," Hood admitted. "The third day in, Donald Stewart, who was the president of the Student Government at the time—SGA, and Hank Black, who was the editor of the *Crimson White,* had made a pac[t] I understand that they were going to break the ice and they were going to come and eat with me."

According to Hood, Stewart and Black arranged the cafeteria tables the night before to ensure that there were no empty tables for Hood to sequester himself. Instead, he would have to choose between Black or Stewart's table.

"What do I do?" Hood wondered, oscillating between the two tables. "I am invited by the White guy to sit at his lunch table and there is no other table. The US Marshals said I had to make a decision. I didn't have time to call Robert Kennedy and find out what do I do in this case. Most of the time that was a possibility. I could always call and find out what I should do. In this case, I sat down [with Stewart] and to me, that was the day the University of Alabama became integrated—on the third day on this campus, which would have been—I think June 13th."

Yet Stewart's seemingly innocuous interactions with Hood had long-reaching ramifications, even for a student as well respected and admired as the SGA president.

In the summer of 1963, Stewart received a phone call from his father informing him that his run-ins with Hood had not gone unnoticed. Apparently, the "fellas" (a phrase Stewart assumes pointed to the Klan) had put his name on a "list." Stewart never figured out what exactly the list was for, though he never had any problems with Klansmen or the like. However, upon receiving word of the "list," Stewart's father urged him to leave the dorm, though he refused.

"I was probably better off there than in my apartment," Stewart laughed, "because if I *was* on the list, at least I had the National Guard."

CHAPTER 13

Old Wounds Healed

October 10, 1996, and September 16, 1998

The legacy of George Wallace is not the schoolhouse door. The legacy of George Wallace is one of God and change.

Vivian Malone and James Hood had not seen the last of George Wallace. In a strange twist of fate, on October 10, 1996, Vivian Malone-Jones was awarded the first Lurleen B. Wallace Award of Courage, an award presented to an Alabama woman who best exemplified the spirit and fortitude of the state's first female governor—who also happened to be George Wallace's departed wife.

Dressed in a tuxedo, George Wallace—now confined to a wheelchair after a failed assassination attempt in 1972—sat near the lavishly dressed Malone-Jones, the woman who, thirty-three years prior, he had attempted to block from entering a school. The dinner served as a strange reunion and was comprised of speeches from an assortment of people, including Fred Gray, an African American civil rights litigator who began by thanking a number of people, including George Wallace.

"I had the distinction of first meeting [Wallace] when he was the second judge, later representing him in the Alabama legislature while he was governor, at which period of time," Gray joked, "I filed a few lawsuits against him."

Next to the podium was Robert F. Kennedy Jr.—bearing a striking resemblance to his father. "I came here tonight specifically because I know my father would've wanted to be here if he were alive," Kennedy began. "Because this is really the closing of a circle that's spanned 35 years, two generations in Alabama history and American history and to me, it has really broad significance."

While Wallace listened attentively, his most deserving critic had yet to take her turn. After several more speeches, the guest of honor, Vivian Malone-Jones, was called to the podium to receive her award, along with a standing ovation.

Dressed in white with her hair cut short, she began by offering a heartfelt thanks to Governor Wallace and his family, as well as her husband, Dr. Mack Jones, who had supported her throughout her ordeal. "It was difficult for me to be [at the University of Alabama], but it was even more difficult for him to come through all of those guards and all of the policemen and all of the things that were going on at that time, to come over and take me out during that period of time," she began. "And especially during a time when I was ostracized by the majority of students on campus."

Malone-Jones painted a more negative impression of her experiences than was originally reported, recalling specifically the struggles of her first day of classes.

"I remembered that the professor made a statement, said, 'Anyone who doesn't want to be in here at this point in time can leave.' About half the class left. These were very trying times."

The audience listened in perfect silence as she continued to recount her tale, at last arriving upon the subject that interested people most—including the governor. "I'm often asked, 'What do you think of the stand George Wallace took?'" she began. "I've always maintained that I felt that it was not right, but the part that is so good, and that has been mentioned by several of our speakers tonight, is that Governor Wallace also recognized that this was not the right thing to do, and extends, tonight, a hand of friendship to say that I was wrong, but let's do better next time. Let's learn from our past mistakes."

She concluded by graciously thanking the Wallace Foundation once more for working with her to establish a scholarship for African American students. "I know how difficult it is these days for young people to go to college," Malone-Jones added.

Yet it had been far more difficult in June of 1963, when Malone dared do it first.

❋

James Hood, too, came to forgive George Wallace.

On September 16, 1998, the recently deceased Wallace lay in repose in the Montgomery State Capitol, his body frail and shriveled from years of confinement to his wheelchair. Approximately twenty-five thousand had come to pay their respects—"nearly as many blacks as whites," one newspaper was sure to note. Yet among these thousands sat one man whose presence perhaps meant more than any other.

Despite their many differences, fifty-six-year-old James Hood had come to pay his respects. He had met Wallace on at least one occasion following the stand in the schoolhouse door, a meeting in which a repentant Wallace reportedly confided to him, "Whom the gods would destroy, they first make mad with power"—less an excuse than an attempt to come to terms with his past discretions.

By 1980, Wallace claimed himself a born-again Christian, paving the way for his racial "rehabilitation" by publicly admitting his wrongs and trying to make up for them.

Speaking before the mourners at First United Methodist Church, Dr. Lester H. Spencer said, "The legacy of George Wallace is not the schoolhouse door. The legacy of George Wallace is one of God and change."

It was a generous prediction, though far too optimistic. Despite decades of public service and a life allegedly redeemed, most Americans had but one image of George Wallace seared into their memories. Nevertheless, on the day of Wallace's funeral, James Hood softened that image, stating, "If any man understands the true meaning of pain and suffering, it is George Wallace."

Hood, too, had known suffering. While Malone graduated from the University of Alabama in June of 1965, Hood wouldn't last beyond the 1963 summer session; this, in part, the result of a controversial opinion article Hood published in the *Crimson White* in which he criticized civil rights demonstrators, urging them to clear the streets and enter the classroom as he had.

"Why doesn't the Negro race wake up and go about this thing in a more intelligent way?" Hood critiqued. "It is my firm belief that through the process of education the sit-ins and swim-ins will be unnecessary. There must be more time spent in the classroom and less time wasted on picket lines."

Hood's "wake up" line—the source of some of the trouble—had been crossed out in the original draft, though was eventually readded prior to printing. Yet equally interesting is what remained omitted. In his published editorial, Hood called his education-as-a-pathway-to-equality theory a "long range" solution, though in his earlier draft he had called it "far-fetched and long-ranged." Did Hood initially believe his theory truly to be "far-fetched" or was it simply a last-minute edit? While it's easy to speculate, the original notes—notes shared between Hood and *Crimson White* editor Hank Black—offered rare insight into Hood's thought process, though they provided few conclusions.

While Hood's editorial acknowledged that he fully understood that his criticism of the movement would likely make him "unpopular with the masses of [his] people," perhaps he felt compelled to write it in an attempt to be better liked by the white students. Hood published the editorial on June 27, just sixteen days after his enrollment, and while during this time students such as Donald Stewart and Hank Black had reached out to him, the majority of students preferred to steer clear—a lack of acceptance with which an extrovert like Hood likely struggled.

On July 1—just days after the publication of Hood's article—attorney Arthur Shores wrote to the young student, informing him of the irreversible damage he'd caused by his editorial. Shores—who had proved integral to the University of Alabama's desegregation attempts beginning with Autherine Lucy—knew the importance of the students' ability to remain tight-lipped on the race issue, though Hood failed to recognize his ever-expanding audience. Shores rightly predicted that Hood's article would only intensify the issue, and he advised the young student to stay silent.

Just two weeks earlier—following their successful registration—Hood had informed the press that he and Malone would offer no further comment and instead would focus their energy on their primary purpose—receiving an education. Yet perhaps the first lesson Hood learned was to listen to his own advice. Rather than burying his head in his books, he soon found himself in the crosshairs of the same civil rights activists he had once inspired. Hood's outspokenness was not only the result of a lack of tact, but perhaps a reflection of his deeply felt isolation.

Decades later, former *Crimson White* reporter Bob Penny remarked, "I've always thought Jimmy Hood wanted basically to be everybody's friend," adding simply, "and that never works."

It certainly hadn't for Hood, who—with little understanding of the reach of his voice—found the backlash from his editorial soon spiraling out of control.

Hood's editorial for the school paper was soon reprinted in newspapers throughout the nation, causing many civil rights demonstrators to reevaluate just what they thought of James Hood. In an effort to return to the civil rights movement's good graces, later that summer Hood found himself attacking university administration at a Gadsden rally—remarks deemed libelous in nature and grounds for expulsion. Perhaps learning from Autherine Lucy's experience, Hood smartly transferred to Wayne State University in Detroit rather than face the consequences that were sure to come. While the young student also cited his personal health and the diminishing health of his father as additional reasons for leaving, the possibility of expulsion likely loomed heaviest of all.

Many remained troubled by Hood's quick exit, particularly given his long-fought battle for admission. According to Jefferson Bennett, after he and Dean Blackburn heard an audio recording of Hood's alleged libelous statements, they returned to Bennett's office, closed the door, and cried—fully acknowledging that there was nothing they could do to spare the student the expulsion sentence that surely awaited him. All of their careful preparations had been squandered, or at least it felt that way.

Hank Black, who originally published the piece, was equally troubled by Hood's departure and for many years shouldered some of the blame.

"I was uncomfortable from time to time," Black admitted, "particularly around Jimmy's leaving the university that summer. If we had not printed [the controversial editorial] or handled it the way we did . . . well, I don't know."

Black believed Hood's statements at the Gadsden rally were likely his attempt "to right the wrong that he had done" by publicly denouncing the movement weeks prior. "I felt bad about it," Black explained, acknowledging that his desire to be involved in a "real story" may have momentarily clouded his editorial judgment. "On the other hand, it was [Hood's] personality, and he did it. But we were kids."

Hood and Black made peace years later, proof of which was found on the inscription Hood made out to him in the front flap of Black's copy of E. Culpepper Clark's book on the subject of the university's desegregation.

"To: Hank," Hood's inscription began. "The friendship and impact you have contributed to my life will be with me forever. May God continue to bless you."

Hood and Malone's enrollment at the University of Alabama had little to do with Tuscaloosa's civil rights movement. While the state and federal government fought the desegregation battle, local figures watched on from a distance.

During Malone's time at the University of Alabama, she steered clear of the local movement, having minimal interaction with the recently formed but little-known Tuscaloosa Citizens for Action Committee. In a 1987 interview, Malone-Jones confirmed that she "did not go out and march or demonstrate or any of that," preferring to concentrate on "staying at the University of Alabama and graduating from the University of Alabama, which was my goal at that point in time."

Yet Malone-Jones believed the local movement and her own education had overlapping goals, even if she and the leaders of Tuscaloosa's black community weren't "working together on a daily basis."

"They were still dealing with lunch counters and all of the other things, accommodations," Malone-Jones continued. "When I went to Tuscaloosa, I couldn't even go to a hotel downtown. That was still a problem there. I still couldn't eat in any place in Tuscaloosa. Those things still had to be taken care of." In her view, they were fighting the war on two separate fronts. While the Tuscaloosa Citizens for Action Committee took their fight to the streets and the courts, Malone waged hers in the classroom.

"I think [black community members] were supportive in any way that I needed them. It's just that my needs were taken care of, so I didn't need to have to go to the black community and ask them, you know, to come in and help me, because basically I had protection of the federal [government] and the city police, and the campus and university police." Malone-Jones added, "They did call, they wrote. They did all the supportive things you could expect anyone to do . . . I don't remember all the names, but there were a sufficient number of people there I could call if I needed them, and many of them came to my graduation."

While Hood and Malone served as beacons of hope for the local civil rights movement, the Tuscaloosa Citizens for Action Committee took no credit for the students' success. Instead, they simply made themselves readily available, fully cognizant that the students had their job to do, and they had theirs.

"[Hood and Malone] gave us hope," remembered local civil rights activist Ruth Bolden. "And it gave us pride that we had accomplished something. But we had a long way to go."

PART THREE

The Movement

TUSCALOOSA, ALABAMA

Summer 1964

CHAPTER 14

The Rise of Reverend Rogers

1954–64

He was really encouraged by Dr. King to go.

In the winter of 1964, a change befell Tuscaloosa. The small southern town was less than a year removed from Wallace's stand, but already the local African American community was beginning to feel empowered. While the past decade had witnessed various efforts at improving race relations—including the formation of the Human Rights Council, the first integrated meeting group in Alabama, as well as the Ministers' Alliance, a contingency of local reverends dedicated to seeking peaceful solutions—the city's civil rights movement gained the most momentum at the hands of the Tuscaloosa Citizens for Action Committee.

While many were involved with Tuscaloosa's civil rights movement prior to the arrival of Reverend T. Y. Rogers, an even greater portion of the African American community was spurred to action following his entrance onto the scene. This shift to activism was not the work of a single person, but the result of a concerted effort on the part of many. Nevertheless, when the tall, lean twenty-eight-year-old man arrived in Tuscaloosa to answer the call for First African Baptist Church's need for a reverend, many came to listen.

While the church deacons knew little of T. Y. Rogers, they wholly trusted his recommender: Dr. Martin Luther King Jr., whose recommendation ensured that the town wasn't merely getting a reverend, but a civil rights leader as well.

❁

Theophilus Yelverton Rogers was born and raised in Coatopa, Alabama, a small, rural town seventy miles southwest of Tuscaloosa. He was the eldest of three, a mostly quiet young man, described by his youngest sister, Bettye Rogers Maye, as "older than his years." Rogers Maye was five years younger than her brother, and even at an early age she viewed him as "a serious-minded person."

"He didn't do a lot of playing around with my sister and I the way I guess many siblings did," she explained. Instead, he could often be found with his ear tilted to the radio, listening intently to the day's news. "We didn't have television growing up, but he loved listening to the radio," Rogers Maye continued. "I can remember when the National Democratic Presidential elections would be on. He would always want to listen to the radio to see what was going on, to see who was winning and that kind of thing."

Rogers's interest in politics continued to grow, and after graduating from high school in 1952, he left Coatopa for Montgomery's historically black university, Alabama State, where he double majored in political science and music. Yet his religious upbringing also drove him toward dedicating a life to God, and it wasn't long before his interests shifted to the ever-blurring region between politics and religion. In 1954, the eighteen-year-old Rogers found himself chairman of his university's chapter of the Student Christian Association, and in an effort to embrace his new role, he invited an up-and-coming Montgomery reverend named Martin Luther King Jr. to speak to his organization. The reverend agreed. It was likely there, in the halls of Alabama State University, that T. Y. Rogers first met the man who not only inspired his journey into the ministry, but also set his compass to Tuscaloosa a decade later.

King seemed equally impressed by the young student, and in 1956, after the Montgomery bus boycott expanded into a movement, a time-strapped King asked Rogers to serve as an assistant pastor at Dexter Avenue Baptist—an enormous vote of confidence for the recent college graduate with no formal ministerial training. Humbled, Rogers graciously accepted, admitting later that while he and King shared much in common, their similarities in conviction and oratory proved both a blessing and a curse.

"There were times when I would have to do counseling and answer questions, and keep down the conflicts within the organization, because he couldn't be there all the time," Rogers explained, noting some of his responsibilities as assistant pastor. "And I had to do it as [King] would do it, because, you see, I wasn't projecting my own self. I was projecting Martin Luther King into the church situation. I was always in the background, although I may have been doing it, because I was trying to do it as he would have done it."

Eventually, his projections of King proved problematic, making it difficult for some to differentiate between the assistant pastor and his mentor. For many of the congregants at Dexter Avenue Baptist, Rogers's King impersonation seemed a bit too spot-on—a kind of mimicry rather than mentoring—costing the Coatopa native a bit of credibility as he lingered in the shadow of King's spotlight.

"There was a time when it irked me," he admitted. "When I got to the seminary, people who knew [King] would say, 'My goodness, you sound just like him, you talk like him, you think like him.' And then I'd say to myself, 'My goodness. I've got to develop T. Y. Rogers and let's cut off Martin Luther King.'"

Rogers struggled in finding his own pastoral voice, though he later conceded that imitating King—consciously or otherwise—was not such a terrible strategy. "I got enough sense to realize that if Plato had students who developed themselves according to their teacher, and imitated him, and emulated him, and that other great men had men that they admired, I should have someone, also."

Rogers's initial pastoral studies under King were mostly informal, a mentorship in which the more experienced reverend simply offered his pupil unrestricted access to the many resources at his disposal. Rogers flourished under the arrangement, though sensing a need for Rogers to carve his own path, King recommended his pupil to Pennsylvania's Crozer Theological Seminary for the 1957 school year. King himself had graduated from Crozer just six years earlier, and Rogers was pleased to follow King's lead. Throughout his own three years at Crozer, Rogers remained in close contact with his mentor, returning to Montgomery during school breaks to assist King, and corresponding with him during the school year.

On August 31, 1957, King struck a fatherly tone when writing to Rogers at the start of the school year, encouraging him to call on occasion, adding also that he would be greatly missed at Dexter Avenue Baptist.

Nearly three years later—on June 19, 1960—King congratulated Rogers on his recent graduation, though his response had long been delayed. In an April letter to King, the soon-to-be graduate noted having caught wind of a new pastoral position opening at Dexter Avenue Baptist, hinting to King that he was interested in the position.

King responded by informing Rogers that while he maintained great faith in the young man, he was reticent to recommend him for the position. This was not due to a lack of faith in Rogers's abilities, but because King recognized the difficulty in convincing Dexter's church members that their once-assistant pastor was now ready for the new position.

Despite the minor setback, King's unwavering confidence in Rogers remained, and four years later, after Rogers gained additional pastoral experience in Pennsylvania, King played an active role in recruiting him to a church, and a town, far more suited to the young reverend's talents.

To this day, members of the Tuscaloosa African American community continue to debate precisely how active a role Martin Luther King Jr. played in Rogers's arrival in their city. Yet what is known for certain is that King had long played a role in determining Rogers's future, first urging him to attend Pennsylvania's Crozer Theological Seminary (as King had), and then urging him to return south upon his graduation.

"My parents and I didn't want him to come back because he was doing so well, and there was so much danger in the South," remembered Bettye Rogers Maye, T. Y. Rogers's youngest sister. "I remember Dr. King came to my parents' house to talk to Mother and Daddy about T. Y. coming back, and I said to Dr. King, 'If my brother comes home, he's going to get killed.'"

"Oh, Bettye, don't say that," King tried. "T. Y. wouldn't want you to think like that."

"He's going to get killed if he comes back," the young girl insisted, though her premonition did little to sway her brother, who leaped at the chance to assist his mentor.

His mission soon shifted to the South, Tuscaloosa, in particular.

While calling Rogers's arrival "fortuitous" and "quite beneficial," the Tuscaloosa Citizens for Action Committee president, Reverend Willie Herzfeld, remained firm that Rogers's entrance into Tuscaloosa's civil rights scene was simply the result of his interest in becoming the church's pastor. "I don't believe it was a part of any master plan by Dr. King or any of the persons in the Southern Christian Leadership Conference," he added.

Yet others disagree, believing King's recommendation *was* part of a "master plan," one that encouraged high-ranking members at Tuscaloosa's First African Baptist Church to install not only a pastor but also a civil rights activist with the abilities to spur the city to action.

In a 1987 interview, Rogers's wife, LaPelzia, attempted to put the matter to rest. "He was really encouraged by Dr. King to go [to Tuscaloosa]," she explained, noting how King believed her husband's arrival would build a "good foundation . . . especially since [United Klans of America's Grand Wizard] Robert Shelton was there."

In his own view, Rogers believed First African Baptist's desire to bring a civil rights activist into their fold was "more a subconscious reason than a conscious one."

"They realized that there were problems in Tuscaloosa which they hadn't been able to deal with at all," he explained, "and they knew also that if Dr. King would recommend somebody, that more than likely [that person] would be involved."

In an even greater show of faith, on Sunday, March 8, 1964, Dr. King attended Reverend Rogers's ordination service at Tuscaloosa's First African Baptist Church, preaching for an end to segregation and making it clear that Rogers was the right man to lead that particular charge.

"There are those who will say a minister should not participate in the struggle against segregation—that he should only preach the gospel," King explained to the overflowing crowd. "But a minister who won't stand up for the rights of his people is not worthy to be a minister of the gospel."

Following the service, King was asked if Tuscaloosa would play a role in the upcoming civil rights drive, to which he replied, "Tuscaloosa is very definitely included in the over-all plans."

CHAPTER 15

The Clash at the Courthouse

January–April 23, 1964

They did not believe that the whites of Tuscaloosa would take such a stand, that they would actually beat Negroes in the streets.

By the winter of 1964, local African Americans already had a hunch that T. Y. Rogers wasn't like Tuscaloosa's other reverends; not only did he leave his pulpit, he left it to march in the streets. He dedicated much of his first winter in Tuscaloosa to amassing his force. Civil rights activist Olivia Maniece remembered well Rogers's door-to-door-salesman approach.

"I became involved because T. Y. was my pastor, and he talked very closely with all of his members individually about his plans," Maniece explained. She recounted how she and a friend were chatting one Saturday evening when Rogers arrived at her home, engaged them in conversation, and announced, "You know, there are so many inequalities here in Tuscaloosa. You know, I'm thinking of getting an organization together, talking with the ministers, and maybe we can do something about it."

The prospect was eye opening to Maniece. "At that time, I don't think anybody in Tuscaloosa had thought to do anything," she explained. "And it really caught both of us by surprise. . . . All we said was, 'That's a good idea.'"

Rogers's first test came in April of 1964.

In the days prior to the dedication of Tuscaloosa's newly constructed county courthouse—in which a time capsule had been inserted into the cornerstone nearly a year prior—a biracial committee met to discuss a matter that weighed heavily on the minds of Reverend Rogers and other Tuscaloosa Citizens for Action Committee (TCAC) members. They believed the "Colored" signs— which had long been a staple in the Jim Crow South—had no place in the state-funded courthouse. According to local businessman George LeMaistre, present at the meeting, the biracial committee agreed that there should be no discriminatory signage, promising to forward the recommendation to the local board of revenue for approval.

Days later, on the afternoon of Sunday, April 12—as rain thundered across Tuscaloosa's dark skies—Governor George Wallace stood firmly in Judge W. C. Warren's second floor courtroom to commemorate the new courthouse. Hundreds filed in for the dedication, though as one paper noted, "It looked like a large part of the crowd was more interested in the governor than in the facilities being dedicated."

Following the previous summer's stand in the schoolhouse door, Wallace's star had continued to rise. In November of 1963 the governor announced his intentions to challenge President Kennedy in the Democratic primary, though Kennedy's assassination just days later shifted Wallace's gaze to the newly sworn-in President Johnson instead. The following April, fresh from receiving a surprising one-third of the vote in Wisconsin's Democratic primary, Wallace returned to Tuscaloosa to give the town a glimpse of the man many believed could take the White House in the next election. In his remarks, Wallace called the courthouse a "temple of justice which personifies and typifies the spirit of the people who live in Tuscaloosa County." Appealing to the crowd, he added also that Tuscaloosa was his "second home," and that his wife, future governor Lurleen Wallace—a Tuscaloosa County native herself—"would like to move the state capitol back here." The hometown crowd cheered, and after touting his accomplishments for a few minutes more, Wallace shifted gears to take aim at the proposed civil rights bill, which had already passed through the House and was now locked in a filibuster in the Senate.

"If this bill passes in its present form there will be no need for new courthouses or even a capitol building in Alabama," he predicted. "The people here will have no power or authority."

The troops had been rallied, while across town, Rogers was rallying his own.

The following Thursday, TCAC made it known that Wallace's so-called temple of justice did not apply to black people. Feeling they'd been duped by the biracial committee (which Rogers referred to as a "salt-and-pepper" committee), TCAC members called for the removal of "all discriminatory signs and practices" within the courthouse by April 23. The letter was received by Probate Judge David Cochrane, along with a promise that if TCAC's demands were not met, the group would "resort to other methods to secure this end"— a thinly veiled threat of direct action that Rogers later clarified to mean "some form of demonstration."

Rogers revealed his media savvy, noting, "Unless they are removed, we have no alternative but to protest in a fashion that will demonstrate to the people of Tuscaloosa County and the world that we are protesting the conditions." In truth, Rogers had plenty of alternatives, though in his search for a fight worth waging, the county courthouse seemed suddenly like fertile terrain. "We felt that this was a good time to dramatize our situation," Rogers later reflected.

Having served under Martin Luther King Jr. in the midst of the Montgomery bus boycott, Rogers had witnessed firsthand how media coverage of a direct action strategy could do much to propel a movement. While he now had a loyal following and a worthy cause, he still lacked the attention he desired. One of the interesting facets of the civil rights movement was that it was often viewed as a war consisting of many simultaneous battles. While Selma, Montgomery, and Birmingham seemed to have done their part, Tuscaloosa (with the exception of the university's desegregation attempts) had remained mostly quiet. Reverend Rogers hoped to change that.

As Rogers and TCAC put the finishing touches on their letter to Judge Cochrane, Wallace returned to Tuscaloosa yet again, this time speaking to a packed crowd at the University of Alabama where he reiterated the dangers of the Civil Rights Act, warning that its passage would "change our whole concept of life."

"If it is passed it will mean the federal government will take over everything—" Wallace assured, "businesses, homes, farms, labor unions and state and local governments."

Less than a week later, on Tuesday, April 21, the county board of revenue voted unanimously to reject TCAC's requests. Undeterred, Rogers informed the press that he had no choice but to make good on his promise for a demonstration, announcing a march scheduled for Thursday, April 23—less than forty-eight hours later.

When Reverend Rogers attempted to obtain a marching permit, Tuscaloosa's police chief, William Marable, refused. If TCAC insisted on marching, Marable made clear, then the Tuscaloosa Police Department would have no choice but to arrest them. A line had been drawn in the sand. Now it was only a matter of waiting to see which side would blink first.

The answer: Police Chief Marable.

Fearing the very real possibility of violence, the police chief eased his stance by allowing the group to march provided they did so in pairs and "did not block any street, sidewalks, doors or storefronts." Rogers agreed to the terms, and the two men—believing they had averted disaster—returned to their constituencies to report what was to happen next.

The first documented mass meeting in Tuscaloosa's civil rights history had occurred just days earlier, on Monday, April 20, 1964. While the march to the courthouse was still three days away, hundreds packed into First African Baptist Church to hear precisely what plan Reverend Rogers had concocted to fight the city's insistence on discriminatory signage. Never before had a reverend so boldly bucked Tuscaloosa's white establishment, and the excitement of the African American citizens was palpable. While the majority of the black community struggled to fully embrace the city's previous efforts at creating a movement, since his arrival into town three months earlier, Rogers's indefatigable spirit had become infectious, particularly among the city's youth and lower classes.

While African American reverend Willie Herzfeld had been attempting to organize a similar movement since 1961, he had been met with heavy opposition every step of the way. "Very few members of the community offered any kind of support," Herzfeld explained. "In fact, members of the Tuscaloosa Citizens for Action Committee who had been attending meetings and working in the organization prior to the election [of Governor Wallace] in Montgomery, refused to even speak to us." He went on to note that even his neighbors were afraid of associating with him in public. "Yes, I guess I was the loneliest man in the city of Tuscaloosa at that point," he concluded.

Rogers remembered that upon his own arrival in Tuscaloosa, a weary Herzfeld confessed, "Look, I'm tired. I have worked, and they have not accepted me. They have left me when I needed them most. Maybe you are not tired and you can do something. Whatever you want to do, I'm with you in it."

Rogers was grateful for the support, though as both men pointed out, the most likely reason for Rogers's increased approval may have had little to do with his indefatigable spirit, but rather with whom that spirit was affiliated. As a Lutheran in a predominantly Baptist town, Reverend Herzfeld was incapable of drawing the same crowd as Rogers. "The Baptist churches reach more people," Rogers agreed. "So instead of having a Lutheran or a Methodist, we need[ed] a Baptist minister."

Rogers fit the bill, and his confidence, coupled with his connections to King, convinced the community of his ability to succeed where others before him had failed. "I think there was a feeling, underneath, that I was going to do this," Rogers later reflected. "From the beginning, people sort of looked to me to become the leader. But I think at the first mass meeting, on April 20th, when I spoke about the then pending march on the downtown Tuscaloosa courthouse, I think this was the real turning point."

In Rogers's view, the turning point had been his ability to earn the African American community's trust, and two nights later, on the eve of the first march, they confirmed this by gathering in even greater numbers at the church. Yet this time, an estimated twenty white supporters were present as well, along with a pair of conspicuous detectives. Rogers described the Wednesday night crowd as "hanging from the rafters" with excitement, adding that when they sang "We Shall Overcome," the crowd was so great that even those standing outside the church joined hands and sang along.

Weaving through the masses, Reverend Rogers eventually made his way to the pulpit of First African Baptist and began setting forth his case for the need for a demonstration. The first piece of evidence: the biracial committee's reneging on its promise to refrain from posting any discriminatory signage.

"As soon as Gov. Wallace headed for Tuscaloosa," Rogers chided, "signs went up all over the place."

The crowd murmured in agreement.

Rogers informed them that they must be prepared to go to jail if necessary, that they should remember to pack their toothbrushes.

"So go ahead and do your handclapping and singing tonight," said Rogers, "because tomorrow we are going to stand with dignity . . . and march in a quiet and orderly fashion to the courthouse building. We are coming here tomorrow without hatred in our hearts and without violence. We are not going to strike back, but will go in a spirit of Christian love."

Yet Rogers refused to extend any such "Christian love" to further line the pockets of local white business owners. Their march would also signal a boycott of downtown stores—adding an economic blow to their otherwise symbolic demonstration. Reverend T. L. Hutchinson, in charge of the boycott, asked the packed church, "Why spend our money with our white brothers when they don't appreciate us. If I am able to buy a one dollar article on one side of the store, I should be able to buy a 10 cent cup of coffee on the other side."

The crowd agreed.

Never before had Tuscaloosa's African American community been willing to risk arrest in such great numbers, but on the night of April 22, they took Rogers's advice: they packed toothbrushes.

By 10:30 A.M. on Thursday, April 23, hundreds of African American students exited the chapel at nearby Stillman College and began assembling alongside Rogers at First African Baptist. The college later reported that approximately half of its 524 students were present at the march, making up a large percentage of the crowd. Word of the march had circulated throughout town by a variety of means, including church announcements, radio broadcasts, and Rogers's ability to plug the march throughout his many comments in the local newspaper. The various streams of publicity ensured a healthy turnout, and soon after the Stillman students arrived, marchers began moving toward the courthouse two abreast, as Marable stipulated. The well-disciplined demonstrators marched in silence, one newspaper reporting that there was "no stir of amusement or happiness among the Negro marchers as they approached the courthouse." While local police and firemen watched, so too did hundreds of other citizens, a sea of white faces peering out at the marchers with equal silence. The mood was described as "calm but tense," and while the *Tuscaloosa*

News reported no problems other than the arrest of one white overzealous demonstrator—a twenty-six-year-old Stillman English instructor named Bill Chase—Reverend Rogers remembered it quite differently.

Rogers hadn't expected violence from police. After all, the fix was supposedly in, and—from Rogers's perspective—he and the police chief had come to a careful agreement that he believed both sides planned to honor. Yet for whatever reason (be it provocation on the part of the demonstrators or simple miscommunication) it wasn't long before the marchers blocked the steps of the courthouse, forcing Marable to take action as promised. The détente was over.

"Move, nigger," Rogers remembered a few policemen calling, a provocation that was soon followed by a minor scuffle aimed at demonstrators. Rogers noted being hit and cattle prodded, though the newspapers failed to report any of these details, only going so far as to describe a few demonstrators being "herded down the [courthouse] steps."

While upset by this first taste of violence, the police action seemed only to reaffirm the African American community's resolve, solidifying them in a manner Rogers had previously witnessed during the Montgomery bus boycott. If there was a burden to be carried, it would be shared.

"They did not believe that that could happen in Tuscaloosa," Rogers explained years later, after having endured far greater instances of violence. "They did not believe that the whites of Tuscaloosa would take such a stand, that they would actually beat Negroes in the streets."

Rogers noted an alleged agreement previously decided by the white establishment that the city would go to great lengths to avoid a situation that might resemble the beatings that had occurred in Birmingham's Kelly Ingram Park the previous summer. He believed this information empowered his cause, serving as a blanket of protection.

"They had agreed previously, along with the other agreements, that were there to be demonstrations, they would permit demonstrations, and that there would be no police dogs, no fire hoses, no cattle prods, or any of this stuff," Rogers reflected. "It was permitted and they would protect the demonstrators as much as they could. There would be no Birmingham, in other words."

Yet the minor instances of violence that broke out at the courthouse seemed to indicate the possibility of future violence as well. When Marable and Rogers later discussed what precisely had spurred the unexpected violence, the police chief faulted Rogers for violating their agreement.

"Well, we had to disperse you," Rogers claimed Marable informed him. "You weren't supposed to stop. You were blocking an entrance [to the courthouse]. And I told you before, preacher, that I would bust your head just as quick as anybody else's."

Marable felt betrayed by the marchers' halt on the courthouse steps, and in an effort to balance the allegiance of his men with his obligations to the demonstrators, he decided to remove the demonstrators by force (though Rogers's and the newspaper's accounts disagree as to just what degree of force was employed).

Another uncertainty is who placed the "Colored" signs in the courthouse to begin with. George LeMaistre placed the blame on "some of the more zealous supporters of Wallace," believing a few renegade supporters had simply done as they had always done, placing the signs accordingly.

Recalling his presence at the biracial committee meeting, LeMaistre agreed, "I got the same understanding that [TCAC] did—that there would be no signs."

Not everyone in town was pleased with the arrival of Reverend Rogers. As expected, much of the white community was nervous about his direct action approach—a strategy that had never been tried in Tuscaloosa in any serious way prior to his entrance upon the scene. Grand Wizard Robert Shelton of the United Klans of America offered the most extreme view of Rogers's meddling, asking, "Who is T. Y. Rogers, to come into this community and put himself in the position of telling a merchant what he will do and what he won't do? Who is he, to come in and negotiate?" He called Rogers's march to the courthouse a "show of ignorance," arguing that the participants "had no knowledge of what they were actually doing. It was excitement for them, they were given an opportunity to be in the limelight."

Further, the thirty-five-year-old Klan leader claimed that Rogers and his "associates" were little more than "pawns or tools of this Communist conspiracy to bring about the turmoil, the animosity, and the ill will among the two races of people. Certainly it's not to the advantage of the Nigra."

He disagreed with TCAC's proposed removal of the courthouse's discriminatory signs, not only philosophically, but on another level as well. "There's a health problem involved," argued the Grand Wizard. "Certainly, no person wants to cast himself into the same segment or movement of society that has such a high rate of carrying diseases, such as the Nigras."

He condemned what he believed to be Police Chief Marable's soft response to the marchers, adding that if the Klan had attempted any such demonstration, they would have been stopped immediately.

"Anytime a group of white people are together, it's classified as a mob," he complained. "But when there's a group of Nigras together, it's a demonstration. Why is this phraseology used?"

Shelton's grumblings continued throughout the summer of 1964 and beyond. While he had dealt with other threats to Tuscaloosa's white community, he had never dealt with a threat like Rogers.

Autherine Lucy, February 1956. (Courtesy of W. S. Hoole Special Collections Library, The University of Alabama)

The weekend mobs, Saturday, February 4, 1956. (Courtesy of the W. S. Hoole Special Collections Library, The University of Alabama)

The Monday morning mob, February 6, 1956. (Courtesy of the W. S. Hoole Special Collections Library, The University of Alabama)

Buford Boone, editor of the *Tuscaloosa News*. (Courtesy of the W. S. Hoole Special Collections Library, The University of Alabama)

Dean of women Sarah Healy. (Courtesy of the W. S. Hoole Special Collections Library, The University of Alabama)

University of Alabama President O. C. Carmichael, 1953–57. (Courtesy of the W. S. Hoole Special Collections Library, The University of Alabama)

Special assistant to the president/administrative vice president Jefferson Bennett. (Courtesy of the W. S. Hoole Special Collections Library, The University of Alabama)

Attorney General Robert F. Kennedy and University of Alabama President Frank Rose. (Courtesy of the W. S. Hoole Special Collections Library, The University of Alabama)

University of Alabama dean of men John Blackburn. (Courtesy of the W. S. Hoole Special Collections Library, The University of Alabama)

Vivian Malone and James Hood registering for class, June 11, 1963. (Courtesy of the *Tuscaloosa News*)

Governor George Wallace faces off against Deputy
Attorney General Nicholas Katzenbach, June 11, 1963.
(Photograph by Warren K. Leffler. Courtesy of the U.S.
News & World Report Magazine Photograph Collection,
Library of Congress Prints and Photographs Division,
Library of Congress, LC-DIG-ppmsca-04292)

University of Alabama student Vivian Malone, summer session 1963. (Courtesy of
the W. S. Hoole Special Collections Library, The University of Alabama)

March to the Tuscaloosa County Courthouse, April 23, 1964. (Courtesy of the Tuscaloosa Sheriff's Department)

Police Chief William Marable (front left) in front of First African Baptist Church. (Courtesy of the William Marable II Family)

Attorney General Robert F. Kennedy, Police Chief William Marable, and Ethel Kennedy. (Courtesy of the William Marable II Family)

Reverend T. Y. Rogers and Police Chief William Marable (background), June 10, 1964. (Courtesy of the William Marable II Family)

Presidential candidate Robert F. Kennedy speaking at the University of Alabama, March 21, 1968. (Courtesy of the Alabama Department of Archives and History, Jim Peppler Collection)

Reverend T. Y. Rogers (front left), Andrew Young (behind Rogers), and Reverend Jesse Jackson (front right) serving as pallbearers for Dr. Martin Luther King Jr., April 9, 1968. (Courtesy of the Alabama Department of Archives and History, Jim Peppler Collection)

CHAPTER 16

The Myth of Marable

May–June 8, 1964

I'm here to enforce the law, whatever the law is.

Throughout May of 1964, Tuscaloosa's civil rights movement continued to gain momentum, culminating in a weeklong demonstration of marches and boycotts scheduled for the first week of June. The newly installed Reverend Rogers had wasted little time organizing demonstrations in opposition to what he believed to be the city's segregationist policies, carefully selecting his targets and organizing allies. On the other side, Police Chief William Marable struggled with an altogether different battle—granting Rogers just enough leeway to bend the rules without allowing the city to break into violence.

The summer provided the ideal time for Rogers to wage his assault. No longer held captive by the monotony of the school day, local high school– and college-aged African Americans were destined to play a critical role in the Tuscaloosa movement, dedicating their summer to a far different type of education. While their mothers and fathers could hardly afford to take time off from work for demonstrations, many of the younger generation could. As an added incentive, for some, their involvement was not only aimed at effecting social change, but ensuring a social life as well, one in which friends could gather daily to take part in a common goal.

On Monday, June 1, this social atmosphere only increased when an unexpected celebrity arrived in Tuscaloosa to rally the crowd. At 8:00 P.M. African American comedian and activist Dick Gregory arrived from Chicago to attend a mass meeting at First African Baptist Church. He was met with great fanfare, the Tuscaloosa audience further committed to its cause at the urging of such a well-known figure.

Rogers and Gregory proved an unlikely duo. The reverend and the comedian rallied the crowd, mixing seriousness with lightheartedness and inspiring everyone in their midst. Further, Gregory's presence served as proof to the local foot soldiers that the Tuscaloosa crusade could have ramifications elsewhere—a realization that motivated many in the crowd that night.

"Some of you are willing to go to jail for what's wrong," Gregory joked. "You ought to be willing to go to jail for what's right."

Throughout the first week of June, while African American teenagers began testing their limits, white segregationists also began testing theirs.

On Thursday, June 4, fourteen-year-old African American Jenifer Merriweather and friends were observing a downtown demonstration when they were suddenly sprayed with a scalding concoction known as mustard oil. According to Dr. J. Woodruff Robinson, a local African American doctor, the oil created a "burning sensation on the arms, face, and eyes," and while Robinson couldn't identify the liquid, given the rise in its use throughout town, he was becoming abruptly familiar with it as cases began to add up.

While some demonstrators risked their personal safety at lunch counters, nearly a hundred others faced similar risks marching downtown. On Friday, June 5, while demonstrators held signs aimed at ending discriminatory hiring practices, a few of the marchers were sprayed, once more, with mustard oil. This time, two men were arrested for the crime—twenty-nine-year-old Hubert Hinton Jones and twenty-six-year-old Billy Wayne Mansfield.

Undeterred, the marches continued Saturday morning, a slow drizzle streaking the sky as a crowd at half-strength marched on. The fifty or so marchers continued to protest what they believed to be unfair practices in Tuscaloosa, proof of which was confirmed when both Jones and Mansfield—the mustard oil sprayers in question—were released on bond just hours after their arrests.

Harvey Burg—a young man sent to Tuscaloosa by the Law Students Civil Rights Research Council—remembered the day he attempted to procure the mustard oil to test its availability. "I had the audacity to walk into the drug store one day where they were selling the mustard gas and asked for some," Burg recalled.

As a young white man in the South, Burg fit the part of the segregationist, and the mustard oil was made readily available.

On Monday, June 8, the demonstrations continued—nearly a week old and still moving at full speed. They had become a daily occurrence, a plague for the local police, and by Monday morning, Police Chief Marable's patience was running thin.

As marchers began filing out of First African Baptist Church, they were quickly met by police, Marable citing a violation in the city's parade ordinance. The city's law enforcement officials—particularly Marable—were desperately seeking out strategies to halt the marches while maintaining the peace. Thanks, in part, to the cool headedness on both sides, no arrests were made, and all violence was successfully diffused. Yet the interaction served as further proof that the police and demonstrators found themselves trapped in a potentially explosive situation, prompting many to believe that it was only a matter of time before somebody lit the fuse.

While the 1960s were filled with powerful men locked in harrowing stand-offs, these men's private views of one another only occasionally corresponded with the public perception. Throughout the Cuban Missile Crisis, President John F. Kennedy and Soviet Chairman Nikita Khrushchev appeared to be enemies of the highest order, though privately they seemed far more empathetic of the tight spot they shared—attempting to prevent nuclear war while facing immense pressure from advisors to do otherwise. Conversely, Deputy Attorney General Nicholas Katzenbach and Governor Wallace's relationship proved far easier to deduce—to put it mildly, they didn't like each other.

Reverend Rogers and Police Chief Marable's relationship seemed to fall somewhere in the middle. Despite the rare threat of head busting, Marable and Rogers's relationship maintained far more civility than allowed by most southern police chiefs and their rabble-rousing reverends. Further, Marable's sympathies rested neither with the segregationists nor TCAC; he viewed himself simply as a defender of the law—a philosophy Rogers likely admired. How successful Marable was at maintaining this neutrality is a matter of debate, though to his credit, he often gave demonstrators the benefit of the doubt, occasionally even going so far as to turn a blind eye to TCAC's illegal marches. When it served the city's purposes, Tuscaloosa city ordinance defined a parade as any group of two or more; however, in some instances, Marable had allowed demonstrators to march in groups of five (though he was well aware of the transgression, even admitting so to the local papers). The police chief appeared to be picking his battles, viewing the occasional march as a minor concession and far better than the possibility of violence.

Rogers maintained a respect for Marable as well, describing the police chief as "very cordial," and remembered that during their first interaction, Marable had informed him, "that the Negroes were very happy in town and that I was intelligent and knew how to conduct myself and that I wouldn't get the town embroiled in a stew." Rogers added that the police chief laid down the ground rules from the start: "He told me what to do and what not to do, in so many words. And we had a very cordial relationship from that point on, until we had a break a little later."

The "break" was likely the result of Bloody Tuesday—a strong-armed approach to policing that lingered just days away.

Yet Reverend Willie Herzfeld recounted a moment the day following their bloody battle in which Marable extended a much-needed olive branch—responding to the demonstrators with far more compassion than he had shown previously. As Herzfeld described, in an effort to prevent yet another illegal march, the police chief met with the reverends to negotiate a peaceful resolution on the street outside a local church. When the negotiations began to unravel, the fire trucks rolled in, further instigating a scene. Everyone looked to Marable to make the call. Would he take a page from Bull Connor's playbook and order the fire hoses turned on the demonstrators, or would he try a different solution?

As his officers watched on, Marable opened his mouth to speak.

"Water down the damn streets," he said, sparing the demonstrators. "It's hot as hell out here."

In a recent interview, Police Chief Marable's son, Bill Marable, offered unique insight into his father's time as police chief throughout the civil rights movement. Citing the liberal use of water cannons and billy clubs by southern law enforcement, Bill Marable reported that his father "was determined that this wasn't about to happen in Tuscaloosa.

"His position all along was, 'I'm here to enforce the law, whatever the law is. I didn't write it, I may not agree with it, but it's the law that's on the books, so it's the law that I will enforce,'" Marable explained. "His whole department was behind him in that respect. I'm not saying that they were as pure as the driven snow in some of their views toward the black community, but they did follow Dad's instructions and what have you, so there was good rapport there."

Later, many would question the sincerity of the Tuscaloosa Police Department's promise to keep the peace, though to the department's credit, Tuscaloosa did experience far less violence at the hands of law enforcement than many southern towns.

Bill Marable credited this lack of violence to two factors, the first being his father's unwavering respect for all people. "It was always Mister or Missus, yes ma'am, no ma'am, thank you," Bill Marable recalled, reflecting on the mantras of his childhood. "You opened doors for ladies. Those were the basic qualities he instilled in me and my sister.

"We didn't have all the luxuries like a lot of kids in school," he continued, "but we had the essentials, and we knew right from wrong, respect for others, and that was how we were raised, and that was how he treated everybody. He treated everybody with respect. I think that's one of the reasons why the folks in the black community had so much faith in his ability and the law enforcement community. . . . He was basically that kind of person."

Tuscaloosa civil rights activist Nathaniel Howard Jr. concurred, characterizing Marable as "a pretty straight fellow."

"He was a good fellow," Howard explained. "A religious man. He respected a minister. He just respected religion."

Reverend Herzfeld seconded the claim, crediting Marable with "[having] a lot to do with the curtailing of potential violence comparable to other cities."

The police chief's grandson, William II, offered a similar assessment. "Every time he talked with someone—and it may have been a janitor or a trash person or anything—he would always speak with them as if they were very important. Someone he looked up to," William explained. "As a kid, that's how I viewed it. As if the person he was talking to was more important than him. . . . Like he was always introducing me to the greatest people in the world by the way he was treating them."

While Marable's fair treatment of all people undoubtedly played a role in curbing racial violence, a second factor—his near constant communication with the community at large—proved equally valuable.

"Tuscaloosa was not a large place and people knew people, and he would take every opportunity he could to speak to city groups or church groups or whatever they were to tell them what his position was and what he was trying to do," Bill Marable explained. Police Chief Marable regularly took calls from Reverend T. Y. Rogers, though in the interest of fairness, took calls from Grand Wizard Robert Shelton as well.

"Sometimes Shelton would call," Marable remembered. "Essentially, Dad would just tell him to chill. 'We don't want any of this stuff. Go out into your field and burn your crosses, but we don't want any guns and we don't want any lynchings.'"

"Their chief complaint was, I believe, that they felt that Dad was on the side of the blacks," Marable continued. "Dad tried to emphasize over and over and over and over, 'It's not my job to interpret a law one way or the other. . . . My job is to keep the peace and enforce the law for all the folks, and that's what's going to happen.' And essentially, the peace was kept."

Rogers and Shelton concurred with this assessment of the chief, Shelton arguing that it was a waste of taxpayer money for Rogers to demand police protection, while Rogers—fully aware of Marable's soft spot for peace—often provided Marable prior notice of demonstrations in an effort to buy the police chief the necessary time to prepare for an appropriate response.

"Before we initiated any direct action," Rogers later confirmed, "we always talked with the police and tried to find out what the regulations were, and what violations we would be making."

By understanding the likely end result at the start of each demonstration, both Rogers and Marable eliminated the possibility of making themselves look foolish on film.

Following Marable's death in 1992, his grandson, William II, found himself newly curious about the pictures that had long coated his grandfather's basement walls. He had yet to fully grasp his grandfather's legacy, though the photographs offered a few much-needed clues into the police chief's past.

"I remember loving it as a kid, seeing these pictures," William recalled. "And as I was going through these pictures, I pulled out a black-and-white photo during civil rights, and I turned on the back of it and it said, 'The Civil Rights March, the Reverend T. Y. Rogers.'" William had never heard of any T. Y. Rogers, and the picture prompted an array of questions, many of which would eventually lead him to a secondhand understanding of his grandfather's role in Tuscaloosa's civil rights movement.

Yet Marable's son, Bill, was a high schooler at the height of the violence. Bill Marable remembered well the troubles his father faced, as well as his reluctance to share the details.

"I was a curious kid. I wanted to learn everything that was going on," Bill Marable explained. "I wanted to cut school and go with Dad and hang out, but he said, 'No, you're in school. You don't need to be in this stuff.'

"At the end of each day I would say, 'What happened today, Dad? What happened today?' I wanted to be the kid in the current events class saying, 'Hey, I got this juicy bit of info here,' but he would share with me only some of the activities."

Bill Marable remembered also the precautions taken to ensure the family's safety. "We had to put a tap on the phone at the house because we were getting threatening phone calls," he explained. As the threats grew more violent, so too did the police chief's concern for his family. "My sister and I had . . . to open the hoods of our cars and check them for bombs because we had received bomb threats for several weeks," Bill Marable said.

In a strange twist of fate, the Marable family's connections to the civil rights movement extended beyond the family patriarch. Police Chief Marable's eldest daughter, Martha, found herself also involved, attending the University of Alabama alongside Vivian Malone. In an even greater display of serendipity— due to the closeness of their last names—on graduation day, the first African American graduate in university history and the daughter of the city's police chief were seated just two seats away from each other as the crowd cheered their shared accomplishment.

The civil rights movement had an equal effect on her younger brother, Bill Marable, who as a child observed his father's commanding presence and decided he, too, wanted to one day serve as an officer of the law. Upon making his intentions known to his father, the police chief shook his head sadly. "You don't want to be a cop," a tired Marable informed his son. "It just ain't worth it anymore."

✳

Yet for all its headaches, policing had its perks as well.

As the head of the city's law enforcement, Police Chief Marable occasionally found himself among celebrities, including the jailhouse rocker himself—Elvis Presley.

"Oh, Lord, there were a lot of Elvis moments," Bill Marable laughed, explaining that every time Elvis performed in Tuscaloosa, his father was typically assigned to the security detail. Marable rarely wore his formal police chief uniform, though on the night he met Elvis's plane he made an exception.

"Chief? You got a uniform?" one of Elvis's aides asked.

"Well, yeah," Marable answered carefully.

"You got a lot of spangle on it?" the man pressed. "A lot of gold?"

"Well, yeah."

"Could we get you to go and put it on?" the aide inquired. "When Elvis gets his picture taken with people, he just likes all that sparkly stuff."

Marable agreed, and the aide placed him in Elvis's limousine, which promptly returned him to his home for the requested wardrobe change.

"My mother was working in the yard, and she saw this football-field-long car pull up," Bill Marable explained. "And I'm out here on my knees digging in the flowerbed, and I say, 'Now what in the world is this?'"

Marable explained how his father leaped from the limousine, running into the house shouting, "Elvis wants some pictures made!"

That same night, after Marable and Elvis's photo shoot, the chief presented the King of Rock and Roll with an officer's badge, making the King an honorary Tuscaloosa police officer.

The police chief met with political celebrities as well, including one memorable meeting with Robert F. Kennedy and his wife, Ethel. When Marable pulled up at the airport in his unmarked squad car, Robert F. Kennedy and his wife got in the car, and he asked, "Chief, you got lights and sirens on this thing?"

"Yes, sir, why?" Marable asked, glancing at Kennedy and his wife in the backseat.

"Hurry up, this woman's got to go," Kennedy explained, and in order to avoid any misunderstanding restated: "This woman's got to *pee.*"

Biting back a grin, Marable nodded, got on the radio and informed the unmarked car ahead of them to "light 'em up" all the way to the President's Mansion, that Ethel Kennedy could not wait.

CHAPTER 17

Bloody Tuesday

June 9, 1964

I don't know that there was a spot from First African Baptist Church all the way down to 15th Street that wasn't bloody.

On the morning of Tuesday, June 9, Police Chief William Marable's efforts for peace were severely tested, as well as his ability to restrain his men from violence. As young African Americans bounded toward First African Baptist Church for another downtown march, a police officer stared on from afar, his stomach knotted with foreboding.

"Something bad is gonna happen today," he predicted. "I just know it is. I have never been involved in anything like this."

The officer's radio squawked at a few minutes past 9:00 A.M., and as the demonstrators entered the church, police were called back to headquarters for "last-minute instructions."

"We got there," remembered civil rights activist Olivia Maniece, "and the church was packed, and there were even people on the outside. There were policemen stationed all down 9th Street, 27th Avenue, all around the church, everywhere."

She went on to describe the exuberant crowd taking part in the usual ritual of songs and speeches, though as the hour approached, Rogers and a few of his fellow reverends attempted to offer their own last-minute instructions.

"They told us briefly what they were going to talk about once they got to the courthouse," Maniece continued. "They said what we might expect on the way, but also how to handle these situations if they occurred." Rogers, much like his mentor, had long stressed the virtues of nonviolence, likely reminding the crowd of its importance prior to the march.

Inside the church, the other reverends continued to rally the crowd, an estimated five hundred people listening intently.

"We're going to lead, you all just follow us," one of the reverends called. "We're going to go on the outside, we're going to form a line, and there should not be more than two persons . . . per row . . . we're not going to break that law. Nobody is going to get out of line."

The drama seemed to be unfolding as planned, though as soon as Reverend Rogers stepped foot outside the church doors, he was immediately confronted by Marable and his men. They faced off in front of Van Hoose Funeral Home, Reverend Rogers maintaining his calm demeanor while Police Chief Marable felt the pressure mounting as white crowds gathered, waiting for his response.

"You have heard my orders that you will not be allowed to march," Marable said. "Do you intend to march anyway?"

"Yes," Rogers nodded.

"You are under arrest," Marable said—hardly surprised by the outcome. The officers reached for the pencil-thin minister, escorting him into a waiting police car. A photograph captured the well-dressed Rogers in mid-step as a baton-wielding officer led him by the arm. His eyes were aimed slightly down, his legs matching the stride of the officer's.

The other reverends were arrested as well, though the crowd of mostly college-aged students refused to be deterred even in the absence of their leaders.

Perhaps surprised by the demonstrators' unwillingness to disperse, the police tried pushing the crowds back toward the church by a variety of means—"elbows, clubs, and electric cattle prods" according to one report. After a five-minute fight that left several marchers bloodied, the majority of demonstrators sought refuge within the church walls, though it hardly proved to be the sanctuary they intended.

"Then the worst period of trouble began," the newspaper explained.

What occurred next would forever alter the course of the local movement, disrupting the careful balance that Marable and Rogers had striven to maintain. After nine days of near-constant protests, the police chief's patience had worn thin, and as the mostly white crowd watched testily from the sidelines, Marable began determining his next move. He could contain, arrest, or attack the demonstrators, though according to Marable, his choice became far easier once the demonstrators began assaulting his men.

While civil rights activists later denied the charge—calling the newspaper reports sensationalized—according to the *Tuscaloosa News,* demonstrators inside the church's foyer began chanting, "We want Freedom, come and get us, we want to go to jail!" As the chanting continued, several others held positions in the church's second story windows and allegedly began flinging bottles and rocks in the direction of the police. The newspaper went on to report a smashed window, as well as demonstrators breaking church chairs and hurling the pieces down at the blue-helmeted police officers anxiously awaiting their orders.

"When the Negroes refused to halt the barrage aimed at the officers, orders were given to turn on the fire hoses," the newspaper reported. "The fire truck was stationed directly in front of the church and the first streams of water were aimed into the second story windows from which most of the articles were being thrown."

Civil rights activist Odessa Warrick has long been haunted by the day the police attacked the church. She'd woken early, preparing herself for violence by wearing two pairs of pants and thick overalls in an attempt to counteract the billy clubs that would surely find her. "The police was out there. The billy clubs was out there. The cattle prods was out there," Warrick recalled. "I had told a lot of peoples, 'Wear tennis shoes, wear shoes with rubber, because where they stick those cattle prods in it won't hurt because the rubber would get it.'"

Yet once the violence broke, Warrick found herself less concerned with cattle prods and more concerned with a well-swung billy club. She fought back against police, grabbing at one attacker's genitals in an attempt to even the fight. "And every time they would beat me on my hands with their billy clubs I would grab them down here," she explained, a hint of pride in her voice. "I would rang 'em. I rang one of them . . . he couldn't do anything, he just fell out. And they said, 'Make that nigger turn me loose! That nigger's killing me! That nigger's grabbing my . . . ,' then they'd come out and say what I grabbed."

Warrick's rage only intensified once the tear gas canisters were launched through the church's prized stained glass windows, and growing desperate, she redoubled her efforts of attacking the men where it hurt most. "Our eyes was full of tear gas and those men beat me and I just . . . I tried to bite it off but I couldn't get my mouth down there to bite it off they was beating me so bad. I left them laying out there in the yard."

"And you want to talk about blood?" Reverend T. W. Linton added, describing his entrance onto the scene at the battle's conclusion. "I don't know that there was a spot from First African Baptist Church all the way down to 15th Street that wasn't bloody."

The newspaper reported the hysteria that followed soon after: African American demonstrators leaping from the church windows and running into the alleyways where they were promptly arrested. The demonstrators scattered, many of them drenched and gagging from fumes. The battle had waged for under an hour, and by 11:15 A.M. the church was cleared, tear gas wafting down the street for several blocks.

"I was observing the entire operation from a distance of about half a block," reported Grand Wizard Robert Shelton, describing the demonstrators as a "massive wave."

"The Nigras, themselves, provoked the incident, by cat-calling the policemen after they pushed them back into the church. The Nigras threw out drink bottles, loose furniture, and other materials that wasn't attached to the inside of the church."

Shelton was quick to defend the police action, arguing that Marable's police force "had no other choice."

"The reporters that were present say, themselves, that the first acts was brought on by the Nigra by throwing out," Shelton continued. "You could see them through the windows, from the inside."

Shelton's interpretation was confirmed by the *Tuscaloosa News,* which reported that an array of items—including bottles, wood, vases, rocks, and cans—had, in fact, pelted the police officers below, noting also that, "several of the policemen threw some of the articles back at the Negroes."

In response to a 2011 newspaper article on Tuscaloosa's civil rights movement, Dick Looser, a thirty-one-year-old reporter in the summer of 1964, attempted to set the record straight on what he believed to be various misconceptions that had perpetuated for over half a century. By Looser's 2011 account, there was no doubt that a small number of African American demonstrators *had* thrown objects at police. He had witnessed the scene firsthand alongside two FBI agents, the three of them observing the scene directly across the street from the church at the time of the violence.

"One [of the objects thrown] was a bottle or a vase that broke on the pavement," Looser explained, "and a shard of the glass caused a small cut on my leg."

He later added that "police retaliated by throwing tear gas canisters through the front door only . . . [n]o tear gas canister was fired through the stained glass window on the right side of the church from the outside."

His proof was in the pictures, one in particular snapped by the *Tuscaloosa News*'s chief photographer, revealing a piece of stained glass "pointed outward toward the cemetery"—evidence, in Looser's estimation, that the glass had been broken from the inside, likely "in an attempt [by the demonstrators] to get air." Sure enough, gracing the front page of the June 10 edition of the *Tuscaloosa News* is a picture of the broken stained glass window, along with an arrow directing the reader to the outward glass.

Yet to this day, the demonstrators present that morning continue to deny the charge of striking first. Rogers, too, denied that any objects were tossed at police. Handcuffed throughout the majority of the battle, he could do little to control the demonstrators even if he'd wanted to. Instead, he watched helplessly as his church was attacked, water crashing through the front doors, windows shattering, his demonstrators running for cover.

"How could it happen in Tuscaloosa?" Rogers wondered. "How could it happen anywhere in the United States?"

After the forty-five-minute battle wound down, an elderly African American man sat on the church's soaking steps, a handkerchief positioned over his mouth and nose. He peered into the ruined structure while police officers in gas masks searched the premises.

The *Tuscaloosa News* noted the "look of disbelief on his face."

It was a feeling shared by many throughout the city.

While these violent incidents had become commonplace in cities like Birmingham and Selma, Tuscaloosa had somehow remained virtually unscathed.

Which left many in town wondering precisely what Rogers had: How could something like this happen here?

As the battle came to a close at First African Baptist Church, Reverend T. W. Linton waited for news at his father's home on nearby McKenzie Court. The minutes dragged on as the young minister willed the phone to ring, praying for good news.

At last, the phone burst suddenly to life, though the news was hardly good.

"You need to get over here quick," a voice called.

Linton hung up the phone and rushed to Howard and Linton's Barbershop, which, due to the number of injuries in the fight with police, had been converted to a makeshift hospital. Linton entered through the rear door, only to be greeted with a disturbing scene—dozens of injured demonstrators lining the floors. The police had previously loaded paddy wagons chock-full of marchers, and those who remained had made their way to the barbershop located just a few blocks south. Linton examined the scene before snapping to action, first demanding the injured be transported immediately to Druid City Hospital and then seeking out a phone to fulfill his primary duty—reporting the crisis to the higher-ups. Rather than using the barbershop phone—which was rumored to be bugged—he turned the corner and headed to a nearby house that belonged to one of his congregants.

Marching swiftly toward the house, Linton heard a familiar voice beckoning him from behind.

"Come here, Minister," a police officer called from atop his motorcycle. "We've been looking for you."

Linton never stopped walking.

"Do you hear me calling for you?"

Ignoring him, a young Linton pressed on toward the house, and upon meeting his congregant at the door he asked to use her phone.

She agreed, and as Linton slipped inside, the woman turned to spot the police officer (known simply as "Motorcycle Red" among the black community) ambling toward her.

She placed both hands on her hips, blocking the doorway.

"Where are you going?" she hissed. "Don't come in my house. That's my pastor and he hasn't done one single thing, so don't come in my house and I mean it." Motorcycle Red waited for Linton to exit while the woman stood guard, eyeing him carefully.

Meanwhile, inside, Linton picked up the phone and placed his first call to African American lawyer Oscar Adams, who upon hearing news of the botched march asked, "Have you called Dr. King yet?"

"No, I called you first."

"Well, call Dr. King," Adams ordered as if it were obvious. "And call Bobby Kennedy on his direct number."

Linton called King first, and after repeating the story, making sure to note the numerous arrests—including the arrest of King's protégé, T. Y. Rogers— King assured Linton that he was sending a bail bondsman to Tuscaloosa to assist.

Linton returned the phone to its cradle before placing his second call— this one to Attorney General Robert Kennedy. Linton repeated the story once more, and Kennedy—no stranger to Tuscaloosa's racial atmosphere following Wallace's stand—was said to have replied, "Listen, I'll take care of it. I'll do what I can. I'll take care of it."

Linton hung up and glanced out the front window to notice that Motorcycle Red had called in reinforcements. Three or four police officers had spread themselves across the front of the house, prompting Linton to exit through the back, bypassing the officers and sneaking into his barbershop just a few houses down.

"I was in here for about three hours," Linton replied, tapping his barber's chair. "Took three hours for the bondsman to get here."

In a 2011 interview, Linton admitted that it seemed somewhat peculiar that a young barber in Tuscaloosa, Alabama, had direct access to the leader of the civil rights movement, as well as the US attorney general. Linton shrugged, "I had [the phone numbers] in my shirt pocket right here," he explained simply, tapping his pocket twice.

Initially, the police estimated fifty arrests, though by day's end the count had nearly doubled. The *Tuscaloosa News* eventually put the number at ninety-four, an approximation confirmed by many present that day. Two booking officers fingerprinted the demonstrators while a police officer guarded the door. Meanwhile, to keep from buoying the spirits of the newly arrested, Rogers and the other reverends were held in separate holding cells, away from their foot soldiers.

Those not carted off to jail found themselves carted off to Druid City Hospital instead. The local hospital was soon inundated with thirty-three injured African Americans ranging in age from fourteen to thirty-eight, though the majority were under twenty years old.

Local civil rights activist Ruth Bolden recalled visiting the injured in the hospital that day. "I don't know how many children were in the hospital, but . . . some was beaten terribly, one girl in particular was just rolling side to side just begging for something. The nurse was so kind and sweet. She said, 'Sweetheart, I can't give you anything else for 35 minutes. I've given you all I can give you for 35 minutes.' They were very kind to the children. One said, 'Regardless of what happened, the police was wrong, because that was those people's church, their place of worship, and the police had no business putting tear gas in it.'" It was the validation Bolden needed—proof that not all white people supported the police action.

While the newspaper reported that Tuesday night remained mostly quiet—little more than a broken windshield and a bottle of gasoline tossed to a porch—African Americans related a far different story. Many of the men were infuriated by what they viewed as an unprovoked attack. As writer Simon Wendt explained, "Not only had police officers attacked one of the last sanctuaries of the African American community; worse, they had brutalized peaceful women and children."

While carloads of black men patrolled the Tuscaloosa streets, guns resting heavily on laps, an African American Korean War veteran named Joe Mallisham eventually calmed their anger, diffusing the situation by promising retribution in a more productive manner—by organizing and defending themselves from future attacks.

It was a promise Mallisham would soon make good on, and many of the men begrudgingly agreed to his terms, handing over their weapons until their blood had time to cool.

Today, the steeple of First African Baptist Church perches high above the West End section of Tuscaloosa, a beautiful brick building tucked alongside a slew of fast food restaurants and just up the hill from Howard and Linton's Barbershop. A historical marker out front notes the church's long standing in Tuscaloosa, though it fails to mention Bloody Tuesday.

"People out of state didn't know about [Bloody Tuesday]," explained Linton, "but we survived it."

Nearly fifty years later, even the survivors are dwindling, as is the story itself. There are few visual reminders of the events of Tuesday, June 9, 1964, though people remember it in other ways.

"You go in [First African Baptist Church] now," promised Odessa Warrick in a 1987 interview, "you can still smell a little bit of that gas."

This was even truer in the days directly following the attack. Rogers described how later that week some of his church members began "wash[ing] the blood off the stairs, although the tear gas was so strong that every few minutes they'd have to run upstairs and stick their heads out of the window."

Nevertheless, by the following Sunday, the congregants of First African Baptist filed into the remains of their church undeterred by the destruction. Their eyes watered as they prayed—a mixture of sadness and the lingering of the gas. Despite the horror, the events of Bloody Tuesday had a silver lining as well. Much like the violence endured during the first march to the county courthouse the previous April, the more recent events further empowered the black community.

"They felt, 'This is what is happening to us, and we're all involved in it,'" Rogers remembered.

At long last, Tuscaloosa's civil rights movement was gaining momentum, though they'd paid their price in blood.

CHAPTER 18

Jamming the Jails

June 10–13, 1964

This town is sitting on a powder keg.

The battle at First African Baptist Church was Tuscaloosa's first major racially motivated clash since the mobs spurred by Autherine Lucy's enrollment at the University of Alabama eight years prior. Yet in the time between, the dynamics had dramatically shifted. While in 1956 a single African American female had faced a lawless mob, by 1964, several hundred African Americans faced the law itself.

"Nobody wants to take action like we did," admitted Tuscaloosa's public safety commissioner George Ryan, "but when the church became a refuge for civil disobedience, it ceases to be a church and becomes a fortress."

While the city would long debate the necessity of the police department's actions, an equally rousing debate was about whether the use of tear gas was intentional—at least such a concentrated supply directed within the church walls. According to civil rights activist Olivia Maniece, present that day, the tear gas within the church was little more than the result of a poor marksman.

"I think what happened is, [the police] were throwing the tear gas at the crowd, and it really went through a window, it broke a window . . . I don't think they were throwing in the church. At first it was not in the church, they were using it on the outside to get the people into the church. But in so doing, they were throwing the canisters, and it broke a window and went inside. They didn't come in and just spray the church, per se, after the people got back in. They were using it to get the people back in," she explained, "and of course, after the window all the doors were opened, so with it being all around the church, naturally it got in there."

Yet Maniece's assessment proved a far more generous interpretation than the one given by other civil rights activists. Reverend Linton blamed the police wholeheartedly. Rather than fulfilling their sworn duty to serve and protect, they had employed instead a kind of billy club and tear gas diplomacy. Upon his return to the church Tuesday morning, Linton recalled seeing white women standing on the sidelines "yelling and pointing out to police the children who were being sheltered by adults from attack," ensuring that not even children were spared.

In response to what would later be known as "Bloody Tuesday," Dr. Martin Luther King Jr. dispatched a close ally, Reverend James Bevel, to assess and assist in Tuscaloosa while Reverend Rogers and other local leaders remained jailed. Rogers was released on Wednesday afternoon, immediately arranging a strategy meeting with Bevel and the remnants of TCAC, primarily to discuss how to raise the necessary funds to release their fellow demonstrators from jail—no easy task given the group's financial constraints.

Over the past year, Reverend Bevel had accumulated a growing list of civil rights achievements, most notably his role in Birmingham's 1963 children's crusade—calling for children to march in the streets of Birmingham despite both President Kennedy and Dr. King's calls to the contrary. Following his brief stint in Tuscaloosa, he would also play a role in organizing 1965's Selma to Montgomery march, though in the days directly after Bloody Tuesday, his energy remained focused on his current task. Speaking to reporters, Bevel made clear the Tuscaloosa Citizens for Action Committee and the Southern Christian Leadership Conference's shared intention to "continue to address ourselves to the grievances of a segregated city," adding that there was a "good possibility" Dr. Martin Luther King Jr. would soon come to Tuscaloosa as a result of the recent violence.

It was an announcement the city commissioners and police department had long feared. Many believed King's presence would spur further violence, particularly by giving the United Klans of America a reason to come out from hiding. For Police Chief Marable, an already volatile situation was quickly worsening—seemingly karmic retribution for the previous day's mishap.

The job of springing the demonstrators from the city jail fell squarely on Reverend Linton. He and King's bail bondsman made several trips downtown to see to their release, though the city's procedural red tape hardly made it easy on them.

When the bondsman attempted to sign the first bond, he was quickly denied.

"Why?" asked the bondsman. "I'm licensed to sign a bond anywhere in this state for up to $100,000.00."

"Well, you aren't going to sign one here," the official informed him. "You have to have property bonds."

In order for the bond to be approved, the signer had to own property other than the one he lived in—a local regulation that made the bondsman's jobs all the more difficult.

"So we got organized with people all over the county, business people, and we sat down and talked about who had property," Linton remembered. "And we began to send people over to have bonds signed."

While Reverend Rogers was released by Wednesday afternoon, his twenty-four hours in jail were, in the opinion of activist Ruth Bolden, excessive. Following Tuesday's arrests, Bolden marched directly into the jail and asked the woman behind the front desk if she knew where Reverend Rogers was being held.

"I don't know, I don't know," the woman shrugged.

"Would that person know?" Bolden demanded, pointing to a nearby officer.

"I don't know," the woman repeated, playing dumb.

"Well, lady," Bolden declared, raising her voice, "why I'm asking is because he's my minister, and I was told he was placed in a police car about two hours ago. Now if you don't have him here in jail what have you done to him? Have you moved him to the swamp and killed him?"

"I don't know, I don't know."

"Well, I'm going to call the United States Attorney General," she informed the woman. "Somebody's going to tell me where Reverend Rogers is."

As she turned to leave, the woman squeaked, "He's here."

Bolden returned to the desk, asking if she could sign a bond for his release, though her request was denied.

Before leaving, the fiery Bolden offered Tuscaloosa police officers some unsolicited advice: Whether they knew it or not, it was in their best interest to release Reverend Rogers. As she put it, "This town is sitting on a powder keg."

Bolden was hardly exaggerating. While the local newspaper reported otherwise, Bolden remembered the anxiety that gripped the town. "Police was going around with guns stuck out the window in the backseat of the car," she began. "People were throwing rotten eggs and tomatoes on you. I drove down here waiting on a light and three white boys came up behind me and told me I had a flat. So I just turned around and drove back to the police station. I did not have a flat. I guess if I'd gotten out of the car there's no telling what they'd done, pelting my car with tomatoes and rotten eggs or what have you."

"I was afraid," Bolden admitted.

Upon returning home, she called a male friend to stay with her that night in an effort to calm her nerves. Believing her phone to be tapped, she explained, "We had to talk in code. I said, 'Come and bring a lot of sandwiches.' He knew what that meant—guns and a lot of bullets. Well, I had some guns . . . and he came, and we stayed around these windows all night, but [the Klan] didn't come."

Thankfully, after such a terror-filled day, no one was hungry for "sandwiches."

On the afternoon of June 10, after a momentary cooling-off period for demonstrators and police officers alike, Reverend Rogers arrived at Bailey's Tabernacle CME Church and continued to rally the crowd.

"We are going to assemble as long as there is breath in our bodies," he made clear. "We are going to demonstrate until freedom is ours."

Fifty-eight of the ninety-four previously arrested demonstrators were still in jail, though hundreds of others remained eager to follow their lead. Rogers told the crowd that they would be going to jail "indefinitely" and "this time we're not coming out."

Once more, Rogers reached out to the city commissioners, assuring them that he would halt all further demonstrations if they were willing to sit down with TCAC representatives in an attempt to fashion a compromise. It was a tactic Dr. Martin Luther King Jr. had made public a year prior in his "Letter from Birmingham Jail"—pressuring for peace.

Yet Tuscaloosa's city commissioners ignored the request, and as promised, TCAC and its supporters immediately resumed operations, preparing for a second round of marches and placing themselves yet again at the whim of Police Chief Marable.

"When the police say, 'You are under arrest,' we will submit peacefully," Rogers reminded the packed church. "Police Chief Marable assured us there won't be any head knocking. He said they are going to arrest us if we march, but that there would be no trouble if we go along quietly."

Rogers relied on the police chief's word, despite that just days prior Marable had failed to keep a similar promise.

Meanwhile, Marable and the city commissioners remained unclear as to what was to happen next. In no uncertain terms, James Bevel had made it clear that Tuscaloosa was quickly becoming a target for King's Southern Christian Leadership Conference (SCLC)—an organization whose nonviolent approach had nevertheless wreaked havoc on other Alabama cities. While Tuscaloosa's white establishment wanted desperately to avoid the mistakes of Birmingham, they were uncertain of how to do so. Further, the Tuscaloosa situation was particularly precarious in that it was home to the United Klans of America— adding an additional stick of dynamite to an already explosive situation. If the SCLC arrived, surely further violence would follow.

Marable searched desperately for an answer. How could he possibly keep the peace while placating both whites and blacks?

While TCAC continued its efforts to reach out to Tuscaloosa's city commission, the commission denied it'd ever even been contacted. When confronted, Public Safety Commissioner George Ryan saw no reason for negotiations, particularly since, according to him, Tuscaloosa had "no city laws covering segregation." Yet segregation remained an unspoken law, proof of which was seen in the "White" and "Colored" signs posted outside the courthouse bathrooms.

Despite the publicity the movement received as a result of Bloody Tuesday, Rogers's leverage already appeared to be waning, at least to local politicians.

"Frankly, as long as outsiders are trying to tell us how to run our business in Tuscaloosa, I personally see no reasons for negotiations," Ryan continued, though he made no mention who exactly these "outsiders" were.

Mayor George Van Tassel publicly decried Rogers as well, noting, "I no longer consider the Rev. Rogers a responsible leader of the Negro population in Tuscaloosa. In fact, I consider his leadership irresponsible."

The white establishment's attempts to discredit the reverend only confirmed what many African Americans already knew to be true: They had found their leader in Rogers.

CHAPTER 19

The Defenders

Dates Unknown

But it took a lot of guts.

Since Autherine Lucy's close call eight years prior, a small group of Tusca-loosa's African American men—mostly ex-military, Korean War veterans—began holding secret meetings at Howard and Linton's Barbershop, sneaking in the back entrance to maintain their anonymity. Their goal: to set up a highly trained, highly secretive organization to defend the black community in a manner local law enforcement seemed reticent to do.

One of the men present at these meetings—and the one most credited with overseeing the group—was a filling station proprietor named Joe Mallisham. While some note that the Defenders organization was formed as a direct response to Bloody Tuesday, others close to the organization claimed that it had been around—in some capacity—for several years prior, though Bloody Tuesday gave them reason to reemerge. Likely, this disagreement over the organization's roots speaks to its exclusivity. Few were made aware of the group; it was so secretive, in fact, that the name assigned to the organization would not even be used until long after the men had disbanded.

Yet despite reports to the contrary, throughout his life, Joe Mallisham remained firm that the formation of the Defenders was in direct response to Bloody Tuesday. "I organized the first unit to protect us," Mallisham explained. "This was the eve of June 9th. Cuz we didn't have any police protection at the time. From there on [I was in charge]."

After receiving word of the horrors of Bloody Tuesday, as well as the resulting ninety-four arrests, Mallisham called upon a hand-selected group of men, informing them, "We're going to have to do it. We have to protect these folks. We have to protect the marches and demonstrations."

The group soon outgrew Howard and Linton's Barbershop, dozens of young men joining their ranks throughout the summer and fall of 1964. Yet membership was not guaranteed. Mallisham required that his men uphold the highest standards, recruiting only "married war veterans" who were willing to "conform to a rigid code of morality." Further, these men were also expected to pledge their lives to the cause of defending their fellow African Americans. In short, Mallisham demanded they function as modern-day superheroes— citizens by day but Defenders by night.

While TCAC members, local reverends, and a portion of the African American community were aware of the Defenders' work, Tuscaloosa's white citizens remained wholly ignorant of the organization. Even progressive whites who worked tirelessly on behalf of the civil rights struggle were kept in the dark. This was not due to a lack of trust, but a result of pragmatism—the organization functioned most effectively when few were aware of the details surrounding their aims.

Jim Webb, a white graduate student in the psychology department, remembered well the backlash that came as a result of his open support for civil rights, as well as the protection he himself required. After hosting some out-of-town civil rights volunteers, Webb turned on his radio to hear a political ad for a city councilman running for office.

"Listen, my friends," the ad began, "drive by 305 Cedar Crest anytime, day or night; see beer and whiskey bottles in the front yard and street; see blacks and whites going in and out all hours of the day and night. Vote for me, and I will clean this mess up."

"Well, that was my address," Webb admitted, "and Cedar Crest was a fairly busy thoroughfare. I wasn't that upset, but the next day I got a call from my mother, who lived in Memphis, and she said, 'Jimmy, I'm coming down to do some genealogy work. Can I come stay with you?' What can you say?"

The nervous graduate student called his psychology professor, Dr. Raymond Fowler—who had connections in the black community.

"Let me think about it for a few minutes, and let me get back to you," Fowler said.

After a few hours, Fowler returned Webb's call, assuring his student that he had nothing to fear. "I've made some calls, and they have told [Grand Wizard] Bobby Shelton that for this week your house is simply off-limits," Fowler assured him.

The question for Webb was: Who exactly were *they*?

Days later, as Webb and his mother pulled into his drive, the student spotted a few peculiarities.

"As we drove up Cedar Crest and turned up to my driveway, I noticed there was an old junk car with the hood up, and a black man was working on something under the hood," he explained. "As I slowed to turn into my driveway, he looked up and gave an almost imperceptible nod. As I pulled into my driveway, there was a black man up in the telephone pole, working on the telephone wires. He, too, gave me an imperceptible nod. My mother had no idea that she had a safety net of black protectors," he laughed. "She went to her grave never knowing that."

Tuscaloosa's civil rights movement had other white allies, most notably University of Alabama law professor Jay Murphy and his wife, Alberta (an instructor in the political science department, as well as a practicing attorney). Despite their dedicated support, even they remained wholly unaware of Mallisham's secret group. This lack of knowledge was to be expected for the majority of Tuscaloosa's white population, though it was surprising that even the Murphys—who had proven their loyalty time and time again—were left entirely in the dark.

Stan Murphy, Alberta and Jay's son, confirmed that to his knowledge, his mother knew nothing of the group. It would take years before Stan Murphy even learned of the Defenders' existence, describing them as "an armed group of veterans who would guard my mama."

"They just threw a curtain around her," Murphy explained, "and if anyone tried to harm her, she had her own secret service."

Jay Murphy, too, was greatly admired by the movement's leaders. While most known as a beloved professor, he was a well-respected labor arbitrator as well. It was his role as arbiter that first led him to African American Joe Mallisham, a union representative in a dispute with Ziegler's Paints. Murphy heard the dispute while in a restaurant in the McLester Hotel in downtown Tuscaloosa, integrating the place on the day of the hearing. When the hotel manager eyed Mallisham and explained to Murphy that the McLester Hotel was for whites only, Murphy snapped, "We're either going to do this here or we're never going to have it done."

And so, all the men—including African American Joe Mallisham—entered the McLester Hotel. From that moment on, Joe Mallisham—the future leader of the Defenders—knew he had an ally in the Murphy family.

Upon reflecting on his own interactions with Mallisham, Stan Murphy referred to him as "a dear friend" and a "thoroughly decent, brave soul.

"He was very unassuming," Murphy continued, "very modest. Nothing was firebrand about Joe. He was very gentle."

But Mallisham was also very cautious, and while he protected civil rights supporters regardless of color, his primary objective was always to protect the movement's leadership—primarily the reverends.

Ruth Bolden remembered one occasion in which Reverend Rogers's yellow Cadillac was towed to a car lot due to a supposed bad check. Once the check cleared and the car was returned, Mallisham examined Rogers's car from bumper to bumper, paying careful attention to the brakes, no doubt fearing the possibility of tampering.

"[Mallisham] was afraid of an accident," Bolden explained, before correcting herself: "We could call it an accident."

Yet Mallisham's Defenders did far more than the occasional car inspection. Rather, they provided round the clock surveillance, particularly at the Rogers home, which Nathaniel Howard Jr. compared to "a military institution."

Throughout much of the summer of 1964, cars provided a perimeter around Rogers's home, some reports even indicating that the armed guards seated inside demanded identification before letting anyone pass down the street. Other perhaps more apocryphal stories reveal that cars had to blink their headlights twice in order to receive the proper clearance, a secret handshake of sorts.

"One guy was shot at, just grazed his head," remembered Ruth Bolden, adding matter-of-factly, "he forget to blink his lights twice."

But of all the safeguards employed to protect Reverend T. Y. Rogers, one indicator always assured the driver safe passage.

"If you were a black person," Nathaniel Howard Jr. explained, "you could get through."

❋

The Defenders' seemingly over-the-top precautionary measures were not the result of acute paranoia, but rather a fully realized threat. There was little doubt in Tuscaloosa's African American community that if anyone was a target, it was T. Y. Rogers.

"He'd get all these threatening calls," Ruth Bolden recalled, noting how the harassment spared no one—not even Rogers's young daughter.

"He would get such nasty calls from nasty white men telling him what they were going to do, and how they were going to bust her backside in, so they had to carry her to and from school."

Rogers acknowledged the harassing phone calls, though admitted that when his wife answered the phone, he often "felt sorrier for the people who called than I did for her."

"If she got a chance to talk to them, she talked to them worse than they talked to her," he explained. "It stemmed some of the tide, because they finally reached the point, I guess, where they said, 'Well, that lady's crazy, anyway, so there's no point in calling so much.'"

While Rogers agreed that his family received "the usual threats," he also pointed out that his wife had long understood that threats were often the result of a job well done. While serving as assistant pastor, Rogers regularly answered King's personal phone line, noting, "There were times when I would answer his telephone for hours on end, and they would be all threats."

Upon receiving his own threats, Rogers reacted with "[a] little fear, and then a little amazement."

"After all, why would they threaten me?" he asked himself, concluding, "I may be making a bigger dent than I thought I was."

Joe Mallisham, too, remained undeterred by the threats.

When asked if he feared for his life, Mallisham laughingly replied, "No. No. I didn't know what fear was . . . people began to realize that the fear of death was stupid. It's going to come anyway. Sooner or later it's going to come. And that was the greatest fear that was hung over our heads. Once we got over that, it didn't have an impact."

Yet not everyone shared his view.

Odessa Warrick—who had been the victim of violence during Tuscaloosa's lunch counter sit-ins, as well as Bloody Tuesday—didn't rely on the Defenders for protection; instead, she concocted her own private methods for defense. While people around town regularly spotted Warrick faithfully toting her Bible, it was not for piety's sake.

"I used to carry a gun in that Bible," Warrick remembered. "The Lord said watch as well as pray."

Throughout the 1960s, the home of Jay and Alberta Murphy served as Tuscaloosa's version of a Parisian salon. Progressive men and women of all colors gathered there to discuss the issues of the day, as well as to plan strategy. T. Y. Rogers, T. W. Linton, Willie Herzfeld, among others regularly spent time at the family home.

"You never knew who was going to be there," explained Stan Murphy, whose childhood and adolescence was spent among an array of black men and women parading through the house to confer with his parents. Murphy went on to note the effect his parents' "open door policy" had on many of the local leaders, prompting several African Americans to admit that the Murphy home was the first time in their lives that they had felt welcomed in a white person's house.

Well aware of their politics (as well as their hospitable reputation), the University of Alabama also employed the Murphys to host the university's more liberal-leaning guests.

"Any time there was anybody slightly off, they'd call my momma," Murphy laughed, naming Congressman Adam Clayton Powell and Senators Eugene McCarthy, Alan Cranston, and Mike Gravel among other household guests. While the young Stan Murphy had little notion that his household was different from any other, at some point even he began to notice the many crosses left to smolder just outside the living room windows.

"We had quite a few crosses burned in our yard," Stan Murphy began, explaining that the sheer regularity of the cross burnings became more of an irritant than a threat. As a result, Jay Murphy dreamed up a unique way to disarm the Klansmen of their scare tactics.

"At one point my dad got a big galvanized tub and filled it with sand. And he put up a little sign that said, 'You're tearing the yard up, put the cross here.'"

Yet the harassment continued. Each night, as the lights went off inside their home, the telephone kept them awake.

"We're right outside your house," a voice hissed. "We're going to kill your wife; we're going to kill your son."

Deciding he'd finally had enough, one night Jay Murphy replaced the phone to its cradle and was moved to take action. For several years he'd endured the onslaught of threats, and while he'd become mostly jaded by the combination of crosses and telephone calls, he knew this routine was unsustainable.

"So apparently what my dad did was, he went down to see Bobby Shelton," Stan Murphy recounted, "and he introduced himself and said, 'I don't know you, nothing personal, but this is what's been happening. And I'm going to hold you personally responsible. And I just want to let you know that if anything happens to my wife or my son, I'm going to come down here, and I'm going to blow your God-damned head off. You understand?'"

Stan Murphy smiled before continuing.

"That was the line—'I'm going to blow your God-damned head off'— which my father was thoroughly capable of doing. He was a magnificent pistol shot. I grew up in a house full of guns, which was odd because there was no one in town who was more of a Zen Buddhist Quaker pacifist than my father. To be that and also a fairly avid gun collector and a great pistol shot was an odd combination. But he took very seriously his duty to protect his family, and I have absolutely no doubt that he would have done whatever was necessary."

According to Stan Murphy, an emergency Klan meeting was called, in which Robert Shelton informed the other Klansmen of the threat.

"The consensus reached," Murphy recalled, "was that very probably the professor was actually going to come down and blow [Shelton's] God-damned head right off."

While it wasn't enough to halt the threats entirely, the Murphys received no threatening phone calls that night.

Murphy recalled also how he and his father often went hunting, putting on quite a show of loading the guns into the car and driving away.

"And we'd go to gun shops and pawnshops, buying guns and swapping guns," Murphy continued, noting that while they certainly enjoyed these activities, his father was actually sending the town a message.

At the time, Stan Murphy was still too young to fully understand the message his father was sending to the community, though he made sense of it years later: "The Murphys are very, very well-armed people."

When asked if he believed his parents feared for their lives, Murphy replied, "They may have, but I was absolutely oblivious to that. If they had any fear at all, it was never communicated to me."

Murphy continued: "But it took a lot of guts. The more you think about this stuff, it took a lot of physical courage to do what they did in this era. And in a different kind of way than for black folks who were involved. There were expectations over there, but when white people would do it, there was almost a traitorous aspect to it. There was something particularly offensive when white people did it."

It was a sentiment the Klansman turned FBI informant, Gary Thomas Rowe, echoed decades before.

"[The Klan] felt contempt for fellow Southerners who submitted without any kind of fight—legal or physical—but they despised most of all the whites who voluntarily sought the companionship of Negroes and actively worked for integration."

When he reflected on this tumultuous time in Tuscaloosa, Stan Murphy voiced a particular disdain for the local white leaders who could have done more but didn't.

"If the civic and business community had said, 'We're not having this race bullshit anymore. We're not going to have a courthouse with segregated restrooms . . . it's illegal and it's offensive, it's dangerous and we want to stop it,' then it never would have happened. There never would have been a fight. There would have been no need for a demonstration."

Yet with few exceptions, white leaders refused to speak out, including those in the religious community. Their shared silence made it abundantly clear that the fight for Tuscaloosa needed to be waged on other fronts—in the streets, in the courts, and if necessary, in the Murphy's living room.

CHAPTER 20

Testing Tuscaloosa

June 30–July 7, 1964

What is the great attraction of lining up and trying to make trouble and get into a restaurant?

With the July 2 passage of President Lyndon Johnson's Civil Rights Act, a new world began emerging throughout the South. Fully aware of the political ramifications of the act, Johnson was rumored to have mumbled to an aide, "We have lost the South for a generation." It was a problem President Kennedy had himself foreseen. Robert Kennedy later remarked that his brother "felt that maybe that [June 11 Civil Rights] speech was going to be his political 'swan song.'"

The legislation altered the course of the country in many ways, including empowering the Justice Department to file suit against discriminatory practices occurring within public accommodations. Thus the law's reverberations were felt in restaurants, movie theaters, and public swimming pools throughout the country. For many African Americans, the playing field appeared to have been leveled at last, prompting them to participate in a methodical feeling-out process of testing the limits of the federal government's ability to enforce such a law. It was a new day for southern blacks, one in which the law appeared to be on their side—a great departure from past experiences in which the roles of judge, jury, and executioner often fell squarely on local white men with little federal oversight.

Yet even before the July 2 passage of the Civil Rights Act of 1964, TCAC and other like-minded organizations had already begun using courtrooms as a means to their ends. While TCAC had previously filed an injunction demanding that race designation signs be removed from the Tuscaloosa County Courthouse, it was not until June 30—just days before Johnson signed the act into law—that the city received official word of the federal court's ruling in TCAC's favor. Just a year prior, local dignitaries had attempted to preserve history by inserting a copper box into the cornerstone of the newly constructed courthouse, though as the future revealed, the courthouse itself was destined for history.

In a small report taking up no more than three inches of front-page news space was the story that many TCAC members recalled as the happiest moment throughout the movement—a court ruling supporting their cause. District Judge Seybourn H. Lynne had made clear that he viewed the discriminatory signage as a violation of the Fourteenth Amendment, noting, "The maintenance of signs . . . is itself discriminatory, whether applied to separate entrances, restrooms, drinking fountains or any other facilities provided for public use."

Now able to move about freely within a government building, African Americans found a new lease on the movement, yet far more important than their ability to share a restroom was the precedent established by Lynne's ruling—that a southern judge in a southern town could put the law before his own self-interest. However, this was far from the first time Lynne proved to be the thorn in the segregationists' side. A year earlier, he had issued the injunction barring Wallace from physically blocking Hood and Malone from registration—a ruling that won few popularity contests for the then fifty-five-year-old southern judge.

On Tuesday, June 30, Lynne's popularity among southern whites diminished further as he mandated the removal of discriminatory signage in the Tuscaloosa County Courthouse. Throughout the day, county officials continued their work as usual, though by nighttime, a far different group crammed inside the courthouse doors.

❈

Just hours after the signs were removed, the Tuscaloosa County Courthouse filled with members of the White Citizens for Action Committee—a pro-segregationist group with affiliates throughout the South. James L. Frazier, president of the Tuscaloosa branch, urged citizens to take a page out of TCAC's playbook and employ economics as a tool to combat this most recent transgression.

Frazier argued that if Tuscaloosa's white population united in the same way African Americans did, then they could regain control of the situation.

"The primary purpose of WCAC is to put the economic pressure on local Negroes and let them run the outside Negro agitators out of town," he reminded the crowd. The "outside Negro agitator" in question was none other than T. Y. Rogers—a perfect scapegoat, though his impact was relatively minor in comparison to President Johnson's civil rights legislation, which would be signed into law just forty-eight hours later.

Yet for many members of the White Citizens for Action Committee, Reverend T. Y. Rogers represented everything the group despised. While WCAC didn't admit disliking *all* African Americans, they did sour to intellectual types (a code phrase for Communists) who they believed were gaming the system on the taxpayer's dime. Rogers's status as an "outside agitator" further infuriated WCAC's members, despite the fact that he'd actually been born and raised in Alabama, and even received his undergraduate degree at Alabama State. However, WCAC much preferred focusing on Rogers's few years in Pennsylvania, where he went to receive his pastoral training, as well as oversee his first church, Galilee Baptist. Yet to the average white Tuscaloosan, this brief stint outside the state wholly qualified him as an outsider—proof enough that Rogers didn't understand the city's long tradition of so-called peaceful coexistence between the races.

As Frazier wrapped up his meeting in Tuscaloosa, back in Washington, legislators were putting the finishing touches on the long-awaited Civil Rights Act of 1964. President Kennedy had first announced plans for major civil rights legislation on the night of the University of Alabama's successful desegregation, though it took over a year to pass the act in both the House and Senate. Despite his hard work, Kennedy would not live to see it to fruition; Lee Harvey Oswald made certain of that.

The assassination of President John F. Kennedy the previous November spurred a mixed reaction on the University of Alabama campus: many students mourned the fallen president while the more callous among them were said to have celebrated his death. Vivian Malone recalled witnessing "people on campus shouting and you know, so happy that the president was assassinated." A minority of Tuscaloosa's public school students was alleged to have shared a similar reaction, cheering and clapping their hands upon hearing news of the bullets fired from atop a Dallas book depository.

Yet eight months after his death, the force of Kennedy's bill lived on.

On Tuesday, July 2, at a few minutes before 6:00 P.M., the residents of Tuscaloosa prepared for their Fourth of July holiday weekend. Meanwhile, in the East Room of the White House, an expressionless President Johnson took the opportunity to address the nation, reminding Americans that racial discrimination was not only against the Constitution but against American principles and morality as well. He summed up the legislation by explaining that it ensured that all Americans would be "equal in the polling booths, in the classrooms, in the factories, and in hotels, restaurants, movie theaters, and other places that provide a service to the public."

Moments later, flanked by Dr. Martin Luther King Jr. among others, the thirty-sixth president of the United States fulfilled the promise that, due to Kennedy's untimely death, his predecessor could not—legislatively ushering in an era of equality with a sweep of his pen.

While the Civil Rights Act of 1964 certainly looked good on paper, not all African Americans were so easily convinced of the Justice Department's ability to enforce it. While Attorney General Robert F. Kennedy had previously proven himself a champion of civil rights, his new task of patrolling an entire country for its discriminatory practices was daunting.

Nevertheless, Congress was willing to give the attorney general the opportunity to try. Before the ink had begun to dry, civil rights activists began testing the law for themselves, while Robert Kennedy began testing the limits of the federal government.

The first test occurred in Kansas City, Missouri, where at precisely one minute after President Johnson's signature, thirteen-year-old Gene Young marched dutifully into the barbershop in the Muehlebach Hotel and was abruptly denied service—the first of many failed attempts at ending discriminatory practices in public facilities. Yet the following morning, after further negotiations, Young returned for the haircut he'd previously been denied, and this time, he received it. Similar tests were tried simultaneously in Albany, Georgia, and Atlanta, among various other southern locales.

Equally quick to action was Alabama governor George Wallace, who publicly rejected the legislation. President Johnson, believing his gubernatorial allies in Tennessee and Florida might engage in some "off-the-record conferences" with Alabama's stubborn governor, soon discovered that Wallace would have none of it. While Wallace graciously invited former governors LeRoy Collins of Florida and Buford Ellington of Tennessee to pay him a visit any time, he would not hear of any "off-the record conference"—halting Johnson's plan to apply pressure by way of the governors.

"My position on this bill is well known," Wallace replied bluntly to the former governors.

Johnson was undoubtedly irked. Wallace's belligerent stand the previous summer had propelled him to become the self-proclaimed defender of segregation, making his submission to the Civil Rights Act all the more important to Johnson. If Wallace could be swayed to submit, other southern states would surely fall into line. Yet quite characteristically, Wallace refused to budge, complicating matters further and positioning himself for round two in the fight for states rights—a position in which the former Golden Gloved boxer was beginning to feel quite comfortable.

Throughout July of 1964, the South became a legislative testing ground—both in Tuscaloosa and beyond. After weeks of endless marches and protests, Tuscaloosa's Fourth of July weekend was expected to serve as a much-needed respite for both the city's police officers and its citizens. Yet by late afternoon on July 4, twenty-five African Americans purchased tickets to a movie at Tuscaloosa's Capri Theater, entering the theater for the first time. Aside from the white moviegoers who abruptly left upon their entrance, the theater's integration occurred without any racial fireworks. One can imagine the electric atmosphere buzzing within the Capri—the African Americans seated inside the cool, damp theater, listening to the film click over the reels while the smell of popcorn wafted from the nearby concession stand. For the majority of white Tuscaloosans, attending a matinee at the Capri was little more than an enjoyable afternoon diversion, yet for the twenty-five African Americans experiencing it for the first time, it bordered on the sublime.

Meanwhile, less than a mile away, Reverend Rogers and Reverend Hutchinson integrated Morrison's Cafeteria, a restaurant that likely never would have served its African American clientele prior to the passage of the act. For the first time, civil rights activists not only had moral law on their side, but federal law as well, and they were eager to partake in everything they had long been denied.

Harvey Burg, who in the summer of 1964 was sent to Tuscaloosa on a grant from the Law Students Civil Rights Research Council, fondly recalled one courtroom interaction in which Reverend Rogers attempted to express his desire to take advantage of the newly opened facilities.

When a white lawyer derisively asked Rogers, "What is the great attraction of lining up and trying to make trouble and get into a restaurant?"

Rogers was quick to reply, "You know something, you guys were fighting so hard to keep us out, we just figured you must have had something magical in there."

Emboldened by their Fourth of July successes, the tests continued well into Sunday, July 5. Eight African Americans bought tickets for an afternoon showing at the Bama Theater, while another pair ate lunch at Morrison's. While neither group had problems getting into their desired locations, both had problems getting out. A crowd of angry restaurant-goers confronted Morrison's African American patrons, while a patron inside the movie theater reported that the integrationists were "escorted out of the building by six white men."

White men began picketing both the Bama and the Capri theaters, waving signs indicating that whites should refuse to patronize businesses that kowtowed to the Civil Rights Act. Many of the protesters were rumored to be Klansmen themselves, holding signs spouting racial slurs such as "Pay a buck, see a coon."

While a handful of local whites ignored the picketers and enjoyed the movie, they often returned to the parking lot to find their vehicles the victims of vandalism—windows shattered and tires punctured. The vandals were making an example not only out of the African Americans who dared test the new legislation, but also whites who were willing to go along with it.

TCAC's prior request for an injunction against Tuscaloosa city officials "interfering with 'peaceful demonstrations'" hit a standstill on June 22, when Judge Clarence Allgood of Birmingham requested additional time due to a "heavy docket." Yet the hearing resumed on Monday, July 6, further proof that civil rights was moving forward both in the streets and in the courtroom.

TCAC received even more hopeful news the following day, when field workers from the Southern Christian Leadership Conference infiltrated the streets of Tuscaloosa and Selma. During a Monday night press conference, Dr. Martin Luther King Jr. remarked that the SCLC would "assess the situation in the two cities to determine what, if any, direct action is necessary."

King explained his decision to send SCLC representatives quite simply: "The problem in Selma and Tuscaloosa is to see that mob rule does not take over implementation of the civil rights bill."

He continued: "The action we take in those cities will depend on the resistance and conditions we find. If we find it necessary to go to the streets to dramatize injustice, we will demonstrate to bring the issue to the open."

King publicly praised Birmingham, Montgomery, and Huntsville—among other Alabama cities—for acclimating to the civil rights bill so quickly. And while it was no secret that the SCLC had dedicated the summer to focusing its attention on Alabama, the organization's next target seemed to have narrowed between Tuscaloosa and Selma.

Under slightly different circumstances, it's quite possible that Tuscaloosa might have taken Selma's position in the annals of civil rights history. However, its selection over Tuscaloosa as the SCLC's next civil rights battleground was likely the result of Selma simply requiring more attention. Couched in the heart of the Black Belt, the town of thirty thousand was far more acquainted with violence than Tuscaloosa's African American citizenry. While Tuscaloosa had endured a few minor scuffles (the exception being Bloody Tuesday, which was far worse than a "scuffle"), it had become evident that Selma was in more immediate need of the SCLC's vast organizational resources.

As if the Southern Christian Leadership Conference needed further provocation to come to Selma, on Monday, July 6, SCLC national coordinator and future congressman John Lewis and fifty supporters were arrested outside Selma's Dallas County Courthouse for attempting to register to vote. These sorts of unprovoked mass arrests were far more rare in Tuscaloosa, and Selma's continued troubles at the hands of law enforcement made it the default choice.

Selma and Tuscaloosa simply maintained far different philosophies on how to enforce the laws. While Tuscaloosa police chief William Marable made what many believed to be a sincere effort to keep the peace, Sheriff Jim Clark of Selma offered no such sincerity. As he proved again and again, Clark was far more concerned with keeping segregation intact than with keeping peace.

The SCLC's decision *not* to bring the fight to Tuscaloosa was likely a result of the city's restraint; King didn't believe the city's situation so dire that it required his full attention. While many have questioned if Tuscaloosa's close proximity to the headquarters of the United Klans of America also played a role in the decision making, it seems a likely possibility, though there is scant evidence to confirm this.

A final factor for the SCLC's decision might reside in its confidence in Reverend T. Y. Rogers himself. Dr. King seemed to have placed his trusted ally in his stead, and owing to his full faith in Rogers, perhaps the SCLC and its leader believed they could more easily allocate resources where they were most needed—eighty miles south of Tuscaloosa, in a small, southern city called Selma.

On July 7, the tests continued throughout Tuscaloosa, African Americans successfully being served at Kress and Woolworth's and the Hotel Stafford. While four African Americans were also served at Tom's Snack Bar on Greensboro Avenue, they were "forcefully ejected" by four white men. Likewise, the Admiral Benbow Inn also refused service, though the setbacks were hardly setbacks at all. Rogers fully understood that not every business would submit to the law so quickly, though by testing the playing field, he had a better sense of his targets. The tests were run with an efficient yet tactical precision, Rogers lining up an additional five restaurants for Tuesday afternoon.

For some integrationists, TCAC's success with local restaurants caused an unexpected side effect—full stomachs. Some new patrons simply couldn't fathom the thought of eating any more—not even for the cause of civil rights.

"They would just ask for a hamburger," explained Ruth Bolden, "just to see if they was going to let them do it. They weren't really hungry."

Bolden described one instance in which comedian Dick Gregory accompanied them, assuring his stuffed lunch mates that when he left Tuscaloosa he was going to leave behind "a lot of fat women."

Yet TCAC's initial successes were tempered by failures. Newspapers reported that by the end of Tuesday, only six of thirteen tested dining establishments had complied with the law—just under 50 percent. However, in a bit of encouraging news, the final movie theater holdout—Druid Theater—admitted six African Americans without incident.

The changes were coming at a quick pace—far too fast for many southern whites struggling to adjust to the swift shattering of the color barriers. Tuscaloosa police officers began stationing themselves outside of restaurants in order to enforce the law.

Meanwhile, business owners were conducting their own tests—seeking out creative ways to circumvent the newly enacted federal law, including locking their doors. In early July, a group of African Americans arrived at Ed's Drive-In to find the doors locked, despite the white people dining inside. Other restaurants took this strategy a step further by closing down entirely. Even Tuscaloosa's Druid City Hospital snack bar found a way to bypass the law—closing down just as African Americans arrived for service.

Throughout the South, segregationist-minded restaurateurs were learning many hard lessons on the economic consequences of preserving the status quo, one in particular: It was hard to feed one's family by refusing to feed somebody else's.

CHAPTER 21

Movie Mayhem

July 8–10, 1964

We nearly mobbed Jack Palance.

While they had experienced some minor successes in dining establishments throughout town, in July of 1964, African Americans took their fight to the movies. After Tuscaloosa's Bama Theater endured a few integration attempts—one successful, one not—the Druid Theater became the next target, the latest battleground for segregation. In the first weeks of July 1964, the Druid Theater became for Tuscaloosa what Foster Auditorium had been the year before—a last stand of sorts, a final breaking point, and once again, white segregationists refused to back down without a fight.

On Wednesday, July 8, seventeen African Americans purchased tickets for a 7:40 P.M. showing, and while there were no incidents inside the theater, upon their exit, a mob over two hundred strong greeted them. The African American moviegoers peered out the theater's windows, eyeing the pair of taxis that would take them to freedom, if only they could make it safely inside. The police attempted to form a ring around the theater's entrance, though this did little to keep the white mob from hurling slurs and debris as the moviegoers made their break toward the cars. While one young moviegoer was hit with a brick, the cabs received damage as well—one earning a broken windshield, the other a dent. Although a third cab was called to pick up the few remaining African Americans, the Deluxe Radio Cab Company refused, believing the situation too volatile to risk damage to its fleet. The remaining moviegoers were left loitering in the lobby for nearly an hour, awaiting an exit strategy while the mob continued to grow in size and fury. The police managed to contain the mob, though they offered little assistance in escorting the African Americans home.

Odessa Warrick was one of those trapped inside the theater that warm summer night. According to her, a few of the boys peered outside the theater and noticed the windows broken out of their cars—a clear sign of the violence that was sure to follow. "We was scared so we called Joe Mallisham," Warrick explained.

Soon after, a pair of cars screeched to a halt in front of the theater, the trapped moviegoers leaping inside amid a flurry of bottles and rocks. The cars pulled away while the mob leaped into their own cars, giving chase.

Aside from a brief interaction at the bus station, the newspaper noted, "no further incidents or outbreaks were reported." Yet this did not mean the night was over. Joe Mallisham, one of the getaway drivers, peeled down Ninth Street with two terror-stricken teens in the backseat. He wove down the streets, Klan cars in hot pursuit, before turning down a road in the west end of town.

"We turned in there, and that road was lined with black folks because word had gotten out that the Klan was going to come in," Mallisham remembered. "Once we got through, the Klan started in, but they didn't make it. They met a barrage of gunfire [from African Americans] right there."

No injuries were reported, though according to Mallisham, it was not for lack of trying. Had the battle continued, he predicted, "There would have been bloodshed all over this town."

Buford Boone, who had faced down mobs before, knew firsthand how destructive their wrath could be to a city's reputation. He had earned a Pulitzer Prize for addressing this very issue in regard to the Autherine Lucy incident, as well as echoing the call for peace once more in the days preceding Wallace's stand in the schoolhouse door. Yet his refrain seemed needed once more in the wake of the newly passed Civil Rights Act. Boone employed the reach of his newspaper yet again to urge the law-abiding majorities to speak out against their vocal opposition. He implored the peaceable public to remind city commissioners that they were "tired of having the ugly cloud of mob rule hanging over our lives." Likewise, he told Tuscaloosans to stand squarely behind Police Chief Marable, assuring the troubled chief "that we respect law, understand [the] difficulties of his job, and that we support police efforts to control all mob elements, of whatever color."

The white men who made up the mobs found themselves in an equally tight spot. While they despised integration in all its forms, many were conflicted about having to make their views publicly known at the expense of endangering white, southern police officers. It was a microcosmic Civil War—brother against brother, friend against friend—and to complicate matters further, many police officers themselves remained sympathetic to the segregationist point of view. Yet with Marable at the helm, the officers were expected to preserve order indiscriminately—whether they wanted to or not. Throughout the summer, issues of honor and duty were entangled with personal views. Each officer had to decide where his allegiance lay: Do I enforce a law with which I disagree, or turn a blind eye to crimes that best serve my personal interests?

Wholly unaware of the previous night's riot, on Thursday, July 9, actor Jack Palance, his wife, and their three children entered the Druid Theater for the 9:00 P.M. showing of *The World of Henry Orient*—a comedy starring Peter Sellers, Paula Prentiss, and Angela Lansbury. Palance, whose movie career would span half a century, became best known for playing the rugged cowboy in films such as *Shane, The Godchild,* and more recently, *City Slickers* and *City Slickers II.* The California-based actor and his family were in town to visit his wife's aunt and had decided to take in a movie. The Palances had just settled into their seats while unbeknownst to them a mob had begun to gather beyond the theater walls. Hardly half an hour had passed when word spread that Palance's Tuscaloosa appearance was a ploy to "encourage compliance with the Civil Rights Act"—a motive that did not sit well with the already on-edge town. They had heard stories of actors like Marlon Brando pulling similar stunts in neighboring towns and were determined to ensure that the liberal, Hollywood elite kept their noses out of their city. As a result, by 10:00 P.M. a crowd estimated between six hundred and one thousand—mostly white teenagers—had surrounded the theater, waiting for the outsiders to exit.

Rumors continued to swirl, some arguing that Jack Palance was African American himself, while others countered that he was a white man but had escorted a black woman into the theater. The truth was that Palance and his wife—both white—along with their three white children, had come to the Tuscaloosa theater for no purpose other than to enjoy the show. While it seemed logical that a family might enter a movie theater solely for that purpose, in July of 1964, logic often took a backseat to rumor.

University of Alabama graduate student and *Crimson White* reporter Bob Penny recalled he and a friend being inside the theater that night, though their focus remained not on the screen, but on the strange occurrence just a few rows behind them.

"We kept noticing these two or three figures who sat down behind the Palance family and began harassing [Jack Palance]. He turned around and said something to them. Then, one of them said, 'You a big, bad, tough guy in movies, ain't that right?'"

In a huff, Palance entered the lobby to report the disturbance to an usher, though he'd hardly stepped foot into the light when he spotted hundreds of white faces jeering him from just beyond the movie theater windows. Theater manager Richard Young fell into the role of movie hero that night, taking it upon himself to guard the actor and his family in his office while awaiting police. Later, he confirmed the Palance family's singular motivation for entering the theater that night.

"Palance appeared puzzled over what was going on outside," Young remembered. "He said he had no knowledge that the Civil Rights law was being tested here, and he had come to the theater for only one reason—to see the movie, 'The World of Henry Orient.'"

However, none of this information was made available to the growing crowds outside. Instead, they continued hurling bricks at the theater, smashing the marquee and cash register in the process—actions that served only to embolden them further. After objects began being tossed at police officers as well, the officers responded with fire hoses and tear gas. It seemed an encore to Bloody Tuesday, though this time, whites demonstrators became the target.

Growing increasingly nervous, Penny approached the nearest police officer and said, "We need to get out of here. Can you give us safe passage?" to which the officer tasked with containing the mob barked, "Find your own goddamn passage."

They did, the pair of white moviegoers rushing out of the theater amid a storm of jeers and rocks. While the college students escaped, Palance and his family remained trapped inside.

Moments later, a new hero emerged—Police Chief Marable—who rushed to the family's rescue by providing the getaway car. Marable's grandson, William II, recalled his grandfather telling him it was "the one time he got to throw somebody around." Marable tossed the movie star and his wife into the backseat of the car, along with their children, and leaped through the back window as one of his officers drove the car to safety.

The Palance family escaped unscathed, though their rental car did not. The newspaper reported that not only had the tires been slashed, but also every piece that could be broken free, including the antenna and windshield wipers, was torn from the car. Most intriguing of all, however, was what the newspaper described as a "paper sign" clinging to the remains of the car.

It read: "The Knights of the Ku Klux Klan Is Watching You."

Only in the aftermath did Tuscaloosans begin to make sense of the scene. It had occurred almost spontaneously—traveling at the speed of whispers—and immediately captivated the attention of hundreds of teenagers, all of whom were curious to witness the effects of the Civil Rights Act firsthand.

The great irony, of course, was that what was likely the city's largest and most dangerous mob in its history had formed not due to any particular action on the part of African Americans but rather in response to a white family's ill-fated decision to enjoy a movie in downtown Tuscaloosa. Equally ironic was the interview Palance gave local reporters just hours prior to the scene, in which he boasted that Tuscaloosa seemed "real friendly."

"One thing is that the people here are not timid," he observed. "They will come right up and say, 'Hello.'"

In an interview given the following day, Palance changed his tune, telling the Associated Press that during his brief stay in Tuscaloosa he "feared for his life, as well as those of his wife and three children."

He also revealed new insight into the harassment he received from within the theater, confirming what Penny had observed from his vantage point just a few rows back. Upon entering the theater, three white men took seats directly behind the family, accusing Palance of "being paid by the National Association for the Advancement of Colored People and the Congress of Racial Equality."

When the harassment continued, five men now lurking behind him, Palance stood, turned to face them, and said, "You're scaring my children," before leaving the theater and moving to the lobby.

"We got the shock of our lives," Palance admitted. "At least 1,000 people were standing looking in. There was a howling, hooting, jeering mob."

Yet for all their unrestrained gusto, the pro-segregation mob failed to recognize one critical detail, a detail Palance was happy to make clear at the expense of the city: "There were no Negroes either inside or outside the theater."

While the United Klans of America never took responsibility for either the rumors or the mob violence, Grand Wizard Robert Shelton admitted that he had been present throughout the incident.

"Well, I, with some of my key personnel, attempted to steer the crowd away," he explained. "We realized that it was a tense situation."

He, too, blamed the mob's reaction on a rumor run amok, faulty information passed from one teenager to the next, eventually building to near disaster. Yet he soon contradicted his own theory, contending that perhaps Palance *did* have a pro–civil rights agenda after all, or at the very least a pro-Palance agenda.

"It seems strange," Shelton admitted, "but I've found from experience that a movie star will go to any extent for publicity."

In Palance's view, the charges of his so-called ulterior motives—including a pro–civil rights agenda—were groundless. In the days following the incident he asked reporters, "Do you think I'd be crazy enough to come down here with my children, if that were so, and risk my children's lives?"

Despite Shelton's unfounded accusations, his statements soon made clear a pattern that had begun to emerge—whenever there was trouble in Tuscaloosa, the Grand Wizard was often nearby. While Shelton remained an ever-present force, he was always careful to remain within the law. This proved problematic for Marable who never found a reason to arrest him.

"I have talked to Chief Marable often enough to know that he has no respect for Bobby Shelton whatever," local businessman George LeMaistre admitted in the summer of 1964. "If he felt he could have made a case against him, he would have been glad to do so. Not because of the personal feeling, but he doesn't want to make a case in court against him that he cannot prove, I'm sure. It would be bad to let Shelton prove himself to be right and the Chief to be wrong."

In the aftermath of the event, only three white men were arrested for the Druid Theater disturbance, though the month prior, ninety-four African Americans had been hauled off to jail for far less.

The day following the Druid Theater riot, a hotheaded Buford Boone found he could hold his tongue no longer.

"Tuscaloosa's mob hospitality was extended last evening to a movie and television personality of note," Boone's editorial began. "And our ugly picture is being projected all over the world today. We nearly mobbed Jack Palance."

Boone urged Shelton to "desist in all provocative activity," adding diplomatically, "And we have some requests of Mr. Rogers."

Serving as power broker, Boone asked Rogers to ensure that African American children didn't find themselves casualties in the fray. White teenagers had already proved the damage they were capable of exacting, and as Boone pointed out, "[a] mob like that last night, if turned on a group of Negroes of the same ages, could present us with an awful problem. Any further tests should be conducted by mature people."

Boone concluded by asking Rogers to "terminate his organization's boycott of downtown merchants," explaining, "they cannot move to meet his demands without ruin."

Rogers had several demands of the white business establishment as well, though his primary request was simply that African Americans be considered for jobs. He wasn't demanding that white proprietors embrace African Americans with open arms, simply that they view them as prospective employees. It was an argument of economics first set forth by Booker T. Washington nearly seventy years prior, in which the Tuskegee University leader noted, "The opportunity to earn a dollar in a factory just now is worth infinitely more than the opportunity to spend a dollar in an opera-house."

To put it another way: Spending power was the surest way to bring about social change.

Proof of this was seen throughout the city. As a result of the boycotts, Tuscaloosa's businesses began suffering. Business owners found themselves trapped in a Catch-22—comply with the law and risk boycott by the Klan, or disobey the law and risk boycott by African Americans. No white business was safe, and livelihoods were on the line.

Yet in other regions of the country, the integration of drug stores and lunch counters proceeded with relative ease. "We've been integrated for years," explained Milton Elsberg, president of Drug Fair stores. "It's never hurt us a bit. I think if everyone doing business in the South could just be convinced that civil rights are here to stay, that if all of them opened up, none would be hurt."

Not all chain stores maintained such a progressive viewpoint, however. One executive for Kress department stores went so far as to acknowledge that in the Deep South "local custom" often dictated store policy. Geography played a role, one Kress executive explained, noting that while Kress could—hypothetically—create a national policy to desegregate its stores, such a policy would likely result in a dramatic loss of business. The executive added, "We know the tenor of the South."

Despite Boone's pleas, Friday's tests were met with little success. Civil rights activists attempted to integrate six restaurants throughout town, though all refused to serve them. While Boone was perturbed by both sides' unwillingness to budge, he was particularly angered by Shelton. Boone believed the Klan's strategy of pressuring businesses to disobey federal law was counterproductive to business as well as the city at large. As was the case in the Autherine Lucy incident, as well as the stand in the schoolhouse door, the newspaper editor continued offering his support for law and order—even if he didn't publicly agree with the laws themselves. So infuriated by the Klan's tactics, Boone returned once more to his own best weapon—the power of the press.

"It reached the point where the business community was about to submit to the rule of the Ku Klux Klan," Boone explained later. "They were afraid. And I wrote the first editorial and put it on the editor's desk and said, 'I'm not going to let a bunch of cutthroats take over this community if I can help it.'"

His editorial criticized Shelton and his organization, calling the Grand Wizard's Klansmen "grownup juvenile delinquents" as well as "gorillas, un-caged but waiting to bite." The Grand Wizard fired back, demanding a full apology for what he deemed "false, libelous and defamatory editorials," in-cluding Boone's charge that he was "sickly looking" and resembled "an owl."

In this instance, Boone's penchant for the pathos-based argument seemed to have backfired. His usual carefully constructed prose gave way to a ven-omous rebuke, offering characterizations of Shelton and his Klansmen more likely to be found in a schoolyard than the front pages of a newspaper.

After a week of taking shots at Shelton, in his Sunday editorial a freshly calmed Boone took a giant leap back, returning to his usual rhetoric and calling for calm, urging citizens to consider what Jesus might do: "What He counseled never has been matched in wisdom and in love."

He was appealing to an audience he feared alienating—the God-fearing southerner.

Yet not all God-fearing southerners agreed.

In a letter to the editor, C. Duke Case attempted to traverse the tightrope employed by many southern moderates.

"I do not agree with the civil rights law," he made clear, "but more than that I detest the radical minority who are bringing discredit upon our city. It is ridiculous to boycott or picket a merchant because he was chosen, by some-one out of his control, to be integrated and because he obeys this law. Now is the time more than ever to support these merchants. It is equally ridiculous for those merchants, frightened by the threat of boycott, to still refuse ser-vice. They do us more harm as they invite the Attorney General's office into our city to make an example of us."

Tuscaloosa had already lost one round to Attorney General Robert Ken-nedy the previous summer, and the city hardly wanted to try him again.

Through his letter, Case seemed to hone in on the city's primary prob-lem: Fear.

"Not of the Negro," he was quick to add, "but of the white radical. This, or any other, community cannot live in fear. It will wither."

In a final chastisement to his fellow southerners, Case noted, "It is disturbing to me as a white man to see the Negro population orderly, disciplined, and following their leaders while the white radicals meet our police and elected officials with mob violence."

The city's white moderates were being forced to choose between race and radicalism, and for many, like Case, the choice was becoming clear.

CHAPTER 22

Boycotting Buses

August 1–September 12, 1964

The company would just as soon be shut down by a boycott as by a strike.

Tuscaloosa's civil rights movement began and ended with the buses.

In the spring of 1962, Reverend Willie Herzfeld had just settled into the bleachers of a high school baseball game when a breathless Stillman College student ran toward him.

"Hey, Reverend Herzfeld," he called, "come and see the students on the bus."

A curious Herzfeld did as he was told, starting slowly toward a halted bus to investigate the problem. Prior to the arrival of Reverend T. Y. Rogers, Herzfeld was often considered the foremost civil rights leader in town, though his efforts had been met with resistance. Nevertheless, when called to "see the students on the bus," he did so wholly unaware of the future implications of his choice.

Upon his arrival, Herzfeld viewed a seemingly ordinary scene—a bus filled with African American college students. The only difference: there was a white woman as well, and none of the black riders were willing to give up their seats.

As a result of their unwillingness to move, the white bus driver refused to move also. The stalemate continued for several minutes, and despite Herzfeld's attempts to diffuse the situation, neither party appeared willing to budge.

After Herzfeld's failed negotiations, the bus eventually squealed forward, driving to a nearby bus station where waiting police abruptly hauled the African American riders to jail.

According to Herzfeld, the jailed students provided a momentary glimpse of a local civil rights movement, though African Americans' enthusiasm soon withered away. Many were toeing the line, but none were willing to cross it. For Herzfeld, two more frustrating years would pass before Reverend Rogers and his followers found the courage to march on the courthouse.

Yet the bus incident provided the spark, and as a result, the first incarnation of the Tuscaloosa Citizens for Action Committee began to take shape, Reverend Herzfeld voted in as president. While Herzfeld remembered the crowds at some meetings reaching into the hundreds, he admitted that they were "not concerned with mass meetings so much." Instead, they were concerned with "getting something off the ground"—a goal Herzfeld never quite managed on his own.

Two years later, Reverend T. Y. Rogers managed to do just that, combining a diverse strategy of meetings, marches, boycotts, and demonstrations to spur a movement in a matter of months. Throughout the spring and summer of 1964, Reverend T. Y. Rogers and TCAC did more to further equality throughout Tuscaloosa than in any previous period in the city's history. And after enduring a police beating and the movie theater mobs, Rogers felt empowered to set his sights on one final summer objective: the local bus system.

As a result of over a dozen alleged incidents of "harassment, intimidation and arrest of Negroes riding on city buses," in an August 1 letter to city officials, Reverend T. Y. Rogers made clear his intent to boycott the Druid City Transit Company's bus system. Nearly a decade prior, a similar battle had waged in Montgomery, and having received a rare, behind-the-scenes look at the operational duties of a successful boycott, Rogers was at long last ready to put those lessons to good use. Tuscaloosa's own bus battle was far slower in the making than Montgomery's; this was likely the result of the bus company's seemingly progressive policy of "non-segregated seating" as well as the "fair and impartial treatment of all passengers." The policy looked good on paper but struggled to hold up when put to the test.

Throughout Tuscaloosa, foot traffic increased while bus traffic declined. After just two days of boycotts, a Druid City Transit Company spokesperson admitted that due to a "highly effective" campaign, the company would halt bus routes "where it is both unsafe and unprofitable for the company to operate."

It was both a victory and a setback for the movement. While TCAC had telegraphed its ability to bankrupt the buses, the people most hurt by the boycott were African American riders themselves, who made up 90 percent of the total passengers.

Fearing financial loss, after just two days of boycotts, the Druid City Transit Company redirected its routes—proof of TCAC's effectiveness. As he had done during his previous boycotts, Reverend T. Y. Rogers made a list of demands. In a letter to transit manager J. J. Hunt, Rogers made six demands, including the firing of one particular bus driver who had allegedly fired shots at an African American rider, as well as a promise of protection from white patrons. Further, and perhaps most importantly, Rogers called for the employment of African American drivers as well as the assurance that "prompt action be taken against all drivers committing acts of omission or commission of company policies." Rogers requested also that any pending lawsuits against African American riders be dropped and that the company's non-segregationist policies "be made public for all the community to know."

The ultimatum was clear: If you want our business, you need to say so publicly.

Druid City Transit Company attorney H. Vann Waldrop found himself at a loss while attempting to placate what seemed to him like impossible demands. "We have done all we can do," Waldrop explained. "The company has dismissed the driver involved in the shooting incident. We have no power to press charges against the man. Also, none of our drivers has police powers to enforce any laws. The Negroes know that we can't meet these demands. It looks as if the city may be without a transit system if conditions don't improve."

By the third day of the boycott, business was down 60 percent and representatives from the Druid City Transit Company were already exploring the possibility of a Friday halt to all bus lines. The boycott proved to be a stake through the heart for the transportation company, confirming, once more, that economics could effect social change.

In an effort to cut costs, not only did the company limit its routes, but it also shrunk its workforce by half, a mere seven bus drivers at work as opposed to the fourteen at the start of the week.

At 11:00 A.M. on Wednesday, August 12, while empty buses crawled across the city, hundreds gathered at the Tuscaloosa County Courthouse to recognize local law enforcement for its efforts to maintain peace and order in a continuing volatile situation.

Chamber of Commerce president Jack Warner presented plaques of appreciation to Police Chief William Marable, among others. Even Alabama football coach Paul "Bear" Bryant braved the storm clouds to present an award to university police chief Allan O. Rayfield, who just years before had stood alongside Mrs. Carmichael as the president's wife faced down a crowd of angry protesters as the result of Autherine Lucy's admittance.

Leveraging his soon-to-come praise, the day prior to receiving his award, Chief Marable spoke to the local Rotary Club, thanking them for the upcoming appreciation day, though admitting also that appreciation alone would do little to maintain order within the city. He noted that the public's support needed to be ongoing, adding that from a practical standpoint, "the shortage of manpower, low pay scales, and the need for more equipment" were all additional worries that needed to be addressed in order to preserve the peace.

A month earlier, in the July 10 issue of the *Tuscaloosa News,* a front-page political cartoon drew attention to the economic toll of enforcing the law. In it, an overburdened taxpayer with the phrase "Tuscaloosa Economy" on his chest is shown squeezed in the jaws of a vice, one side of which reads, "Mob Pressure" while the other reads, "Legal Compliance." On the left side of the frame, a white hand labeled "Extremists" tightens the jaws further.

Marable was well aware of the financial strain, and after providing the Rotary Club with a wish list of resources, added, "Most of all, we need you. All the men, money and equipment we can get don't mean a thing without your support."

Marable's experience had taught him that mobs would always outnumber law enforcement, and the simplest way to diffuse one was to prevent it from forming in the first place.

The night of Thursday, August 13, marked a temporary end to bus service in Tuscaloosa. The drivers returned their buses to the garage once more, stepping forth from their swinging doors for what they believed was the last time. All twenty drivers and six mechanics were laid off as the company suspended operations throughout the city.

The Druid City Transit Company's decision to halt service was the result of having taken in a mere $150—an amount so miniscule it failed even to offset operational costs. The lack of bus service caused a momentary spike in taxi service, though many regular bus riders soon learned they could hardly afford the fare.

The end of the city's bus service reinforced white citizens' bitterness toward TCAC, many of whom believed its tactics were a disproportionate response given the circumstances. Halting an entire city's bus service due to a few minor incidents seemed unwarranted, and few were willing to side with the movement's actions. Yet what many citizens failed to realize was that the bus boycott was not simply the result of a few minor incidents. Rather, Rogers and the Tuscaloosa Citizens for Action Committee were drawing attention to what they believed were calculated discriminatory practices that had long festered within the town. Coupled with the recent surge of civil rights successes, TCAC remained motivated to continue its pressure on the source of the wound.

Since July, many white southerners had endured what they considered the usual inconveniences associated with the Civil Rights Act—including sharing restaurants and movie theaters—but now that their buses had been taken away, it began to have a more direct effect, at least for the small minority of whites who still rode the buses.

In a letter to the editor, local citizen Frank Huttlinger noted, "only by continued cooperation can either group maximize the return from their respective inputs of capital and labor." In an effort to ride the line of neutrality, Huttlinger continued, "it would seem that the demands of the TCAC that the bus company immediately hire a Negro bus driver are perhaps unreasonable in view of the present union contract." However, he also acknowledged that bus riders were "entitled to travel in safety, even if this means the presence of law enforcement officers on certain buses."

Huttlinger's cool-headed call for "continued cooperation" seemed right, but in the midst of Tuscaloosa's heated environment, the implementation of any such compromise appeared to have become all but impossible.

As if taking Huttlinger's advice, on the morning of Saturday, August 15, Reverend T. Y. Rogers, along with Reverend T. W. Linton and Reverend Willie Herzfeld, met with the Druid City Transit Company manager J. J. Hunt and attorney H. Vann Waldrop in an effort to come to terms to end the crippling boycott. Yet as the meeting dragged on, it became apparent that Rogers refused to back down, while Hunt and Waldrop cited an inability to submit to demands beyond their control. Their primary sticking point: Rogers's insistence the company hire an African American bus driver.

Waldrop and Hunt explained that their company's union contracts required them to rehire the original drivers first, though Rogers remained unmoved by the explanation.

"Federal law says that we can't hire Negro drivers at the present time even if we wanted to," explained Waldrop. "If and when the company hires additional drivers, they will be employed without regard to race, creed or color."

Rogers refused the argument, reminding Hunt and Waldrop, "Since the company gets 90 per cent of its business from the Negro community, it should hire Negro drivers."

Logically, it made sense, yet according to Waldrop, by doing so the company would be in violation of its contract. If they dared hire a single African American driver prior to rehiring the white drivers, they would likely face a strike from the white drivers.

For the Druid City Transit Company, it was a lose-lose situation.

"The company would just as soon be shut down by a boycott as by a strike," Waldrop explained wearily.

Exasperated transit manager J. J. Hunt added, "We have never had a single application from a Negro seeking employment as a bus driver."

As patience continued to wear thin, both sides stepped away from the negotiating table having come no closer to resolving the conflict.

On Monday, August 24, the Druid City Transit Company strongly hinted that it planned to move its infrastructure entirely out of Tuscaloosa.

While the 1955–56 Montgomery bus boycott endured 381 days prior to the city's submission, in Tuscaloosa 1964, it took a little over two weeks for the bus company to fold. TCAC's overwhelming success was likely the result of several factors, including a community fully invested in the cause, as well as a ridership wholly dependent on African Americans. Yet equally important is the apparent change to the psyche of white southerners. Something seemed to have changed in the nine years separating the Montgomery boycott from Tuscaloosa's own effort, and while difficult to pinpoint, it was undoubtedly linked to city leadership and law enforcement agencies—both of which seemed less invested in the fight in Tuscaloosa.

While TCAC and the bus company officials tried a few additional half-hearted attempts at compromise, there was little progress. Both sides seemed to have been pushed as far as they were willing, and transit manager J. J. Hunt found himself caught between a rock and a hard place. He couldn't afford to violate the union contracts, but he also couldn't afford not to hire an African American driver as Rogers demanded. His company had become collateral damage in a civil rights battle, and there was little he could do. Yet Rogers—who believed something could always be done—had little sympathy for the man, and in his August 24 letter to Hunt and Mayor Van Tassel, offered no alternative solutions.

"If you are unable to meet this condition," Rogers said simply, "we are unable to patronize your buses."

While the Druid City Transit Company had a policy against hiring African American drivers, ironically, the Tuscaloosa County school system did not. At the start of the 1964 school year, the primary qualifications for hire of a bus driver were a valid driver's license as well as that the license holder be between the ages of sixteen and fifty—a wildly lenient qualification that allowed fifteen upperclassmen to drive the buses for the underclassmen.

Also of note was that the color of one's skin was irrelevant; proof of which was made clear that very school year when of the seventy-two hired drivers, twenty-three were black.

As the bus drivers barreled into town, Tuscaloosans watched their long, hot, tumultuous summer come to its close. From April through August, the city had endured a battery of racial tests beyond its wildest dreams, though as the seasons changed, so too did the atmosphere.

This time, local African Americans had made their stand and won.

CHAPTER 23

Remembering Reverend Rogers

March 25–29, 1971

There will be no curtain call for T. Y. Rogers Jr.

March 25, 1971, was an unseasonably cold night in Georgia. With a low of 32 degrees, much of the city was tucked safely in their homes, though Reverend Rogers remained hard at work deep into Thursday night and early Friday morning. While the young reverend remained TCAC's leader and continued serving as head pastor at Tuscaloosa's First African Baptist Church, he and his family had recently relocated three hours east to Atlanta, bringing him closer to his work as a director of affiliate chapters of the Southern Christian Leadership Conference. Rogers's fine work in Tuscaloosa had been recognized at the national level, and in the wake of King's death, he was encouraged to take a leadership role within his mentor's former organization.

Rogers's new city of Atlanta had accumulated two inches of rain earlier in the day, and this, coupled with traces of snow, provided dangerous driving conditions, particularly for an already notoriously fast driver. Just three blocks from home, Rogers reportedly spun out on an icy stretch of road sometime after midnight, colliding with an abutment, and he reportedly died soon after.

It was a hard blow to the civil rights community, though it hurt most in Tuscaloosa.

On the night of his death, civil rights activist Ruth Bolden woke to a ringing phone.

"I was in the bed," Bolden remembered. "It was after midnight, I think, and Minnie Thomas called and said, 'Girl, your pastor was killed by a car wreck tonight,'" adding mysteriously, "[But] you know it wasn't no car wreck."

Bolden called her nephew, who knew Rogers well, and was surprised to find his reaction to be far calmer than she imagined. The young man had recently spent time with Rogers and had sensed what he considered to be peculiar behavior from the reverend.

"I believe T. Y. felt his death," Bolden's nephew informed his aunt that night. As proof, he recounted a recent conversation in which Rogers had been unexplainably drawn to a patch of nearby flowers.

"He kept talking about those white lilies," the nephew informed Bolden, as if some secret meaning might be deduced from the encounter.

Bolden, hardly comforted by her nephew's words, grieved throughout the sleepless night. And when the sun rose the next day, she found herself fully incapable of driving to work.

The following morning, the *Tuscaloosa News* reported, "the man who almost singlehandedly led the civil rights drive which wiped away racial barriers in Tuscaloosa" had died unexpectedly at the age of thirty-five. He was four years younger than King.

Tuscaloosa's First African Baptist Church was at a loss as to how to proceed without its reverend. Rogers, who had taken his place at the pulpit 474 times over the past seven years, was conspicuously absent on the morning of Sunday, March 28. Instead, Rogers's center chair was now draped with a black ribbon to honor him. One reporter described "a faint sob coming from somewhere among the pews" while "the 19 pipes of the organ slowly breathed to life and the people raised their voices in 'Onward Christian Soldiers.'"

A crowd 250 strong pulled tight in the pews as Deacon Roosevelt White attempted to comfort the congregants.

"Fields that were green a few days ago are brown now," he began, adding later, "Yes, we are sad, but let us not stop here. Death to the righteous is like a cloud that shuts out the noon-day sun. It has a silver lining."

Yet for many it was difficult to envision any semblance of a silver lining.

By the afternoon service, the crowd had nearly doubled, an outpouring of five hundred from the local community and beyond who long remembered Rogers's efforts on their behalf.

"We must join our hands and press on," preached Reverend E. J. James Jr. "There still are mountains to be climbed."

Stillman College's Maxwell Barnes offered a similar message: "T. Y. Rogers had a lot of unfinished business on earth, especially in Tuscaloosa."

Rogers had indeed died with unfinished business, though the SCLC remained committed to finishing it for him. In the weeks prior to his death, Rogers had worked tirelessly to organize a march from Eutaw to Montgomery in an effort to draw greater attention to race problems in the public schools. In many ways the demonstration was to mirror King's Selma to Montgomery march, in which Rogers—as well as Reverend T. W. Linton and dozens of other Tuscaloosans—had taken part. Although the Eutaw to Montgomery march was not a true march—rather than asking demonstrators to walk the entirety of the 125-mile route, a bus transported them to various stops along the way—it still managed to fulfill its mission of drawing attention to the problem. In the days following Rogers's death, SCLC director Albert Turner said, "We are determined to carry this march out as a tribute to the Rev. Rogers. We are now calling it the T. Y. Rogers Memorial March against repression."

Reverend T. Y. Rogers's final journey to Tuscaloosa began with a four-hour detour to Reverend Ralph Abernathy's West Hunter Street Baptist Church in Atlanta. After an additional two-hour delay at the Atlanta airport, Rogers's body eventually found its way to Birmingham, where it was driven an hour south to Tuscaloosa and was laid in state in the chapel of First African Baptist. However, Rogers's late arrival did little to deter his many supporters from paying their last respects. Throughout the night and deep into the dawn, an unknown number of well-wishers shuffled past the casket to offer their farewells.

On Monday, March 29, twelve hundred flocked into First African Baptist's chapel while another three hundred craned their necks from the outside steps. Throughout its 105-year history, the church had likely never seen such a crowd; its numbers far surpassing even Bloody Tuesday. Many well-known civil rights figures were in attendance, including Reverend Ralph Abernathy, who presented the eulogy, as well as Rogers's mentor's father, Reverend Martin Luther King Sr.

"Let it be known that the weak sting of death cannot kill T. Y. Rogers Jr.," cried Abernathy while standing in Rogers's usual place at the pulpit. "Let it be known that no grave can hold his dynamic, invigorating personality.

"There will be no curtain call for T. Y. Rogers Jr.," he added, reminding the grief-stricken crowd of the harsh reality of the situation. "He is dead. That is a fact of history. We just must never let his work go unfinished."

Yet many in the black community remained far less willing to let it go.

Having endured King's assassination less than three years prior, a portion of the local African American community had grown cynical, incapable of believing that a simple car crash was enough to bring down their fallen hero. Many suspected foul play, including Ruth Bolden, who heard rumors that as Rogers left his Atlanta office in the early hours of Friday morning, two blinking lights were spotted in the distance—perhaps a signal to warn a would-be assassin of his approaching target. She had also heard rumors of Rogers being beaten—allegedly by a right-handed man—and that the car crash was a cover-up to destroy evidence.

"They said he ran into the abutment of a bridge," Bolden explained. "But nobody believed that. He was a good driver."

Local civil rights activist Nathaniel Howard Jr. found no credibility to the rumors, nor did he concur with Bolden's assessment of Rogers's driving.

"I used to ride with T. Y.," he explained, "and I used to take the wheel from him sometimes because you would think he was on the Atlanta speedway. I'd say, 'T. Y., why are you driving so fast?' [and he'd reply] 'Gotta go.' He had that type of attitude."

Howard continued: "When I got the news that he had gotten killed, I had an idea what had happened. T. Y., used to leave First Baptist Church and come to my daddy's barbershop right down the hill on 27th Avenue, by the graveyard . . . he would barely stop the car. I said, 'T. Y., if somebody came down a side street you're creamed, man. That's the end of you,' [and he'd say] 'Well, I've got to go where I've got to go.' He was kind of pompous in that sense of driving a car. . . . It's lucky T. Y. didn't get killed crossing the railroad track [near Howard and Linton's Barbershop] . . . He would drive almost blind at 50, 60, 70 miles per hour."

Seven years prior, Rogers admitted his propensity for speeding, describing one incident in which a Tuscaloosa police officer pulled him over for "doing about 50 miles an hour in the 20-mile zone."

However, Ruth Bolden wasn't alone in her struggle to grasp the untimely nature of her reverend's death. According to Rogers's youngest sister, Bettye Rogers Maye, her family, too, shared the troubling feeling that foul play was at work.

In the hours leading up to his death, Rogers was busily putting the finishing touches on his Eutaw to Montgomery march scheduled to take place in the coming days. "He must have called us that Thursday [March 25] and told us that he was going to start this march, that there was going to be a lot of opposition, but that they were going to march," Rogers Maye recalled. "According to his secretary in Tuscaloosa, he called her that night, the night of the 25th, and told her to tell the people of Tuscaloosa to be ready to join the march when he came through. *That whatever happened to him,*" she stressed, "the march was going to take place."

According to Rogers Maye, Rogers's wife, LaPelzia, recalled that her husband had mentioned, quite vaguely, that he was "facing some opposition about the march and had to meet with a group of people to get things straightened out."

LaPelzia received the phone call later that night, informing her that her husband had died in a car crash. She immediately notified Rogers's family in Coatopa, at which time Bettye Rogers Maye and her parents boarded an early morning bus to Atlanta, Rogers Maye adding, "we just weren't up to driving."

The family arrived at Atlanta's Grady Memorial Hospital, only to be told that the body had already been transported from the morgue to a nearby funeral home. Rogers's wife, parents, and sister followed the trail, and upon their arrival at the funeral home, were asked to wait.

"We assumed that we were going to be carried into a holding room where the body was, but when they carried us in to see my brother, he had already been embalmed. He was dressed in funeral home attire, and he was in the casket." Rogers Maye estimated that all of this had taken place by around 11:00 A.M. the following morning—less than twelve hours after Rogers's death.

"My sister-in-law had not been told of any of this information," Rogers Maye noted, adding that the embalming occurred without the family's consent.

Equally disconcerting was what the Rogers family found at the junkyard.

"[T. Y.'s] car was flattened like a pancake," Rogers Maye continued.

Local police drove them next to the scene of the accident, where the family's suspicions continued to grow.

"There were no skid marks on the street," Rogers Maye explained, and after further examining the tree he was alleged to have hit, Rogers's sister was surprised to find that there were few indications that any accident had occurred there, noting that even the tree's vines remained undisturbed.

When Rogers's father attempted to retrieve his son's belongings, he was further shocked to learn that the police hadn't recovered any; Rogers's briefcase and cars keys had gone mysteriously missing. Stranger still, the police noted that Rogers hadn't been wearing any shoes.

According to Rogers Maye, the Federal Bureau of Investigation shared the family's misgivings, representatives from which asked permission to exhume Reverend Rogers's body following the funeral because, as Rogers's sister put it, "it was obvious that T. Y. had been killed, and that it was not a car accident."

Yet Rogers's parents and wife were against the exhumation. After observing what they believed to be an incomplete investigation into the assassination of Dr. Martin Luther King Jr., the Rogers family found little sincerity in the FBI's actions, explained Rogers Maye. This lack of trust, coupled with the family's raw and deeply embedded grief, made the thought of cooperating with authorities quite difficult.

"My mother was just out of her mind," Rogers Maye explained. "She said, 'There's no need to dig my son up, just let him go.'"

According to Rogers Maye, at the family's request, the federal agents dropped the case before it even got started. A recent request through the Freedom of Information Act yielded no FBI record for Reverend Rogers.

"I have no idea who may have been behind it, you know," Rogers Maye added, "but yes, we always felt [his death had not occurred naturally]."

In the years that followed, Rogers Maye struggled to overcome a bitterness directed toward both whites and blacks—whites for the role a few might have played in her brother's death, and blacks for never fully appreciating her brother's sacrifice. She paid regular visits to T. Y.'s grave, often whispering, "I just want to know what happened to you."

During one nightly visit to the cemetery, she paid her respects to her brother (who the family fondly called "Junior") before heading back to her car in the dark.

"I got to my car and hit the ignition, but the car wouldn't say a word," she explained. "I hit it again. It wouldn't say a word. I remember saying, 'Junior, I am not afraid of you. Stop messing with my car, I'm ready to go home.'"

And then, with one final foot to the gas the car purred to life, a baffled Rogers Maye driving home in peace.

While there were many complications surrounding his death, T. Y. Rogers's legacy remains far less complicated. By most accounts—barring those set forth by white segregationists—Rogers was a quiet and thoughtful leader whose abilities to organize, inspire, and carry out carefully prepared demonstrations allowed for a wave of civil rights victories throughout the summer of 1964 and beyond. Yet not even Rogers's inner circle was without its own minor grievances.

"People have their own way of evaluating a person," explained Nathaniel Howard Jr. "Sometimes they evaluate a person because they are vindictive about a person's ability or his popularity or what have you. The only thing that I thought was a little discouraging about T. Y. was that he was a little too precocious. Just a tad. He was a little too flamboyant, so to speak. He didn't do enough research on protests from the people, or try to find how this happened."

Joe Mallisham of the Defenders agreed. "T. Y. was a man of action, [but] he didn't think things through. One [time] I publicly and openly criticized him. He didn't want anybody to get close to him, as far as leadership was concerned."

LaPelzia Rogers concurred, noting that her husband placed the majority of his faith in the movement's foot soldiers rather than its leaders. "T. Y. trusted the so-called small people because they were his base and standing behind him. They had nothing to lose," she explained. "They were his biggest help. The ministers, you have the ones who actually worked with him, but as far as his trust, it was actually the little people."

Although distance separated them, many of the leaders of Tuscaloosa's civil rights movement continued to keep in touch. A few years after Rogers's arrival, Herzfeld took a post in California, though he and Rogers reunited during the weekend of King's funeral.

"We had a real fine visit, and a kind of reunion of those of us who had shared so much of the Tuscaloosa history and had written so much of the Tuscaloosa

Civil Rights story," Herzfeld recalled. Upon reflecting on their shared time together, he added, "I think that we wrote the story together, and it's not a question—at least not to my mind—there was no question as who was more prominent.... I was beside T.Y. and he was beside me, right up until the time I left Tuscaloosa."

While Herzfeld and Rogers shared an enthusiasm for the movement, many of their fellow clergymen did not. Rogers attributed his initial chilly reception to an intellectual gap between himself and other local religious leaders.

"I came from Alabama State College and from [Crozer] Seminary. I had an educational degree and a professional degree, and the majority of the Baptist ministers in Tuscaloosa do not," Rogers explained simply.

But this rift was created by a generational gap as well. Rogers was a young, vibrant reverend whose connections within the civil rights movement provided him a unique and ever-expanding network. Contrarily, many of Tuscaloosa's African American reverends were far older and possessed far less experience with civil rights dealings, and in particular, with King and Rogers's direct action strategy. Many had grown up in an era where extreme racial violence occurred with even greater regularity, and they knew full well just what dire consequences could come as a result of a black man speaking his mind. Their misgivings toward Rogers were expected; they didn't want to be associated with such a radical man of God.

Yet as Rogers's stock began to rise, so too did those willing to support him. Although, as LaPelzia Rogers was sure to note, the bulk of his supporters came not from the middle class, but the working class—African Americans with little to lose and an entire world to gain.

While many have noted similarities between Rogers and King, civil rights activist Theresa Burroughs—a friend to both men—denied the claim. "There was no similarity between the two, only their quietness. Their stillness," she remembered. "They could just be so quiet and so still, you know. Sometimes when people are kind of nervous and have nervous energy they just keep moving. Not really going any place but just fiddling. But they were just so still, and so quiet . . . that's the only similarity that I can remember between the two of them.

"T.Y. was just T.Y.," she added later. "That's all I can say."

Yet Rogers's wife, LaPelzia, had little trouble identifying similarities between the two men. "[T.Y.] had that type of personality, and King was his biggest hero, you know. I couldn't say that he really emulated King—because that has to be a gift from God—but [Rogers] most certainly was in sync with all of his ideas."

Nevertheless, much like Burroughs, LaPelzia Rogers struggled to articulate the source of her husband's power. "Only thing I can say is that there was just something about him. He just had it in him."

LaPelzia also noted that Rogers's successes had come at a cost, admitting that her husband "got old fast . . . by quite a few years."

"Physical problems," she explained. "It was just one of those things that he put up a front, but every once in awhile, you know, he would come down and he was concerned, and you could see that he was worried."

Perhaps the true mystery of Reverend T. Y. Rogers isn't who he was, but how history has managed to overlook him. The same might be said of the Tuscaloosa movement, and in particular, some of the movement's more memorable demonstrations. In a 2009 issue of the *Tuscaloosa News,* one report called Bloody Tuesday "one of the most overlooked tales of the civil rights era."

Employing the language of a Zen koan, the article philosophically asked: "If billy clubs and axe handles crack skulls, and there is no national media around to document the atrocity, did it really happen?"

Those who demonstrated alongside Rogers throughout the summer of 1964 remain equally perplexed by how the city's history has mostly been forgotten.

In the summer of 1987—twenty-three years after Rogers's arrival onto the Tuscaloosa scene—University of Alabama PhD student Alan DeSantis interviewed several surviving members of the Tuscaloosa Citizens for Action Committee in an effort to better understand the inner workings of the movement. And at the conclusion of nearly every interview, he was sure to ask the most perplexing question of all: Why was Tuscaloosa overlooked?

While Birmingham, Montgomery, and Selma all received full credit for their roles throughout the civil rights movement, according to DeSantis, no one remembered Tuscaloosa for anything more than Governor Wallace's 1963 stand in the schoolhouse door.

The question caused Ruth Bolden to take pause.

"I just don't know what to say about that," she admitted, later adding, "I don't know why we didn't get our bigger cut in the picture."

Nathaniel Howard Jr. blamed it on a "lack of knowledge, or a lack of being aware of the impact."

"You have to blame the black community, too," he explained. "You have a certain responsibility to see that whatever happened is told to the people. . . . I would fault them for it. We are to blame, too. You are supposed to pass it on, and it's been left out."

While Odessa Warrick seemed to agree that a lack of knowledge was partly to blame, she blamed this lack of knowledge on the town's size.

"Tuscaloosa is a small city," she explained, "and [historians] never have time to stop here and find out what went on in Tuscaloosa."

When LaPelzia Rogers was asked a more personal question—if she felt her husband, in particular, had been overlooked—she wholeheartedly agreed. When asked why, she replied, "Well, you can ask yourself the same question about any other black leader that hadn't been able to be known nationally like King was. . . . There are a whole lot of great black people who just don't get mentioned because most of the [historians] are white."

Mallisham added that "petty jealousy" also played a role in the reshaping of civil rights history. "You had Andrew Young, Julian Bond, Jesse Jackson, Ralph Abernathy—all of these fellows constituted Reverend King on the [SCLC] executive board. They're the ones who got the glory for a lot of things that transpired elsewhere.

"The movement was like a joint establishment," he continued. "You've got one phase over here and one phase over here and one phase over here and one phase over here, and that's what people didn't realize. Atlanta was a base for one thing, Birmingham another base, Little Rock another base and Mobile another base.

When asked if Tuscaloosa functioned as a "base" as well, he replied that it hadn't, that "it wasn't supposed to be.

"It was the nerve," he explained. "Because Robert Shelton was here, this was the nerve."

While Tuscaloosa may seem to have been relegated to the footnotes of history, this was never Reverend Rogers's take on his town. In August of 1964, while in the midst of the bus boycott, T. Y. Rogers was asked for his own impressions of Tuscaloosa. "My image of the city now is different from what it was when I came to Tuscaloosa," he began. While he always believed that the African American community wanted to act, he believed they were tied down by an "elite" group of African Americans who were being "manipulated by the whites downtown."

But throughout the summer of 1964, Rogers noted a change of heart, that this "elite" group of African American leaders was beginning to realize that "it is bound up with the masses, and that what affects the masses unfavorably affects them.

"Regarding the whites," he added, "I felt, in the beginning, that [Tuscaloosa's] white community was completely closed; that the University of Alabama was a closed community and the intellectuals out there were intellectuals in part only, that they were not participating in the main stream of intellectual thought in this country. My image now is that there are many intellectuals at the university who are not only concerned about what is going on socially in our city, but who are willing to give money and to participate as best they can."

He summed up the complications of Tuscaloosa's populace in this way: "So now we have a small group of liberals, who are willing to move; a larger group of moderates, which does not want to move but will move within the confines of the law."

Yet despite any and all opposition that TCAC and Rogers would face in the years that followed, the reverend remained undeterred in his central conviction: "Negroes in Tuscaloosa," he predicted, "can and will stick together."

CHAPTER 24

The End of an Era

1964–71

That which unites us is, must be, stronger than that which divides us.

While Autherine Lucy's 1956 attempt at desegregation ended in chaos, it proved a necessary step toward future desegregation efforts, proof of which was made clear seven years later by Governor Wallace's stand in the schoolhouse door. Wallace's stand, too, left an indelible mark, serving as a barometer for a nation's struggles with race. While both of these events maintain clear timelines, the city's civil rights movement remains far harder to trace. Undoubtedly, the summer of 1964 proved a pivotal time for Tuscaloosa's civil rights movement, though TCAC and Reverend Rogers continued its battles through 1971. Even after Rogers's death, the city's African American community continued gaining ground—his departure offset by America's changing landscape.

In May of 1965, nearly two years after the stand in the schoolhouse door, *Crimson White* student reporter Dan Williamson noted that Tuscaloosa "must have the most unique civil rights situation in the world." The senior had come to this conclusion from drawing upon the culmination of his four years of experiences at the university and its city. His article went on to describe the major players—Grand Wizard Robert Shelton ("full of snap and quick to answer"), Reverend T. Y. Rogers ("easy to talk to and he answers slowly, softly, deliberately"), and Police Chief William Marable ("friendly and frank")—a diverse cast of characters, all of whom possessed competing interests.

"To summarize," Williamson reported, "the situation in Tuscaloosa is mixed and confused: a sort of unnatural quiet for the time being."

Yet Vivian Malone drew a far different conclusion. Just weeks after Williamson's assessment, Malone donned cap and gown and became the first African American student to graduate from the University of Alabama. In her waning days at the university, she offered a rare public statement since first entering the school two years prior.

"On the whole it's been quite a happy year for me," she told the press. "I have no bitterness." She added that she had not had an "unpleasant experience" at the university and would miss her friends most of all. As further proof of her assimilation, when asked by reporters if she believed Alabama's beloved football coach Paul "Bear" Bryant could walk on water, Malone replied, "Maybe."

Perhaps the most symbolic visit to Foster Auditorium occurred the year following Malone's graduation—on March 18, 1966—when then-Senator Robert Kennedy and Governor George Wallace shared the stage just one day apart. Both were invited to speak at a two-day forum called "Emphasis 66" to discuss that year's theme: "The Student Role in a Democratic Society." Many Alabamians were opposed to Kennedy's invitation to speak at the very site where he and his brother had forced desegregation just three years before. Letters poured into newspapers throughout the state, calling RFK "human garbage" and "a dirty little man who needs a haircut." Kennedy responded to the criticism, explaining: "I'm here because I was invited."

While Wallace's speech was soon forgotten, Robert Kennedy's words would live on—one line, in particular: "That which unites us is, must be, stronger than that which divides us."

Kennedy's call for unity proved a perfect foil for Wallace's more combative tone, and the University of Alabama students responded to his message of peace. They also responded to the senator's poking fun at their governor, including a reference to the schoolhouse door incident in which Kennedy quipped, "I was wondering why they sneaked me in the side door . . . someone was blocking the door out front."

Crimson White reporter Dan Williamson noted that Kennedy's "wit and charm won the audience over to him to an amazing degree." Even when

Kennedy controversially proclaimed "that Negroes must be as free as other Americans . . . not because it is economically advantageous, not because the law says so, but because it is right," the crowd overwhelmed him with cheers. It was a response Kennedy couldn't have dreamed of three years earlier, when a mostly silent student body watched begrudgingly as Hood and Malone breached the color barrier.

In closing (and perhaps taking a final jab at Wallace) Kennedy added: "And it is far easier to accept and stand on the past than to fight for the answers of the future."

Just a few minutes past midnight on June 5, 1968, Robert Kennedy was felled by an assassin's bullet while working through another crowd—those gathered in the kitchen of Los Angeles's Ambassador Hotel. He had just claimed victory over Eugene McCarthy in the California primary—a victory that helped solidify him as the Democratic frontrunner—though he'd never live to follow his brother's footsteps to the Oval Office.

Three months prior to his death, on Thursday, March 21, 1968, Robert Kennedy returned once more to Tuscaloosa. Two years had passed since his previous visit, and this time he returned with a clearer political agenda. Having announced his bid for the presidency just days before, the fresh-faced New York senator arrived into a dreary Tuscaloosa two hours behind schedule. A rain delay had stranded him in Atlanta, though upon touchdown, a two-hundred-car motorcade escorted him from the local airport to the university's Memorial Coliseum where ten thousand loyal supporters eagerly awaited him.

He offered a simple but well-received speech, reiterating his call for unity for which he'd planted the seeds during his previous visit to Tuscaloosa. This time, he linked the need for unity to the 1968 election, employing his usual bit of humor to warm up the crowd.

"I received some bad news and some good news here at the university today," he began, speaking to a packed coliseum. "The bad news is that [Coach] Bear Bryant will not run as my vice president," he joked, a comment that drew applause from the football loving crowd. "The good news," he continued, "is that he is willing to let me run as *his* vice president."

Years prior, Kennedy had urged Bryant to publicly take a pro-desegregation position, though the coach respectfully declined. Yet Bryant's unwillingness to go public had little to do with a lack of admiration for Kennedy or his ideas. According to Bryant's close friend, sportswriter Mickey Herskowitz, Alabama's beloved football coach was "prepared to shock people in Alabama by supporting Kennedy for president in 1968." Herskowitz added: "There was no doubt that he was a Kennedy fan, and that included Kennedy's doggedness in integrating the University of Alabama."

Yet on March 21, 1968, the crowd inside Memorial Coliseum was privy to none of this.

While much of RFK's speech served as an antiwar political stump speech, he managed to work in the race question on at least a few occasions. Hinting at their shared behind-the-scenes work toward achieving peaceful desegregation, Kennedy told the crowd he was "pleased to have a chance to meet Frank Rose again," calling the university's president "an old friend for a long period of time." This was undoubtedly true—their relationship first blossomed over a dinner thirteen years prior, and then again during their careful behind-the-scenes work to thwart Governor Wallace in June of 1963.

Returning once more to the question of race, Kennedy explained, "A few short years ago Americans were divided over issues which at that time seemed immense. Whether a Negro citizen should attend school here at the University of Alabama, whether he should have the right to eat a meal in a public restaurant, and whether he should have the right to vote. But these quarrels are behind us now, dwarfed by the far more serious issues that are facing all of us as Americans."

For Kennedy, the more serious issue—and the one that played better to a southern audience—was his grave reservations about the Vietnam War. Yet even in his criticism of the war, he managed to slip race back into the equation.

"For when a Negro leaves his home to risk death 12,000 miles away," he reasoned, "while we—you and I—live and study in comfort, I want him to find the door of opportunity open when he returns, and I think the people of Alabama want that as well."

The people inside the coliseum seemed to agree, cheering for what just years earlier would have been a wildly unpopular suggestion.

In the days following Kennedy's assassination, reporter Howell Raines reflected on Kennedy's many admirers in Tuscaloosa. "The enthusiasm for Bobby Kennedy was probably more personal than political for most of the students," he began, speculating, "perhaps Kennedy's very unpopularity with the state's older citizens served to increase his stature with the young ones."

Raines went on to describe Kennedy fearlessly making his way among the "hordes of handshakers," how, as ten thousand well-wishers crowded the university's coliseum for a glimpse of the man who had forever altered the racial makeup of their school, "there was that haunting awareness . . . that he was wide open, that one madman could end it all."

On April 4, 1968—exactly two weeks after Kennedy's final speech in Tuscaloosa—Dr. Martin Luther King Jr. was the one left wide open, dying at the hands of a gunman in Memphis, Tennessee. Robert Kennedy—who would be assassinated himself before King's killer was brought to justice— received word of King's death in the moments prior to speaking to a mostly African American crowd in Indianapolis. The audio recording is chilling— Kennedy whispering to an aide, "Do they know about Martin Luther King?" To which the aide mumbled that the crowd did not. Kennedy stood in the back of a flatbed truck, commanding silence.

"I have some very sad news for all of you," he began, breaking the hearts of every African American listener in the crowd.

King's death would have long-reaching ramifications in Tuscaloosa as well. Hours after word of King's death reached the city, a few sporadic instances of violence were aimed at local businesses—broken windows as well as a few hurled Molotov cocktails. Yet the response by Tuscaloosa's African American community proved far tamer than the full-scale assaults that leveled entire sections of Washington, DC; Baltimore; and Louisville; among others. Reverend T. Y. Rogers acted swiftly to subdue the threat of violence in his town by organizing two marches for April 5—the day following King's death. Recognizing marches as the alternative to riots, Police Chief Marable readily issued the parade permits, granting Rogers free rein of the streets.

True to form, the *Tuscaloosa News* reported that while Marable "expressed regret over King's death," his primary concern remained maintaining law and order.

"This points up vividly the responsibility shared by all citizens—Negro and white," preached Marable, "that we must sanely and sensibly appraise our problems and resolve them in the same way." While King's assassination may have saddened him personally, Police Chief Marable understood that his allegiance was first and foremost to his town.

Meanwhile, at the University of Alabama, the Democratic Student Organization's weekly "peace vigil" transformed into a vigil for King. The university's newly formed Afro-American Association took part as well, as did students believed to be from Stillman College (though this cross-collegiate unity was retracted in the following day's edition of the *Tuscaloosa News*). Nonetheless, 150 people took part in the vigil, and while the university had a strict rule "barring nonstudents from demonstrating on campus," Dean Blackburn sensed the need to allow all mourners—from wherever they hailed—to share the moment in peace.

On Saturday, April 6, Reverend Rogers called upon "all citizens who believe in brotherhood of man and human dignity, who detest violence" to gather for a 2:00 P.M. march the following day.

Nearly two thousand citizens—both black and white—answered the call, a crowd far greater than any mob the city had ever produced. After a brief memorial service inside First African Baptist Church, Reverend T. Y. Rogers led the marchers along the route he first attempted four years prior in protest of discriminatory signage—from the church to the Tuscaloosa County Courthouse.

Upon reaching the courthouse, Rogers directed the blame at the same constituency King himself had chastised five years earlier in his "Letter from a Birmingham Jail"—the silent, white majority.

"Speak now, you don't have much time," Rogers urged white America. "Speak now, because cities are burning and black folks are weeping."

While Alabama license plates proclaimed the state the "Heart of Dixie," Rogers countered that Dixie had no heart.

"If Dixie had a heart," he reasoned, "Martin Luther King . . . John F. Kennedy . . . Medgar Evers . . . wouldn't be dead."

In two months time, he would add another Kennedy to the list.

The closeness of Reverend Rogers's relationship to Martin Luther King Jr. was perhaps best exemplified in Rogers's role throughout King's funeral proceedings. While TCAC sponsored a bus to transport Tuscaloosa citizens to Atlanta for the services, Reverend Rogers was not among his flock. Instead, he took his place alongside his newly deceased mentor, a loyal pallbearer who stayed with the mule-drawn wagon along its route from Ebenezer Baptist Church to Morehouse College. Dressed in a black turtleneck, dark jeans and a matching jacket, thirty-two-year-old Rogers fit the part of the youthful pupil, as did Jesse Jackson and Andrew Young—two more of King's young protégés. The three stood out among the more formally dressed pallbearers, perhaps emblematic of the shift from the old guard to the new. In the years to come, both Jesse Jackson and Andrew Young would keep one foot in the political sphere and the other in the pastoral—a one-two punch that allowed them to most effectively continue their fight for equality. To this day, Jackson and Young have continued this fight, while Reverend Rogers's 1971 death stripped him of the opportunity to fulfill his own destiny.

Nevertheless, he made the legacy time afforded him. In the weeks following King's death, Rogers was invited to speak at the University of Alabama—the same institution where, just five years prior, blacks were unable to attend. Speaking to a crowd of forty in Garland Hall, Rogers parsed no words while expressing his frustration: "We have the power to put a man on the moon, but we won't use the power to train a man to stand on his own two feet."

His barbs cut even closer to home when he noted that African American students at the University of Alabama "really aren't treated as human beings ought to be treated." He cited the Greek system's inability to accept them. For Rogers, school admission was a far cry from student acceptance, and in his view, the work had just begun.

The world was changing, and the era, it seemed, was coming to an end.

After serving the Tuscaloosa police department for a quarter century, Police Chief Marable officially retired on April 30, 1976. "I wouldn't necessarily say [he was] forced out," explained Marable II, his grandson, though he did note that his grandfather's political views didn't mesh well with the current establishment. "And his political views were basically how he got to power in the 1960s," he continued, "on his treatment of people. But there were certain people [in local government] whose mentality hadn't changed very much."

Marable had first joined the force in 1951 and steadily risen from patrolman to sergeant to parole officer before serving a five-year stint as a captain.

His levelheadedness as a defender of the law provided him with a distinguished career, though his unwillingness to turn a blind eye or submit to Klan rule made him enemies as well as friends. In April of 1962, upon being named police chief, Marable stated that his goal for the department was to "re-emphasize service to the public and undertake a general progressive program for the department."

For many white Tuscaloosans, the word "progressive" seemed to signal a color-blind enforcement of the law, a seismic shift for a southern town. Marable's role throughout the city's civil rights movement proved critical toward advancing these aims, though he too paid a price with his health.

Upon Marable's death in the early 90s, his grandson cited stress as a contributing factor: "The stress he went through in the 60s and early 70s, I think that was very tough on him."

Meanwhile, Grand Wizard Robert Shelton outlived the police chief by nearly a decade, dying of a heart attack on March 17, 2003, and leaving behind a conflicted legacy all his own. Morris Dees, cofounder of the Southern Poverty Law Center—the law firm that had successfully filed suit against the United Klans of America several years prior—called Shelton "truly an evil man." He noted that in the months preceding her father's death, Shelton's daughter, Cindy, informed Dees that she was "ashamed of his role in violence against those in the civil rights movement." Shortly after Shelton's passing, his son reconciled his father's legacy the only way he knew how: "To me, he was always just my father," he explained, "and that's all that he ever will be."

As time pressed on, the University of Alabama's desegregation story lost another major player. In October of 2005, Vivian Malone-Jones died of a stroke, forty-two years after desegregating the University of Alabama. Not only was she one of the first African Americans to enter the university (following only Autherine Lucy), but she was also the first to graduate. For years, she served in the Environmental Protection Agency, overseeing the Civil Rights and Urban Affairs division until her retirement in 1996. Speaking of her experiences at the University of Alabama, her brother-in-law—the then-lawyer, now attorney general—Eric Holder, remarked, "She had very strong beliefs as a Christian. She always credited those beliefs in getting her through."

After graduating from Wayne State University, James Hood attended graduate classes at Michigan State University before accepting a job with Michigan's law enforcement agency. However, he soon moved on to Wisconsin where he spent many passionate years working with community colleges, declaring in a 1990s interview that he believed community colleges to be "where the need is and where the future of education is." An education advocate throughout his life, he returned to the University of Alabama to earn his doctorate in education, and did so in 1997.

Upon her 1956 expulsion from the University of Alabama, Autherine Lucy found renewed happiness in her marriage to Hugh Lawrence Foster later that year. The pair spent several years in Louisiana and Texas before returning home to Alabama. In 1988—thirty-two years after her unwarranted expulsion—the university's board of trustees overturned its expulsion decision, an act that motivated Lucy Foster to return to the university to earn her masters in education, which she did in 1992, graduating alongside her daughter.

Meanwhile, in the years separating Autherine Lucy's desegregation attempt and the present, the city of Tuscaloosa continued to make history.

In a unique bit of serendipity, in April of 2011—in the midst of my writing this book—Captain Loyd Baker began clearing out files on the second floor of Tuscaloosa's Sheriff's Department when he came across a few yellowed folders crammed in the back of a metal filing cabinet. Curious, he removed them, stumbling across clues to Tuscaloosa's civil rights movement that likely hadn't been viewed in nearly half a century.

In early May I sat down in the chief deputy's office and became one of the first to peruse them since law enforcement had so many years before. I was struck by the artifacts, including an age-worn handbook distributed by the Southern Christian Leadership Conference titled "Freedom for Army Recruits." It opened with a message from Dr. King in which he made clear his primary goal for Alabama's African Americans: "If the Negro doesn't have the right to vote in Alabama," he explained, "then his future is endangered everywhere."

Yet perhaps more revealing than the handbook's pro-voter-registration agenda was the rhetoric it employed. In contrast to the SCLC's usual peaceable prose, the handbook employed a far more belligerent tone, comparing the civil rights movement to a "war," and urging demonstrators to join the "Freedom Army."

"In a regular war people leave home, leave their families and jobs, leave school, or whatever they are doing and go off to fight," the handbook began. "We must do the same thing if we are ever going to be free. We must leave our homes and whatever we are doing and join the rest of the people who will [b]e going off this spring to fight segregation."

It continued: "So this spring, 1964, on a certain date which will be kept secret until the time comes, a call will go out for all those who have volunteered to REPORT FOR DUTY. . . . Schools across the state will be closed because the students will be gone to the army. Women and girls will fight this war as well as the men and boys. Ministers, young people, adults, *everyone* must respond to the call if we are going to be free!"

In Tuscaloosa—under the leadership of Reverend Rogers—many responded with gusto.

On April 30, 1964—just days after TCAC's first march to the Tuscaloosa courthouse—the Alabama Legislative Commission to Preserve the Peace released a confidential intelligence report noting that by the end of May there was likely to be a "massive assault upon the laws of the State of Alabama."

The report went on to note the Southern Christian Leadership Conference, Student Nonviolent Coordinating Committee, and Congress of Racial Equality, among others, were joining forces to test the laws of the state. The report further indicated that while Birmingham was the "prime target," smaller cities would also play a role, including Montgomery, Dothan, Selma, Gadsden, and Tuscaloosa.

The recently discovered sheriff's department files also contained a list of license plates, car types, names, and addresses for those who had parked outside the church on the night of the April 22 rally. Of the one hundred or so names, many would long be associated with the city's civil rights movement, like the Defenders' leader, Joe Mallisham, as well as long-time activist Nathaniel Howard Jr. While the names initially served as a watch list for local law enforcement, nearly fifty years later, when read in a new light, it more closely resembles an honor roll of the men and women who believed strongly enough in their convictions to risk their jobs, their reputations, and their lives.

On a memo describing the events of the mass meeting of April 22, 1964, the reporter noted that in one instance, "Rogers asked the crowd why they were in the church tonight."

The reporter noted a single word breathed into the cool night air, one that had urged so many to do so much when the time and place demanded: "freedom."

The word hummed from pew to pew, from person to person—a promise they were destined to make good on.

A New Beginning

June 11, 2011

At the time of this writing, forty-eight years ago today James Hood and Vivian Malone walked through the doorway of Foster Auditorium and made history. I walked through the same doorway yesterday afternoon and did not. Instead, I was greeted by this message on the wall directly before me:

The University of Alabama Welcomes You To
Foster Auditorium
A New Beginning

To the left of the message is a flat-screen television complete with a touch screen, which curious passersby are invited to touch a link for more information on any number of key players: Autherine Lucy, James Hood, Vivian Malone, John F. Kennedy, Robert F. Kennedy, Nicholas Katzenbach, John Blackburn, Sarah Healy, among others.

Stepping past the screen, I entered the basketball arena where Hood and Malone once registered for classes, though the scratching of pencils on enrollment cards has now been replaced with silence. The school colors were everywhere—red and white run amok—and within moments, my eyes fell upon an enormous American flag dangling from the ceiling. It was not difficult to envision the basketball game played there on Saturday, February 4, 1956, when Alabama decimated the Georgia Tech Yellow Jackets, while an anxious student body plotted the protest that would occur later that night. And it's equally easy to envision Hood and Malone stepping through the auditorium doors seven years later, while student reporter Hank Black trailed behind. The stories are still everywhere—a great swirling of history encapsulated within Foster Auditorium's hallowed walls—if only we are willing to listen.

And yet this morning, as my wife, dog, and I wander once more to the infamous door on this anniversary, we find that we are the only ones. Nearby, I hear the hum of hoses power washing the sidewalks, and I am reminded of the fire hoses in Kelly Ingram Park so many years before. To my left is a cluster of summer-session students jostling toward the quad, but there are no bald-headed deputy attorney generals among them, no arms-crossed governors, no African American students waiting to enter the school.

Today, we are just two people walking a dog on a beautiful Saturday morning in Tuscaloosa. There are no celebrations, no vigils, no moments of remembrance.

My wife indulges me as I take turns playing the parts, me filling in first for Wallace, then Katzenbach, before having my wife stand in. I want to be Hood and Malone, too, so I back up and march steadily toward the door, trying to make sense of how it might have felt on that scorching afternoon as the cameras clicked all around them.

These are feelings I will never grasp, mostly because while the place is right, the time is wrong, and I have the wrong color skin. My own entrance into the University of Alabama several years back occurred without fanfare. I was a name on a roll, nothing more. And in the years to come, as I transitioned from graduate student to instructor, taking my place at the front of the classroom, all of my students—regardless of color—became names on a roll as well. Few of them understood what it took to set this town and its university free, though perhaps their forgetting confirms a secret truth—at long last, our city can be just a city again.

And these days, our doors remain always open.

Notes

Introduction

5. "In more sober days": Gene Roberts and Hank Klibanoff, *The Race Beat: The Press, the Civil Rights Struggle, and the Awakening of a Nation* (New York: Vintage Books, 1995), 138.

Chapter 1

9. On the night of Thursday, January 26, 1956: "Four Crosses Are Burned on UA Campus," *Tuscaloosa News,* February 1, 1956.

9. "a land of quick reactions, of sudden and stunning violences": Carl Carmer, *Stars Fell on Alabama* (Tuscaloosa: The University of Alabama Press, 1990), 15.

10. "organization which is pledged": "3 Crosses Burn; 2 Men Nabbed at University," *Tuscaloosa News,* February 2, 1956; Ann Mitchell, "Keep 'Bama White" (thesis, Georgia Southern College, 1971), 42.

10. a total of eight crosses: "Four Crosses Are Burned on UA Campus."

10. "give them all their respect": Mitchell, "Keep 'Bama White," 5–6.

11. "conduct and marriage record": Ibid., 33.

11. "represented not only herself but her race": Ibid., 34.

11. "send down some basketball players about 7'2'"": Bill McEachern, "Student Reaction to Negro Seems Mostly Resignation," *Tuscaloosa News,* February 2, 1956.

11. In an attempt to diffuse any potential confrontations: E. Culpepper Clark, *The Schoolhouse Door: Segregation's Last Stand at The University of Alabama* (Tuscaloosa: The University of Alabama Press, 1995), 58.

12. "didn't mind the Negrowoman": Bill Gibb, "Negro Vows Court Fight to Get Dormitory Room: Trustee Orders No-Room Action," *Tuscaloosa News,* February 1, 1956.

12. "I don't like it": Ibid.

12. "It's bad enough that she's here": Bill McEachern, "Student Reaction to Negro Seems Mostly Resignation," *Tuscaloosa News,* February 2, 1956.

12. "I'm a died-in-the-wool Confederate": Ibid.

12. "resignation": Ibid.

12. "I figured all along": Ibid.

13. "We don't care how many cross burnings": Clark, *Schoolhouse Door,* 58; Mitchell, "Keep 'Bama White," 36.

13. "impolite and obnoxious": Mitchell, "Keep 'Bama White," 84.

13. "elbowed her way": Ibid.

13. Author E. Culpepper Clark noted the many specific charges: Clark, *Schoolhouse Door,* 59.

13. "By simply being there": Ibid.

13. "every action had its explanation": Ibid.

13. driving Lucy in his Cadillac: Anthony Blasi, *Segregationist Violence and the Civil Rights Movements in Tuscaloosa* (Washington, DC: University Press of America, 1980), 36.

14. "Every gesture made that day": Clark, *Schoolhouse Door,* 59.

14. Writer Anthony Blasi concurred: Blasi, *Segregationist Violence,* 36.

14. "All the criticism leveled against Miss Lucy": Mitchell, "Keep 'Bama White," 86.

14. three additional crosses were burned: "3 Crosses Burn; Two Men Nabbed at University."

14. Meanwhile, a few hours to the southeast in Montgomery: "South's Race Cauldron Boils Stirred by Alabama Bomb Blast," *Tuscaloosa News,* February 2, 1956; Al Lanier, "NAACP Leader's Home Hit by Bomb, Second in Days," *Tuscaloosa News,* February 2, 1956.

15. "segregated travel in Alabama": Lanier, "NAACP Leader's Home Hit by Bomb, Second in Days."

15. "No single racial clash in the South had attracted so many reporters": Roberts and Klibanoff, *Race Beat,* 130.

15. "It was a great day for me": Bill Gibb, "Walking Steps to History," *Tuscaloosa News,* February 5, 1956.

16. Accompanying Lucy was Reverend R. I. Alford: Clark, *Schoolhouse Door,* 61.

16. "as if [Lucy] was going to church": Interview with Joyce Lamont conducted October 12, 2011.

16. "I was all in favor of her attending the university": Ibid.

16. "I was standing there sharpening a pencil": Ibid.

16. "[The Secret Service] stuck out": Ibid.

17. "For two cents I'd drop the course": Clark, *Schoolhouse Door,* 61; Bill McEachern, "Campus Curious, Calm as Negro Starts Class," *Tuscaloosa News,* February 3, 1956.

Chapter 2

18. street sales leaped nearly 75 percent: "World Turned Eyes on UA This Week," *Tuscaloosa News,* February 3, 1956.

18. "Tuscaloosa and the University of Alabama were in the eyes": Ibid.

18. just over 56,000: Wayne Phillips, "Tuscaloosa: A Tense Drama Unfolds," *New York Times,* February 26, 1956.

19. Born in Newnan, Georgia: "Buford Boone," *Encyclopedia of Alabama,* http://www.encyclopediaofalabama.org/face/Article.jsp?id=h-1783.

19. While shying away from the term *liberal:* Mitchell, "Keep 'Bama White," 107; Roberts and Klibanoff, *Race Beat,* 134

19. "boycotted simultaneously": Mitchell, "Keep 'Bama White," 107.

19. "Let us remind": "This Pushing, Pushing Is No Good," *Tuscaloosa News,* February 3, 1956.

19. "Never have we seen a time when an abundance": Ibid.

20. "disturbances on University Avenue": The Sarah Healy Papers, The W. S. Hoole Special Collections Library, The University of Alabama (hereafter Sarah Healy Papers).

20. "There was a large crowd": Ibid.

20. a more conservative estimate: Bob Kyle, "Cross Burns in Center of University Ave.," *Tuscaloosa News,* February 4, 1956.

21. "spoke until their voices gave out": Ibid.

21. "calling for a measure to send Alabama's Negroes": Clark, *Schoolhouse Door,* 63.

21. averaging an hour a day to the task: Ibid.; Mitchell, "Keep 'Bama White," 50.

21. Present was Dean Healy: Sarah Healy Papers.

21. "a small flame at approximately 10:15 P.M.": Ibid.

22. a strong presence in Tuscaloosa, first organizing in 1868: "The Ku Klux Klan Organized at Tuscaloosa," *West Alabama Breeze,* April 4, 1917.

22. efforts of Ryland Randolph: Gladys Ward, "Life of Ryland Randolph" (thesis, The University of Alabama, 1932).

22. with the exception of the summer of 1933: Southern Commission on the Study of Lynching, *The Plight of Tuscaloosa: Mob Murders, Community Hysteria, Official Incompetence* (Atlanta: 1933), 21.

22. "beer party": Sarah Healy Papers.

22. "a truly vicious deadly organization": Ibid.

22. "lynch mob": Blasi, *Segregationist,* 35.

22. "jeered . . . cheered each time a photographer": Bill Gibb, "'Rally' Ends Quietly," *Tuscaloosa News,* February 5, 1956.

23. "occupied by several out-of-town Negroes": "Students Damage Auto," photo caption, *Tuscaloosa News,* February 5, 1956.

23. "Come, Come, Comrade!": D. DePree, "Letter to the Editor: Blame the Party," *Tuscaloosa News,* February 14, 1956.

23. "These degrading incidents": Walter J. Christenson, "Letter to the Editor: Nauseous State," *Tuscaloosa News,* February 15, 1956.

24. "cautioned his followers against violence": Clark, *Schoolhouse Door,* 67.

24. "Mob action can never accomplish anything": Walter Flowers, "Letter to the Student Body," *Crimson White*, February 7, 1956, 1.

24. "99 per cent of you": Clark, *Schoolhouse Door*, 67.

24. "uphold the traditions of this great University": Ibid., 68.

24. "They shouted almost throughout his attempt": Sarah Healy Papers.

24. Although he'd served as an educator all his life: "Education: Goodbye to 'Bama," *Time Magazine*, November 19, 1956.

25. "I don't think they want to hear me": Bill Gibb and Stroube Smith, "Patrol Slips Lucy away from Mob: Apparent Ruse Thwarts Crowd." *Tuscaloosa News*, February 6, 1956, 1.

Chapter 3

26. "These precautions were taken": Sarah Healy Papers.

26. "I just walked through and smiled": Howell Raines, *My Soul Is Rested: Movement Days in the Deep South* (New York: Penguin, 1983), 326.

27. "Lynch the nigger": Clark, *Schoolhouse Door*, 72.

27. "We are never going to be able to get her out of the front door": Sarah Healy Papers.

27. "Autherine, I think we are going": Raines, *My Soul Is Rested*, 326.

27. "There they go, there they go": Clark, *Schoolhouse Door*, 72.

27. "I managed to get in [the car] and locked the doors": Sarah Healy Papers.

28. "hoped that some of them": Ibid.

28. After viewing D. W. Griffith's *Birth of a Nation*: Gary May, *The Informant: The FBI, the Ku Klux Klan, and the Murder of Viola Liuzzo* (New Haven, CT: Yale University Press, 2005), 143.

28. Not only did Chambliss: The Oliver Cromwell Carmichael Collection, The W. S. Hoole Special Collections Library, The University of Alabama.

28. "was the first time I had ever seen Klansmen": Wayne Greenhaw, *Fighting the Devil in Dixie: How Civil Rights Activists Took On the Ku Klux Klan in Alabama* (Chicago: Lawrence Hill Books, 2011), 143.

28. "Many of these people were good": Ibid.

29. "I asked the Lord to give me strength": Nora Sayre, "Barred at the Schoolhouse Door," *Progressive*, July 1984; Raines, *My Soul Is Rested*, 326.

29. "If anybody wants to start something": Roberts and Klibanoff, *Race Beat*, 132.

29. "Well, just like a flash of lightning": Sarah Healy Papers.

30. "Apparently, police had used a ruse": Bill Gibb and Stroube Smith, "Patrol Slips Lucy away from Mob: Apparent Ruse Thwarts Crowd," *Tuscaloosa News*, February 6, 1956.

31. "She was all splattered with eggs and whatnot": Interview with Reverend T. W. Linton, January 5, 2011.

31. "They stayed on 14th Street": Ibid.

31. "We called the police department and they said": Ibid.
32. "paralyzed": Dan T. Carter, *The Politics of Rage: George Wallace, the Origins of the New Conservatism, and the Transformation of American Politics* (New York: Simon and Schuster, 1995), 83.
32. "during the week proceeding [Lucy's]": Sarah Healy Papers.
33. "I advised the president that providing": Ibid.
33. "no plans . . . to order": Associated Press, "Governor Says He's Not Upset over University," *Tuscaloosa News,* February 7, 1956.
33. "leaving it up to the police": Robert Sherrill, "George Wallace: A Potpourri of Style," in *Gothic Politics in the Deep South* (New York: Grossman Publishers, 1968), 276.
33. By some estimates, more than one thousand African Americans: Diane McWhorter, *Carry Me Home: The Climactic Battle of the Civil Rights Revolution* (New York: Touchstone, 2001), 99.
33. "the first black student": Ibid.

Chapter 4

34. "unless we can maintain law and order": Bill McEachern, "'UA on Brink of Disgrace' Carmichael Tells Faculty," *Tuscaloosa News,* February 7, 1956, 1, 2.
34. "He told us things were dangerous": Interview with Joyce Lamont conducted October 12, 2011.
34. "The question now is whether an anarchy": McEachern, "'UA on Brink of Disgrace' Carmichael Tells Faculty," 1, 2.
35. "We owe a great deal to Walter Flowers Jr.": Ibid.
35. "Friday's was ugly": Ibid.
35. "Elements from the outside": "Carmichael Blames 'Outside' Elements in UA Demonstrations," *Tuscaloosa News,* February 7, 1956.
35. "law and order": Ibid.
35. "With all these forces": Ibid.
36. "the rattle of stones": Sarah Healy Papers.
36. "Let's go back to the Union Building!": McEachern, "'UA on Brink of Disgrace' Carmichael Tells Faculty," 1, 2.
36. "Give us some more, give us some more": Ibid.
36. "the area was cleared": Ibid.
37. "In my best judgment": Sarah Healy Papers.
37. "exclude Autherine Lucy until further notice": Clark, *Schoolhouse Door,* 79; Stroube Smith, "Lucy Vows Legal Fight to Return to Campus: 48 Hour Deadline Put on Re-Instatement Bid," *Tuscaloosa News,* February 7, 1956, 1; Sarah Healy Papers.
37. "There is no other": Clark, *Schoolhouse Door,* 80; Sarah Healy Papers.
37. "I do not claim to have saved": Sarah Healy Papers.

37. "It took this University years to recover": Ibid.

37. "Dr. Carmichael left here a broken man": Ibid.

38. "during the present semester": Arthur Shores Papers, Birmingham Civil Rights Institute Archive (hereafter Arthur Shores Papers).

38. In a May 14, 1953, letter: Ibid.

38. "nice man": Interview with Joyce Lamont conducted October 12, 2011.

38. "The hate mail that came": Ibid.

38. Perhaps most revealing of all: The Oliver Cromwell Carmichael Collection, The W. S. Hoole Special Collections Library, The University of Alabama.

39. "refused to share the concern": "Education: Goodbye to 'Bama," *Time Magazine,* November 19, 1956.

39. "I suppose one of the worst things": Sarah Healy Papers.

Chapter 5

40. "And make no mistake": "What a Price for Peace," *Tuscaloosa News,* February 7, 1956.

41. "Not a single University student": Ibid.

41. "I was in the . . . pressroom": "A Voice of Justice and Reason: Buford Boone's *Tuscaloosa News.*" *The Alabama Experience.* University of Alabama Center for Public Television and Radio, 1994.

41. "The recent mob action": "Hope Lies with Students," *Tuscaloosa News,* February 8, 1956.

41. "outstandingly fine in their coolness": Ibid.

41. "Every act of real aggressiveness": Ibid.

42. In a letter dated May 9, 1957: The Buford Boone Papers, The W. S. Hoole Special Collections Library, The University of Alabama; "A Voice of Justice and Reason."

42. his home phone buried under a pillow: Blasi, *Segregationist Violence,* 44.

43. First, Dean Corson set forth his "outsiders have invaded" theory: Clark, *Schoolhouse Door,* 81.

43. "on two occasions 'twenty seconds'": Ibid., 81.

43. "Nothing worse could happen": "Trustees Feared Murder in Barring Negro Coed," *Tuscaloosa News,* February 8, 1956.

43. "most loyal": Clark, *Schoolhouse Door,* 81.

43. "non-commitally": John Hamner, "President May Move to Take Stronger Role in UA Action," *Tuscaloosa News,* February 10, 1956.

43. "The truth was that such a request": Ibid.

43. Angered by Carmichael's tepid response: John Hamner, "Faculty Revolters Plan No New Action," *Tuscaloosa News,* February 8, 1956, 1.

43. "police protection, either civil or military": Ibid.

44. "It is for the long benefit": Mitchell, "Keep 'Bama White," 95.

44. "do all possible by honorable means": Clark, *Schoolhouse Door,* 83.

44. "bespectacled stringbean of a young man": Ibid., 82.

44. Holt was rumored to have: Ibid.

44. "America has been called to greatness": Murray Kempton, "When the Riots Came," in *Reporting Civil Rights: American Journalism, 1941–1963* (New York: Library of America, 2003), 241.

44. "We have a chance to tell the world": Ibid.

44. "The question is not what we may think": Ibid.

45. "If Miss Lucy wanted to go to bed": Langston Hughes, "A Brickbat for Education— A Kiss for the Bedroom in Dixie," in *Reporting Civil Rights: American Journalism, 1941–1963,* 249.

45. "living proof of integration": Ibid.

45. "And, I expect that that alleged": Ibid., 250.

46. "clean, prosperous city": Wayne Phillips, "Tuscaloosa: A Tense Drama Unfolds," *New York Times,* February 26, 1956.

46. "In Tuscaloosa, the Negroes and whites": Ibid.

46. "Negro recreation was given a share": Ibid.

47. "I think most people honestly": Reminiscences of George LeMaistre (1964), on pages 20–21 in the Columbia University Center for Oral History Collection (hereafter CUCOHC).

47. On February 17, newly anointed White Citizens Council: Bill Gibb, "Legal Fight Is Urged to Save Segregation: Dallas Senator Sparks Council Formation Here," *Tuscaloosa News,* February 18, 1956, 1, 3.

47. "confronted the basic dilemma of every liberal": McWhorter, *Carry Me Home,* 103.

47. "different man": Ibid.

48. "Negroes were publically ridiculed by men": Wayne Phillips, "Tuscaloosa: A Tense Drama Unfolds," *New York Times,* February 26, 1956.

48. "racial rumblings" hardly seem a secret: Claude L. Dahmer Jr., "An Analysis of Student Opinion at the University of Alabama toward Current Racial Issues" (thesis, The University of Alabama, 1949).

48. When asked if Congress should support President Truman's: Ibid., 40.

48. However, when asked if a federal antilynching bill: Ibid., 48.

49. "Which of the following statements best expresses": Ibid., 53.

49. From 1974 to 1981, the number of African American: *The University of Alabama Fact Book, 1986* (Office of Institutional Research, 1986).

Chapter 6

53. In a morning phone call to Attorney General Robert Kennedy: Walter Lord, *The Past That Would Not Die* (New York: Harper and Row, 1965), 195.

54. "I think it is silly going through": Sherrill, "George Wallace: A Potpourri of Style," 186.

54. "Just wait'll dark": Lord, *Past That Would Not Die,* 202.

54. A reported 160 US marshals: "Mississippi and Meredith Remember," CNN .com, September 30, 2002, http://articles.cnn.com/2002-09-30/us/meredith_1 _james-meredith-federal-prison-guards-mississippi?_s=PM:US.

54. "The Big Question: What Next?" Relman Morin, "The Big Question: What Next?" *Tuscaloosa News,* October 2, 1962, 1.

54. drove to a retreat two hours east: Gertrude Samuels, "Alabama U: A Story of 2 among 4,000," *New York Times,* July 28, 1963.

54. Measuring in at six feet two inches: "Middleman In Alabama: Frank Anthony Rose," *New York Times,* June 11, 1963, 20.

55. "Frank Rose was a hell of a president": Interview with Donald Stewart conducted February 1, 2011.

55. "Breakfast is the only time in a 15-hour": "Nation's Crisis Crowds In on One Man," *Life Magazine,* June 14, 1963, 77–80.

55. "to do something that O. C. Carmichael": Sarah Healy Papers.

55. "Why in the hell does Frank think": Ibid.

55. "We simply could not let such a thing happen here": Jack Stillman, "Price of Peace Major Concern for Businessmen," *Tuscaloosa News,* June 11, 1963, 1.

56. Five high-profile community leaders attended the first meeting: The Anthony Blasi Papers, The W. S. Hoole Special Collections Library, The University of Alabama; Stillman, "Price of Peace Major Concern for Businessmen," 1.

56. "co-chairmen of a committee without a name": Stillman, "Price of Peace Major Concern for Businessmen," 1.

56. "At the time of Autherine Lucy": Ibid.

56. "lone Negro application": Don Chapin, "Group to Examine, Evaluate the Lone Negro Application," *Crimson White,* October 25, 1962.

56. "This is nothing new": Ibid.

57. "The truth of the matter is": Interview with Wali Ali Meyer (formerly Mel Meyer) conducted December 17, 2010.

57. "So I decided we'd publish it": Ibid.

58. "Ever kill anyone?": Ibid.

58. "There is one adjective": *The Corolla,* The University of Alabama, 1963.

58. When reflecting on his time as a student reporter: Interview with Harris Cornett conducted December 16, 2011.

59. "I was scared to death even to go to Stillman": Interview with Hank Black conducted May 15, 2011.

59. "We met with him and talked about": Interview with Harris Cornett conducted December 16, 2011.

59. After a few meetings at Stillman: Ibid.

59. *Buddy, get out:* Interview with Hank Black conducted May 15, 2011.

59. "I was sweating bullets": Ibid.

59. "no thought on the part of the board of trustees": "'No Thought' of Closing UA Dr. Rose Says," *Crimson White,* November 1, 1962, 1, 3.

60. "The University of Alabama cannot go through": Ibid.

60. "in unity there is strength": "A Mature Movement," *Crimson White,* November 15, 1962.

60. "There will not be another Oxford here": "Blackburn Discusses Oxford, Evaluation, at Palmer Meet," *Crimson White,* November 1, 1962, 11.

60. "Now comes a part of this drama that has never before been publically revealed": Sarah Healy Papers.

61. After filing his application: Samory Pruitt, "A Reflection of Student Desegregation at The University of Alabama as Seen through the Eyes of Some Pioneering African American Students: 1956–1976" (diss., The University of Alabama, 2003), 142–43.

61. "We had walked around the campus": Ibid.

Chapter 7

62. J. Hal McCall—president of the Tuscaloosa: "County Courthouse Box Filled Up and Sealed," *Tuscaloosa News,* June 6, 1963.

62. The day after the time capsule: "Negroes Join In on Talks," *Tuscaloosa News,* June 6, 1963.

63. "In spite of all our efforts to protect her": Sarah Healy Papers.

63. "the president [Carmichael] said nothing to me": Pruitt, "A Reflection of Student Desegregation at The University of Alabama as Seen through the Eyes of Some Pioneering African American Students: 1956–1976," 111.

63. "We talked about football": Sarah Healy Papers.

63. printed a map that marked: "Roadblocks Will Ring UA," *Tuscaloosa News,* June 6, 1963.

63. The perimeter stretched down toward the Black Warrior: Ibid.

64. "Everyone was worried about a bomb": Interview with Harris Cornett conducted December 16, 2010.

64. "I had dated his daughter": Ibid.

64. "George told me a lot": Ibid.

65. "George was an interesting guy": Ibid.

65. "If there is anyone who doesn't want another Oxford incident": Buddy Cornett, "Kennedy Last One to Want Another Oxford—Says Wallace," *Crimson White,* November 15, 1963.

65. "No one looks down on people": Ibid.

65. "[Wallace] really doesn't believe what he says": Sherrill, *Gothic Politics in the Deep South,* 283.

66. "around-the-clock call": "Tuesday Is Set for Enrollment of Two Negros," *Tuscaloosa News,* June 7, 1963.

66. "not more than 50 to 60 per cent": The Reminiscences of George LeMaistre (1964), on page 17, in the CUCOHC.

66. "I remember going to a friend of mine's house": Interview with William G. Marable conducted January 31, 2011.

66. Lingo was described as having the "air of a general": Don McKee, "Troopers' Chief Sees No Trouble at UA," *Tuscaloosa News,* June 7, 1963.

66. "I don't think we're going to have any trouble": Ibid.

66. "The governor will make that decision": Ibid.

Chapter 8

67. "expressing its good wishes and prayers": Associated Press, "Legislature Offers Prayers for Wallace," *Tuscaloosa News,* June 7, 1963.

67. "It was an unusual moment": Ibid.

67. "Governor Wallace knows that regardless": "All of Us Must Listen," *Tuscaloosa News,* June 7, 1963.

67. "We believe his 'last stand' decision to be foolish": Ibid.

68. "If we have violence": Ibid.

68. on Thursday, June 6, the notorious segregationist: Associated Press, "Connor Meets with Wallace," *Tuscaloosa News,* June 7, 1963.

69. "at the ballot box and by economic boycotts": James Mixell, "Stay Clear of Campus, Connor Urges Council," *Tuscaloosa News,* June 8, 1963, 1.

69. "You are not going to whip the integration fight": Ibid.

69. "a big gathering of white men and automobiles": "Our Danger Is Fear," *Tuscaloosa News,* June 8, 1963, 1.

69. "The state of Alabama is not obligated": W. P. Thaxton, "Letter to the Editor: Call for Calmness," *Tuscaloosa News,* June 8, 1963.

69. "low-key": "Exercise in Responsibility," *Tuscaloosa News,* June 10, 1963, 4.

70. "irresponsible rumor and to wild gossip": Ibid.

70. "promptly and regularly": Ibid.

70. "develop a strategy for cooperating": Roberts and Klibanoff, *Race Beat,* 328.

70. Local radio stations: "Stations Here Join for UA Coverage," *Tuscaloosa News,* June 9, 1963, 1.

70. "Only factual and documented reports": Ibid.

70. "So far as we know": "Exercise in Responsibility," *Tuscaloosa News,* June 10, 1963, 4.

71. "The Ole Miss disaster had become legend": Gene and Klibanoff, *Race Beat,* 328.

71. Local journalist and photographer Camille Maxwell Elebash: The Camille Max-

well Elebash Papers, The W. S. Hoole Special Collections Library, The University of Alabama (hereafter Camille Maxwell Elebash Papers).

Chapter 9

72. "Out of an abundance of caution": "Wallace Orders 500 Guardsmen into Tuscaloosa," *Tuscaloosa News,* June 9, 1963, 1.

72. "a small arsenal of pistols, clubs, knives and ammunition": Ibid.

72. "As we drove off toward Tuscaloosa": Gary Thomas Rowe Jr., *My Undercover Years with the Ku Klux Klan* (New York: Bantam, 1976), 83.

73. "tear the school apart": Ibid.

73. "the previous year's rioting": Ibid.

73. "Jesus Christ, we sure hate": Ibid., 84.

73. "We had to pick you up": Ibid., 90.

73. "we support him now, we will support him Monday": "Shelton Predicts Economic Boycotts," *Tuscaloosa News,* June 9, 1963, 1, 2.

73. "But I am asking you other people": Ibid.

74. "I see in Wallace the ability": Ibid.

74. "We were there": Interview with Harris Cornett conducted December 16, 2010.

74. "I have talked to Brother George": Ibid.

74. "That was a surprise to me": Interview with Bob Penny conducted May 15, 2011.

74. "It was a stage show": Interview with Harris Cornett conducted December 16, 2010.

74. "I was one of the murderers": Interview with Bob Penny conducted May 15, 2011.

74. *This was what the Klan:* Ibid.

75. "I don't think [Shelton]": Interview with Harris Cornett conducted December 16, 2010.

75. "two wooden clubs, six loaded pistols": "6 Men Arrested with Weapons," *Tuscaloosa News,* June 9, 1963, 1.

75. "In Montgomery, a former farm boy": "Hoping, Praying, Thinking," *Tuscaloosa News,* June 9, 1963, 4.

75. "mental preparation": Ibid.

75. "The first I knew about it was during the spring of 1963": Interview with Don Siegal conducted November 18, 2010.

75. "feared man . . . an enforcer": Ibid.

76. "Who would like a Bloody Mary?": Ibid.

76. "We got one big problem going on": Ibid.

76. "He told us at that meeting that integration was coming": Ibid.

76. "We went to all the dorms": Ibid.

76. "There wasn't a rock as big as the end of your thumb": Sarah Healy Papers.

76. Glass bottles, a necessary ingredient: Samuels, "Alabama U: A Story of 2 among 4,000."

76. rumors of a Klan force: Ibid.

77. "Folks like Don [Siegal] and others": Interview with Donald Stewart conducted February 1, 2011.

77. "The deal that was expressed": Ibid.

77. "I told them that this was sort": Ibid.

77. "It was a unified effort": Ibid.

78. that barred cameras: "National Spotlight Falls on Capstone." *Tuscaloosa News,* June 9, 1963, 1.

78. no live broadcast: Ibid.

78. "unprecedented": "Stations Here Join for UA Coverage," *Tuscaloosa News,* June 9, 1963, 1.

78. "It is necessary for the governor to be here": Dick Looser, "Tightly Sealed UA Awaiting Governor," *Tuscaloosa News,* June 10, 1963, 1.

78. "declined comment on the wisdom": Ibid.

78. "long be remembered as the time": "Races: The Revolution," *Time Magazine,* June 7, 1963.

79. "My prayer is that all of our people": "Changing Attitudes in the White South," *Newsweek,* June 17, 1963.

79. "the action that I am going to take": Associated Press, "To Risk Arrest, He Says," *Tuscaloosa News,* June 6, 1963, 1.

79. "What happens to George Wallace": Ibid.

79. "I give you my word": Ibid.

79. aggressive tackling of the state budget: "Nations: Where the Stars Fall," *Time Magazine,* September 27, 1963.

79. "first-rate governor": Ibid.

80. relied heavily on federal funding: Ibid.

80. pumped $229 million worth of grants into his state: Ibid.

80. "the greatest disturber": Sherrill, *Gothic Politics in the Deep South,* 255.

80. "more imagination and drive": Ibid.

Chapter 10

81. In anticipation of the governor's stand: Jack Stillman, "Capstone Story Well Covered by News Media," *Tuscaloosa News,* June 12, 1963.

81. "If the treatment accorded me by the students": Ibid.

81. "some of my white friends": Ibid.

81. "subdued curiosity": Ibid.

82. "They wanted to know how": Ibid.

82. "no-violence pledge": Looser, "Tightly Sealed UA Awaiting Governor," 1.

82. "air of calmness": "Air of Calmness Covers Campus," *Tuscaloosa News,* June 10, 1963, 1.

82. "one of the quietest days": "Wallace Orders 500 Guardsmen into Tuscaloosa," *Tuscaloosa News,* June 9, 1963, 1.

83. "Let's not have any mob violence here": Dick Looser, "University Showdown at Hand: Wallace Prepares to Stand in Door," June 11, 1963, 1, 2.

83. "if they had come here": Ibid.

83. For the governor, much of Monday evening: Ibid.

83. "So, we issued him a faculty card": Sarah Healy Papers.

83. "And you know, he did": Ibid.

83. "intelligent enough to realize that demonstrations": "In Our Interest," *Crimson White,* June 9, 1963, 3.

83. "moral grounds . . . we must obey": "Our Own Back," *Crimson White,* June 9, 1963, 3.

83. "I had an enormous amount of angst and conflict": Interview with Hank Black conducted May 15, 2011.

84. Buckley/Goldwater conservative: Ibid.

84. "represented where I was in that swing": Ibid.

84. "Segregation is going, whether we like it or not": William Faulkner, "A Faulkner Letter," *Crimson White,* June 9, 1963, 1, 3.

84. "confederation of older men": Ibid.

85. "Mirabel, plc chief, good man": The Michael Dorman Papers, The W. S. Hoole Special Collections Library, The University of Alabama (hereafter Michael Dorman Papers).

Chapter 11

86. On Tuesday, June 11, James Hood and Vivian Malone: "It Was Quiet Trip into Tuscaloosa," *Tuscaloosa News,* June 11, 1963; Hedrick Smith, "Courtesy and Curiosity Mark Campus Reception," *New York Times,* June 12, 1963, 1, 21.

86. occurred at 7:22 A.M.: Michael Dorman Papers.

86. After several minutes of squawking radio: Ibid.

86. By 7:35 A.M. Attorney General Robert Kennedy OK'd: Ibid.

87. eight hundred miles to the northeast: *Crisis: Behind a Presidential Commitment.* Dir. Robert Drew, 1963.

87. "heed his stern advice": "JFK Watchful . . . Bobby, Too," *New York Journal-American,* June 11, 1963.

87. "The governor cannot block": *Crisis: Behind a Presidential Commitment.*

87. "making a fool": Ibid.

88. "perfectly obvious to all of those newspaper people": Ibid.

88. "I was in the auditorium on the ground": Interview with Bob Penny conducted May 15, 2011.

88. "I wish little George would hurry up": Ibid.

88. "It was time": Interview with Don Siegal conducted November 18, 2010.

88. "I remember my station": Ibid.

89. "the consequences to your state and its fine university": Looser, "University Showdown at Hand: Wallace Prepares to Stand in Door," 1, 2.

89. "This is the opinion of all here": Ibid.

89. Rose wanted peaceful desegregation: McWhorter, *Carry Me Home,* 461.

89. "one of the most impressive men": Allen Barra, *The Last Coach: A Life of Paul "Bear" Bryant* (New York: W. W. Norton, 2005), 279.

89. "It was so hot in Tuscaloosa, Alabama": Camille Maxwell Elebash Papers, script for *George Wallace: A Politician's Legacy.*

89. "Martin Luther King likes to fight these things out in the street": Looser, "University Showdown at Hand: Wallace Prepares to Stand in Door," 1, 2.

90. "Want to say hello to Kerry?": *Crisis: Behind a Presidential Commitment.*

91. "I'm way down here in the Southland": Ibid.

91. "You're going to have to play it a little by ear": Ibid.

91. "We don't need your speech": "JFK Federalizes State Guard after Governor Blocks: Will Be Enrolled Says U.S. Official," *Tuscaloosa News,* June 11, 1963; "Wallace's Statement at Foster," *Tuscaloosa News,* June 11, 1963, 1.

92. "not a show": *Crisis: Behind a Presidential Commitment.*

92. a ketchup-covered lunch of steak and onion rings: "Classes Started, UA Quiet," *Tuscaloosa News,* June 12, 1963, 1.

92. "I couldn't actually see George": Interview with Hank Black conducted May 15, 2011.

92. By 10:58 A.M., Vivian Malone exited the car: Michel Dorman Papers.

92. At 1:40 P.M., General Henry Graham's helicopter: Clark, *Schoolhouse Door,* 229.

93. "aghast . . . for a stunt": Michael Dorman Papers.

93. "*brief* stunt": Ibid.

93. "particularly disgraceful alley cat": Dan T. Carter, *The Politics of Rage: George Wallace, the Origins of the New Conservatism, and the Transformation of American Politics,* (New York: Simon and Schuster, 1995), 148.

93. "It was easy enough to stand in the schoolhouse door": Sherrill, *Gothic Politics in the Deep South,* 281–82.

93. "hit anyone for years": Ibid.

93. "From the outset, Governor": *Crisis: Behind a Presidential Commitment.*

94. "Alabama is winning this fight against": Clark, *Schoolhouse Door,* 230; "Classes Started, UA Quiet," *Tuscaloosa News,* June 12, 1963, 1.

94. at 3:33 P.M.: Michael Dorman Papers.

94. "drew a wolf whistle": Hedrick Smith, "Courtesy and Curiosity Mark Campus Reception," *New York Times,* June 12, 1963, 1, 21.

94. "distaste for any kind of conflict": Mark Kriegel, *Namath: A Biography* (New York: Viking, 2004), 91.

94. "It was a thrill to see Vivian": Ibid., 92.

94. "He was so different": Ibid., 94.

95. Hank Blank followed close behind: Interview with Hank Black conducted May 15, 2011.

95. "Hi, there," one of the registrars smiled: "Races: The Long March," *Time Magazine,* June 21, 1963.

95. "We were sitting here watching it on the news": Interview with Reverend T. W. Linton conducted January 5, 2011.

96. "advance agreement": Ted Sorensen, *Counselor: A Life at the Edge of History* (New York: Harper Perennial, 2009), 278.

96. "no prior agreement": Camille Maxwell Elebash Papers, script for *George Wallace: A Politician's Legacy.*

96. "It worked out pretty well": Ibid.

96. "an uncertain parlay at best": Stephan Lesher, *George Wallace: American Populist* (New York: A William Patrick Book, 1994), 216.

Chapter 12

97. "I think we'd better give that speech tonight": Sorensen, *Counselor,* 278.

98. "I hope when you are Attorney General": McWhorter, *Carry Me Home,* 463.

98. "He asked if I had any problems": Pruitt, "A Reflection of Student Desegregation at The University of Alabama as Seen through the Eyes of Some Pioneering African American Students: 1956–1976," 151.

98. The president changed Sorensen's: Sorensen, *Counselor,* 280–81.

98. "toned down, but its substance remained": Ibid., 281.

98. "two clearly qualified young Alabama residents": John F. Kennedy Civil Rights Address, delivered June 11, 1963, www.americanrhetoric.com/speeches /jfkcivilrights.htm.

99. "If the President tries to enforce": Associated Press, "President Outlines Rights Proposals," *Tuscaloosa News,* June 12, 1963, 1.

99. "one of the most eloquent, profound and unequivocal": Associated Press, "Praise, Criticism Sound for JFK," *Tuscaloosa News,* June 12, 1963.

99. "nominal interest": David Halberstam, *The Unfinished Odyssey of Robert Kennedy* (New York: Random House, 1968), 142.

99. "cautious leader": Robert Dallek, *John F. Kennedy* (Oxford: Oxford University Press, 2003), 68.

99. "It took crises in Mississippi and particularly": Ibid.

99. Nevertheless, Robert Kennedy remained particularly: Sarah Healy Papers.

100. "they were two of the Ten Outstanding Young Men": Ibid.

100. In January of 1955: The United States Junior Chamber Foundation, http://usjayceefoundation.org/history/1950/1954/index.htm.

100. "sort of like a little fraternity": Sarah Healy Papers.

100. "Dr. Rose and I arranged": Ibid.

100. "At that time, the cry in the deep south": Ibid.

100. "We went through a series": Ibid.

101. "No, I don't have a room": Ibid.

101. "The next thing I know": Ibid.

101. "We often opposed each other": Ibid.

101. Likewise, it would send a clear message that Alabamians: Camille Maxwell Elebash Papers, script for *George Wallace: A Politician's Legacy*.

101. "Do you really think we can trust them?": Sarah Healy Papers.

102. "looked like a football stadium after a homecoming game": "Foster Auditorium Looks Like Stadium after Game," *Tuscaloosa News*, June 12, 1963.

102. "And standing in the doorway this morning": Ibid.

102. "I walked the campus": Pruitt, "A Reflection of Student Desegregation at The University of Alabama as Seen through the Eyes of Some Pioneering African American Students: 1956–1976," 179–80.

103. "Hey, Hood, over this way": Paul Davis, "2 Negroes Begin Capstone Classes," *Tuscaloosa News*, June 12, 1963, 1.

103. Snapping his fingers: Ibid.

103. "Little or no change": "Little or No Change," *Tuscaloosa News*, June 12, 1963, 1.

103. "Hood, they got one in Jackson last night": Davis, "2 Negroes Begin Capstone Classes," *Tuscaloosa News*, June 12, 1963, 1.

103. "they didn't want us to see": Pruitt, "A Reflection of Student Desegregation at The University of Alabama as Seen through the Eyes of Some Pioneering African American Students: 1956–1976," 150.

103. "They had to treat me like": Ibid., 150.

103. But the world soon learned of Evers's death: McWhorter, *Carry Me Home*, 464–65.

103. "suffered a muscle spasm": "Coed Faints, Hood's First Class Short," *The Tuscaloosa News*, June 12, 1963.

103. "the spasm was related": Ibid.

104. By all accounts, the brown-eyed, 160-pound: "Students Who Met Crisis," *New York Times*, June 12, 1963, 21.

104. "continued to work his way": "Thumbnail Sketches of Three Students," *Huntsville Times*, June 11, 1963.

104. "one of the things that I also had in the back": Pruitt, "A Reflection of Student

Desegregation at The University of Alabama as Seen through the Eyes of Some Pioneering African American Students: 1956–1976," 141.

104. "as a craftsman": "Students Who Met Crisis," 21.

104. "I want to write a book someday about Negro life": Ibid.

104. "We have a police dog": Ibid.

104. At five feet six and 124 pounds, her small frame: Ibid.

105. "No, some girls came by": "Thumbnail Sketches of Three Students," *Huntsville Times,* June 11, 1963.

105. "well-dressed girl—composed, reserved and quiet": "Negros Described as 'Stoic,' Congenial," *Tuscaloosa News,* June 11, 1963.

105. "fully cognizant that her stay on the campus": Ibid.

105. "Whenever you go to a new place": "Thumbnail Sketches of Three Students."

105. "I was struck by the differences": Interview with Raymond Fowler conducted November 15, 2010.

105. "[When Hood] came into the dormitory": Ibid.

105. "Become the governor of the state of Alabama": *Crisis: Behind a Presidential Commitment.*

106. the students appeared mostly content: Arthur Shores Papers.

106. "I went over and sat down": Interview with Donald Stewart conducted February 1, 2011.

106. "My first couple of days": Pruitt, "A Reflection of Student Desegregation at The University of Alabama as Seen through the Eyes of Some Pioneering African American Students: 1956–1976," 147–48.

106. "What do I do?": Ibid., 149.

107. "I was probably better off there than": Interview with Donald Stewart conducted February 1, 2011.

Chapter 13

108. Vivian Malone and James Hood had not seen the last: "Lurleen B. Wallace Award of Courage," October 10, 1996. C-Span, http://www.c-spanvideo.org/program/BW.

108. "I had the distinction of first meeting": Ibid.

109. "I came here tonight specifically": Ibid.

109. "It was difficult for me": Ibid.

109. "I'm often asked, 'What do you think'": Ibid.

109. "I know how difficult it is these days": Ibid.

110. frail and shriveled: Sue Ann Pressley, "At Wallace Funeral, a Redemptive Tone," *Washington Post,* September 17, 1998.

110. "nearly as many blacks as whites": Ibid.

110. "Whom the gods would destroy, they first make mad with power": Rick Bragg,

"Wallace Remembered, for Who He Was and Who He Became," *New York Times,* September 17, 1998.

110. "The legacy of George Wallace": Ibid.

110. "If any man understands the true meaning": Ibid.

110. "Why doesn't the Negro race wake up": James Hood, "Needed: More Students, Less Pickets," *Crimson White,* June 27, 1963, 4.

110. "It is my firm belief that": Ibid.

110. Hood's "wake up" line: Ibid.; The James Hood *Crimson White* Collection, The W. S. Hoole Special Collections Library, The University of Alabama.

111. "unpopular with the masses of [his] people": Ibid.

111. Arthur Shores wrote to the young student: Arthur Shores Papers.

111. "I've always thought Jimmy Hood": Interview with Bob Penny conducted May 15, 2011.

112. According to Jefferson Bennett: Sarah Healy Papers.

112. "I was uncomfortable from time to time": Interview with Hank Black conducted May 15, 2011.

112. "I felt bad about it": Ibid.

112. "To: Hank": Ibid.

113. "did not go out and march or demonstrate or any of that": Interview with Vivian Malone-Jones conducted by Alan DeSantis on August 15, 1987, The DeSantis Collection, W. S. Hoole Special Collections Library, The University of Alabama (hereafter DeSantis Collection).

113. "working together on a daily basis": Ibid.

113. "They were still dealing": Ibid.

113. "I think[black community members]": Ibid.

113. "[Hood and Malone] gave us hope": Interview with Ruth Bolden conducted by Alan DeSantis on June 16, 1987, DeSantis Collection.

Chapter 14

118. "older than his years": Interview with Bettye Rogers Maye conducted May 17, 2011.

118. "He didn't do a lot of playing around": Ibid.

118. Rogers's interest in politics: "Theopholius [*sic*] Yelverton Rogers Jr.," *King Encyclopedia,* http://mlk-kpp01.stanford.edu/kingweb/about_king/encyclopedia/rogers_theopholius.html.

119. "There were times when I would": The Reminiscences of T. Y. Rogers (1964), on page 7, in the CUCOHC.

119. "I got enough sense to realize": Ibid.

120. On August 31, 1957, King struck a fatherly tone: Clayborne Carson, Peter Holloran, Ralph Luker, et al., *The Papers of Martin Luther King Jr.: Symbol of the Move-*

ment: January 1957–December 1958. August 31, 1957 correspondence between Reverend Martin Luther King Jr. and Reverend T. Y. Rogers.

120. Nearly three years later: Clayborne Carson, Peter Holloran, Ralph Luker, et al., *The Papers of Martin Luther King Jr.: Threshold of a New Decade: January 1959– December 1960.* June 18, 1960, correspondence between Reverend Martin Luther King Jr. and Reverend T. Y. Rogers.

120. King responded by informing Rogers: Ibid.

120. "My parents and I didn't want him to come back": Interview with Bettye Rogers Maye conducted May 17, 2011.

120. "Oh, Bettye": Ibid.

121. "fortuitous . . . quite beneficial": Interview with Willie Herzfeld conducted by Alan DeSantis on August 12, 1987, DeSantis Collection.

121. "I don't believe it was a part of any master plan": Ibid.

121. "He was really encouraged by Dr. King": Interview with LaPelzia Rogers conducted by Alan DeSantis on June 28, 1987, DeSantis Collection.

121. "more a subconscious reason than a conscious one": The Reminiscences of T. Y. Rogers (1964), on page 2 in the CUCOHC.

121. "They realized that there were problems in Tuscaloosa": Ibid.

121. "There are those who will say": "King Talks Here, Calls for End of Segregation," *Tuscaloosa News,* March 9, 1964.

121. "Tuscaloosa is very definitely included": Ibid.

Chapter 15

122. "I became involved because T. Y.": Interview with Olivia Maniece conducted by Alan DeSantis on June 24, 1987, DeSantis Collection.

122. "At that time, I don't think anybody": Ibid.

123. "It looked like a large part of": Bob Kyle, "Rain Christens Courthouse for Throng at Dedication," *Tuscaloosa News,* April 13, 1964, 1, 2.

123. "temple of justice": Ibid.

123. "second home": Ibid.

123. "If this bill passes": Ibid.

124. The following Thursday, TCAC made it known: "'Bias' Is Charged at New Courthouse," *Tuscaloosa News,* April 16, 1964, 1, 2.

124. "salt-and-pepper": "Mixing Leaders Ready to Stage Protest March," *Tuscaloosa News,* April 23, 1964, 1, 2.

124. "all discriminatory signs": "'Bias' Is Charged at New Courthouse," 1, 2.

124. "resort to other methods to secure this end": Ibid.

124. "Unless they are removed": Ibid.

124. "We felt that this was a good time": The Reminiscences of T. Y. Rogers (1964), on page 22 in the CUCOHC.

124. "change our whole concept of life": Rex Sanders, "Governor Brings His Crusade To UA," *Tuscaloosa News,* April 16, 1964, 1, 2.

125. voted unanimously to reject TCAC's requests: "March, Boycott, Planned in City," *Tuscaloosa News,* April 22, 1964, 1, 2.

125. "did not block any street": "Mixing Leaders Ready to Stage Protest March," 1, 2.

125. "Very few members": The Reminiscences of Willie Herzfeld (1964), on page 18 in the CUCOHC.

126. "Yes, I guess I was the loneliest man": Ibid.

126. "Look, I'm tired": The Reminiscences of T. Y. Rogers (1964), on page 11 in the CUCOHC.

126. "The Baptist churches": Ibid., 13.

126. "I think there was a feeling": Ibid., 17–18.

126. "hanging from the rafters": Ibid., 23.

126. "As soon as Gov. Wallace": "Mixing Leaders Ready to Stage Protest March," 1, 2.

127. "So go ahead and do your handclapping": Ibid.

127. "Why spend our money": Ibid.

127. By 10:30 A.M. on Thursday, April 23: "Protest March Free of Violence," *Tuscaloosa News,* April 23, 1964, 1, 2.

127. "no stir of amusement": Ibid.

128. "Move, nigger": The Reminiscences of T. Y. Rogers (1964), on page 25 in the CUCOHC.

128. "herded down the [courthouse] steps": "Protest March Free of Violence," 1, 2.

128. "They did not believe that that could happen in": The Reminiscences of T. Y. Rogers (1964), on page 27 in the CUCOHC.

128. "They had agreed previously": Ibid., 27.

129. "Well, we had to disperse you": Ibid., 28.

129. "some of the more zealous": The Reminiscences of George LeMaistre (1964), on page 9, in the CUCOHC.

129. "I got the same understanding": Ibid.

129. "Who is T. Y. Rogers": The Reminiscences of Robert Shelton (1964), on page 28 in the CUCOHC.

129. "show of ignorance": Ibid., 5–6.

129. "There's a health problem": Ibid., 6.

130. "Anytime a group of white people": Ibid., 38.

Chapter 16

144. "Some of you are willing to go to jail for what's wrong": "Keep on Marching, Negro Comedian Urges Group Here," *Tuscaloosa News,* June 2, 1964.

144. fourteen-year-old: "Demonstrators Hit with Mustard Oil," *Tuscaloosa News,* June 5, 1964; "More Sit-Ins Are Tried Here; Pickets March," *Tuscaloosa News,* June 3, 1964, 1.

144. "burning sensation on the arms": "Demonstrators Hit with Mustard Oil."

144. twenty-nine-year-old Hubert Hinton Jones and twenty-six-year-old Billy Wayne Mansfield: "Two Men Arrested in Racial Incident," *Tuscaloosa News*, June 5, 1964.

144. The fifty or so marchers: "Demonstrators March on Downtown Section," *Tuscaloosa News*, June 6, 1964.

145. "I had the audacity to walk": Interview with Harvey Burg conducted April 6, 2011.

145. parade ordinance: "Marchers Here Turned Back," *Tuscaloosa News*, June 8, 1964.

146. "very cordial": The Reminiscences of T. Y. Rogers (1964), on pages 19–20 in the CUCOHC.

146. "He told me what to do": Ibid., 20.

146. "Water down the damn streets": Interview with Willie Herzfeld conducted by Alan DeSantis on August 12, 1987, DeSantis Collection.

147. "was determined that this wasn't about to happen in Tuscaloosa": Interview with William G. Marable conducted January 31, 2011.

147. "It was always Mister or Missus": Ibid.

147. "We didn't have all the luxuries": Ibid.

147. "a pretty straight fellow": Interview with Nathaniel Howard Jr. conducted by Alan DeSantis on June 27, 1987, DeSantis Collection.

147. "[having] a lot to do with the curtailing": Interview with Willie Herzfeld conducted by Alan DeSantis on August 12, 1987, DeSantis Collection.

147. "Every time he talked with someone": Interview with William M. Marable II conducted February 23, 2011.

148. "Tuscaloosa was not a large place": Interview with William G. Marable conducted January 31, 2011.

148. "Sometimes Shelton would call": Ibid.

148. "Before we initiated": The Reminiscences of T. Y. Rogers (1964), on pages 23–24, in the CUCOHC.

148. "I remember loving it as a kid": Interview with William M. Marable II conducted February 23, 2011.

149. "I was a curious kid": Interview with William G. Marable conducted January 31, 2011.

149. "We had to put a tap": Ibid.

149. "You don't want to be a cop": Ibid.

150. "Oh, Lord, there were a lot of Elvis moments": Ibid.

150. "Chief, you got lights and sirens on this thing?": Ibid.

Chapter 17

151. "Something bad is gonna happen today": "Day Started Quietly and Then Came 'Explosion,'" *Tuscaloosa News*, June 9, 1964, 1, 3.

151. "We got there": Interview with Olivia Maniece conducted by Alan DeSantis on June 24, 1987, DeSantis Collection.

152. "They told us briefly": Ibid.

152. "We're going to lead, you all just follow us": Ibid.

152. "You have heard my orders": "Day Started Quietly and Then Came 'Explosion,'" 3.

152. "elbows, clubs, and electric cattle prods": Ibid.

152. "Then the worst period of trouble began": Ibid.

153. "When the Negroes refused to halt": Ibid.

153. "The police was out there": Interview with Odessa Warrick conducted by Alan DeSantis on July 6, 1987, DeSantis Collection.

153. "And every time they would beat me": Ibid.

154. "Our eyes was full of tear gas": Ibid.

154. "And you want to talk about blood?": Wayne Grayson, "State SCLC Rally Recalls 'Bloody Tuesday,'" *Tuscaloosa News,* February 27, 2010.

154. "I was observing the entire operation": The Reminiscences of Robert Shelton (1964), on page 18 in the CUCOHC.

154. "The Nigras": Ibid., 18–19.

154. "The reporters that were present say": Ibid., 19.

154. "several of the policemen": "Day Started Quietly and Then Came 'Explosion,'" 1, 3.

154. In response to a 2011 newspaper article: Dick Looser, "Letter to the Editor: Civil Rights March Misinformation Abounds," *Tuscaloosa News,* May 1, 2011.

154. He had witnessed the scene firsthand: Interview with Dick Looser conducted May 9, 2011.

155. "One [of the objects thrown] was a bottle or a vase": Looser, "Letter to the Editor: Civil Rights March Misinformation Abounds."

155. "police retaliated by throwing tear gas": Ibid.

155. "How could it happen in Tuscaloosa?": The Reminiscences of T. Y. Rogers (1964), on page 45 in the CUCOHC.

155. "look of disbelief on his face": "Day Started Quietly and Then Came 'Explosion,'" 1, 3.

156. "You need to get over here quick": Interview with Reverend T. W. Linton conducted January 5, 2011.

156. "Come here, Minister": Ibid.

157. Linton called King first: Ibid.

157. "I had [the phone numbers]": Ibid.

157. *Tuscaloosa News* eventually put the number at ninety-four: "City Police Take Arrests in Stride," *Tuscaloosa News* June 9, 1964, 1; "Scattered Violence Reported," *Tuscaloosa News,* June 10, 1964, 1.

157. The local hospital was soon inundated: "Scattered Violence Reported," *Tuscaloosa News,* June 10, 1964, 1.

157. "I don't know how many children": Interview with Ruth Bolden conducted by Alan DeSantis on June 16, 1987, DeSantis Collection.

158. "Not only had police officers": Simon Wendt, "God, Gandhi, and Guns: The African American Freedom Struggle in Tuscaloosa, Alabama, 1964–1965," *Journal of African American History* 89, no. 1 (2004): 37.

158. "People out of state didn't know": Grayson, "State SCLC Rally Recalls 'Bloody Tuesday.'"

158. "You go in [First African Baptist] now": Interview with Odessa Warrick conducted by Alan DeSantis on July 6, 1987, DeSantis Collection.

159. "wash[ing] the blood off the stairs": The Reminiscences of T. Y. Rogers (1964), on page 50 in the CUCOHC.

159. "They felt, 'This is what is happening'": Ibid., 50.

Chapter 18

160. "Nobody wants to take action": "Scattered Violence Reported," 1, 2.

160. "I think what happened is, [the police]": Interview with Olivia Maniece conducted by Alan DeSantis on June 24, 1987, DeSantis Collection.

161. "yelling and pointing out to police the children": Thomas Linton, "'Bloody Tuesday' a Public Crime Unacknowledged," *Tuscaloosa News,* March 1, 2009.

161. Reverend James Bevel, to assess and assist in Tuscaloosa: "Negroes to Chart Strategy," *Tuscaloosa News,* June 10, 1964, 1–2.

161. Reverend Bevel had accumulated a growing list: Randy Kryn, "Movement Revision Research Summary Regarding James Bevel," Chicago Freedom Movement, http://cfm40.middlebury.edu/node/287?PHPSESSID=93ecfd343b560d53c16 658fc46c0bbc6.

161. "continue to address": "Negroes to Chart Strategy," 1–2.

162. "Why?" asked the bondsman: Interview with Reverend T. W. Linton conducted January 5, 2011.

162. "So we got organized with people": Ibid.

162. "I don't know, I don't know": Interview with Ruth Bolden conducted by Alan DeSantis on June 16, 1987, DeSantis Collection.

163. "Police was going around with guns stuck": Ibid.

163. "We had to talk in code": Ibid.

163. "We are going to assemble as long as there is breath": "Negroes Vow They'll March," *Tuscaloosa News,* June 11, 1964, 1.

163. Fifty-eight of the ninety-four: Ibid.

164. "When the police say": Ibid.

164. "no city laws covering segregation": "Negroes Never Asked for Talk, Officials Say," *Tuscaloosa News,* June 12, 1964.

165. "Frankly, as long as outsiders": Ibid.

165. "I no longer consider the Rev. Rogers a responsible": Ibid.

Chapter 19

167. "I organized the first unit to protect us": Interview with Joe Mallisham conducted by Alan DeSantis on July 22, 1987, DeSantis Collection.

167. "We're going to have to do it": Ibid.

167. "married war veterans . . . conform to a rigid code of morality": Wendt, "God, Gandhi, and Guns: The African American Freedom Struggle in Tuscaloosa, Alabama, 1964–1965," 45.

167. "Listen, my friends": Interview with Dr. Jim Webb conducted December 1, 2010.

168. "As we drove up Cedar Crest": Ibid.

168. "an armed group of veterans who would guard my mama": Interview with Stan Murphy conducted December 16, 2010.

169. "We're either going to do this here": Ibid.

169. "a dear friend": Ibid.

169. "[Mallisham] was afraid of an accident": Interview with Ruth Bolden conducted by Alan DeSantis on June 16, 1987, DeSantis Collection.

169. "a military institution": Interview with Nathaniel Howard Jr. conducted by Alan DeSantis on June 27, 1987, DeSantis Collection.

169. "One guy was shot at, just grazed his head": Interview with Ruth Bolden conducted by Alan DeSantis on June 16, 1987, DeSantis Collection.

170. "If you were a black person": Interview with Nathaniel Howard Jr. conducted by Alan DeSantis on June 27, 1987, DeSantis Collection.

170. "He'd get all these threatening calls": Interview with Ruth Bolden conducted by Alan DeSantis on June 16, 1987, DeSantis Collection.

170. "felt sorrier for the people": The Reminiscences of T. Y. Rogers (1964), on page 29 in the CUCOHC.

170 "the usual threats": Ibid., 30–40.

170. "There were times when I would": Ibid., 30–40.

170. "After all, why would they threaten me?": Ibid., 40.

170. "No. No. I didn't know what fear was": Interview with Joe Mallisham conducted by Alan DeSantis on July 22, 1987, DeSantis Collection.

171. "I used to carry a gun in that Bible": Interview with Odessa Warrick conducted by Alan DeSantis on July 6, 1987, DeSantis Collection.

171. Throughout the 1960s, the home of Jay and Alberta Murphy: Interview with Stan Murphy conducted December 16, 2010.

171. "You never knew who was going to be there": Ibid.

171. "Any time there was anybody slightly off": Ibid.

172. "So apparently what my dad did was": Ibid.

173. "But it took a lot of guts": Ibid.

173. "[The Klan] felt contempt": Rowe, *My Undercover Years with the Ku Klux Klan,* 150.

173. "If the civic and business community had said": Interview with Stan Murphy conducted December 16, 2010.

Chapter 20

174. "We have lost the South for a generation": Clay Risen, "How the South Was Won," *Boston Globe,* March 5, 2006.

174. "felt that maybe that [June 11 Civil Rights] speech": Sorensen, *Counselor,* 283–84.

175. In a small report taking up no more: "Signs Removed on Restrooms at Courthouse," *Tuscaloosa News,* July 1, 1964, 1.

175. "The maintenance of signs": Associated Press, "Remove Signs, County Ordered," *Tuscaloosa News,* June 26, 1964.

175. On Tuesday, June 30, Lynne's popularity: "Signs Removed on Restrooms at Courthouse," *Tuscaloosa News,* July 1, 1964, 1.

176. united in the same way: "White Citizens Call for Action," *Tuscaloosa News,* July 1, 1964, 1.

176. "The primary purpose of WCAC": Ibid.

177. "people on campus shouting": Pruitt, "A Reflection of Student Desegregation at The University of Alabama as Seen through the Eyes of Some Pioneering African American Students: 1956–1976," 196.

177. "equal in the polling booths": "President Lyndon B. Johnson's Radio and Television Remarks upon Signing the Civil Rights Bill," July 2, 1964, http://www.lbjlib .utexas.edu/johnson/archives.hom/speeches.hom/640702.asp.

177. Moments later, flanked by Dr. Martin Luther King Jr.: Associated Press, "Rights Bill Goes to President: Signing Slated Tonight," *Tuscaloosa News,* July 2, 1964, 1.

177. Gene Young marched dutifully into the barbershop: Associated Press, "Rights Law Tested," *Tuscaloosa News,* July 3, 1964.

178. "off-the-record conferences": Associated Press, "Won't Enforce Law, Will Fight It, Wallace Says," *Tuscaloosa News,* July 3, 1964, 1.

178. "My position on this bill is well known": Ibid.

178. twenty-five African Americans purchased tickets to a movie: "Theater Mixed Here; No Trouble," *Tuscaloosa News,* July 5, 1964, 1.

179. "What is the great attraction of lining up": Interview with Harvey Burg conducted April 6, 2011.

179. "escorted out of the building by six white men": "Few Clashes Occur Here," *Tuscaloosa News,* July 6, 1964.

179. windows shattered and tires punctured: Ibid.

180. "interfering with 'peaceful demonstrations'": "Court Hearing on Picketing Resumes Here," *Tuscaloosa News,* July 6, 1964.

180. "assess the situation in the two cities": Associated Press, "King Workers Plan Tests Here, Selma," *Tuscaloosa News,* July 7, 1964.

180. "The action we take": Ibid.

180. Couched in the heart of the Black Belt, the town of thirty thousand: Luther H. Hodges and Richard M. Scammon, *County and City Data Book, 1962* (Bureau of Census, Department of Commerce, 1962), 581.

181. "forcefully ejected": "4 Eating Places Integrated Here," *Tuscaloosa News,* July 7, 1964, 1.

181. "They would just ask for a hamburger": Interview with Ruth Bolden conducted by Alan DeSantis on June 16, 1987, DeSantis Collection.

181. "a lot of fat women": Ibid.

181. Newspapers reported that by the end of Tuesday, only six: "Further Tests of Rights Act Planned Here," *Tuscaloosa News,* July 8, 1964, 1.

182. arrived at Ed's Drive-In: "10 Spots Here Refuse Service to Negroes," *Tuscaloosa News,* July 8, 1964, 1–2.

Chapter 21

183. On Wednesday, July 8, seventeen African Americans: "Stones and Bottles Hurled at Negroes," *Tuscaloosa News,* July 9, 1964, 1, 2.

183. While one young moviegoer was hit with a brick: Ibid.

184. "We was scared so we called Joe Mallisham": Interview with Odessa Warrick conducted by Alan DeSantis on July 6, 1987, DeSantis Collection.

184. "no further incidents or outbreaks were reported": "Stones, Bottles, Greet Negroes at City Theater," *Tuscaloosa News,* July 9, 1964, 1–2.

184. "We turned in there": Interview with Joe Mallisham conducted by Alan DeSantis on July 22, 1987, DeSantis Collection.

184. "There would have been bloodshed": Ibid.

185. "tired of having the ugly cloud": "The Price of Our Silence," *Tuscaloosa News,* July 9, 1964, 1.

185. "encourage compliance with the Civil Rights Act": "Gas Used on Mob; City Orders Curfew," *Tuscaloosa News,* July 10, 1964.

186. "We kept noticing these two or three little figures": Interview with Bob Penny conducted May 15, 2011.

186. "Palance appeared puzzled": "Gas Used on Mob; City Orders Curfew."

187. "We need to get out of here": Interview with Bob Penny conducted May 15, 2011.

187. "the one time he got to throw somebody around": Interview with William M. Marable II conducted February 23, 2011.

187. The newspaper reported that not only had the tires been slashed: "Gas Used on Mob; City Orders Curfew."

187. "paper sign": Ibid.

187. "real friendly": Rex Sanders, "Actor's Visit in City Cut Short by Violence," *Tuscaloosa News,* July 10, 1964.

187. "One thing is that the people here": Ibid.

187. "feared for his life": Associated Press, "Feared for Life, Palance Says on New York Arrival," *Tuscaloosa News,* July 11, 1964, 1, 3.

188. "being paid by the National Association": Ibid.

188. "You're scaring my children": Ibid.

188. "We got the shock of our lives": Ibid.

188. "There were no Negroes": Ibid.

188. "Well, I, with some of my key personnel": The Reminiscences of Robert Shelton (1964), on page 16 in the CUCOHC.

188. "Do you think I'd be crazy": Associated Press, "Feared for Life, Palance Says on New York Arrival."

189. "I have talked to Chief Marable": The Reminiscences of George LeMaistre (1964), on page 28 in the CUCOHC.

189. "Tuscaloosa's mob hospitality was extended": "Putting On the Squeeze," *Tuscaloosa News,* July 10, 1964.

189. "And we have some requests of Mr. Rogers": Ibid.

190. "The opportunity to earn a dollar": Booker T. Washington, "The Atlanta Exposition Address," in *The Norton Anthology of African American Literature,* ed. Henry Louis Gates Jr. and Nellie Y. McKay (New York: W. W. Norton, 2004).

190. "We've been integrated for years": "Terribly Dangerous," *Newsweek,* June 10, 1963.

190. "local custom. . . . We know the tenor of the South": Ibid.

191. "It reached the point where": "A Voice of Justice and Reason."

191. "grownup juvenile delinquents . . . gorillas, uncaged": "Lullaby and Goodnight," *Tuscaloosa News,* July 8, 1964, 1.

191. "false, libelous and defamatory editorials": "Robert Shelton Replies," *Tuscaloosa News,* July 10, 1964, 1–2.

191. "What He counseled never has been matched": "May We Pray—And Listen," *Tuscaloosa News,* July 12, 1964.

191. "I do not agree with the civil rights law": C. Duke Case, "Letter to the Editor: Support Stands," *Tuscaloosa News,* July 12, 1964.

192. "Not of the Negro": Ibid.

192. "It is disturbing to me as a white man": Ibid.

Chapter 22

193. "Hey, Reverend Herzfeld": The Reminiscences of Willie Herzfeld (1964), on pages 8–9 in the CUCOHC.

194. "not concerned with mass meetings so much": Ibid., 11.

194. "harassment, intimidation and arrest": "Negro Threat to Quit Buses Made Public," *Tuscaloosa News,* August 3, 1964, 1.

194. "non-segregated seating": Ibid.

195. "highly effective": "Boycott Causes Cut in City Bus Service," *Tuscaloosa News,* August 11, 1964, 1.

195. "prompt action be taken": Ibid.

195. "We have done all we can do": Ibid.

195. In an effort to cut costs: "Entire City Bus Service in Doubt: Outlook Termed Gloomy," *Tuscaloosa News,* August 12, 1964, 1.

196. plaques of appreciation: "County's Officers Praised," *Tuscaloosa News,* August 12, 1964, 1.

196. "the shortage of manpower": "Apathy Biggest Foe, Chief Marable Says," *Tuscaloosa News,* August 12, 1964, 1.

196. In it, an overburdened taxpayer: Mob Pressure Political Cartoon, *Tuscaloosa News,* July 10, 1964, 1.

196. "Most of all, we need you": "Apathy Biggest Foe, Chief Marable Says," 1.

197. The Druid City Transit Company's decision: "Buses Sit Idle at Garage," *Tuscaloosa News,* August 14, 1964, 1.

197. "only by continued cooperation": Frank D. Huttlinger, "Letter to the Editor: Fears Unfounded," *Tuscaloosa News,* August 21, 1964.

198. "Federal law says that we can't hire": Paul Davis, "Boycott Leaders Given Hard Facts by Bus Officials," *Tuscaloosa News,* August 16, 1964, 1, 2.

198. "Since the company gets 90 per cent": Ibid.

198. "The company would just as soon be shut down": Ibid.

198. "We have never had a single application": Ibid.

199. "If you are unable to meet this condition": "Bus Owner Eyes Complete Pullout," *Tuscaloosa News,* August 24, 1964, 1.

199. At the start of the 1964 school year: Sarah White, "School Buses Revving Up," *Tuscaloosa News,* August 27, 1964.

Chapter 23

201. "I was in the bed": Interview with Ruth Bolden conducted by Alan DeSantis on June 16, 1987, DeSantis Collection.

201. "I believe T. Y. felt his death": Ibid.

201. "the man who almost singlehandedly led the civil rights drive": "Rev. T. Y. Rogers Killed in Atlanta Auto Accident," *Tuscaloosa News,* March 26, 1971, 1, 2.

201. Instead, Rogers's center chair: Waylon Smithey, "Memorial Service Held Here for T. Y. Rogers," *Tuscaloosa News,* March 29, 1971.

201. "a faint sob": Ibid.

201. "Fields that were green": Ibid.

202. "We must join our hands and press on": Ibid.

202. "T. Y. Rogers had a lot of unfinished business": Ibid.

202. "We are determined to carry this march out": Ed Watkins, "'March against Repression' Starts in Eutaw," *Tuscaloosa News,* March 31, 1971, 1, 2.

203. "Let it be known that the weak sting of death": "Abernathy Urges Others to Carry On for Rogers," *Tuscaloosa News,* March 30, 1971.

203. "There will be no curtain call": Ibid.

203. "They said he ran into the abutment": Interview with Ruth Bolden conducted by Alan DeSantis on June 16, 1987, DeSantis Collection.

203. "I used to ride with T. Y.": Interview with Nathaniel Howard Jr. conducted by Alan DeSantis on June 27, 1987, DeSantis Collection.

204. "doing about 50 miles an hour": The Reminiscences of T. Y. Rogers (1964), on page 18 in the CUCOHC.

204. "He must have called us that Thursday": Interview with Bettye Rogers Maye conducted May 17, 2011.

204. "We assumed that we were going to be carried": Ibid.

205. "There were no skid marks on the street": Ibid.

205. "My mother was just out of her mind": Ibid.

205. "I have no idea who may have been behind it": Ibid.

205. "I just want to know what happened to you": Ibid.

206. "People have their own way of evaluating a person": Interview with Nathaniel Howard Jr. conducted by Alan DeSantis on June 27, 1987, DeSantis Collection.

206. "T. Y. was a man of action": Interview with Joe Mallisham conducted by Alan DeSantis on July 22, 1987, DeSantis Collection.

206. "T. Y. trusted the so-called small people": Interview with LaPelzia Rogers conducted by Alan DeSantis on June 28, 1987, DeSantis Collection.

206. "We had a real fine visit": Interview with Willie Herzfeld conducted by Alan DeSantis on August 12, 1987, DeSantis Collection.

207. "I came from Alabama State College": The Reminiscences of T. Y. Rogers (1964), on page 14 in the CUCOHC.

207. "There was no similarity": Interview with Theresa Burroughs conducted on January 19, 2011.

207. "T. Y. was just T. Y.": Ibid.

208. "[T. Y.] had that type of personality": Interview with LaPelzia Rogers conducted by Alan DeSantis on June 28, 1987, DeSantis Collection.

208. "one of the most overlooked tales of the civil rights era": Tommy Stevenson, "Tuscaloosa's Bloody Tuesday," *Tuscaloosa News,* February 22, 2009.

208. "If billy clubs and axe handles crack skulls": Ibid.

209. "I just don't know what to say about that": Interview with Ruth Bolden conducted by Alan DeSantis on June 16, 1987, DeSantis Collection.

209. "lack of knowledge": Interview with Nathaniel Howard Jr. conducted by Alan DeSantis on June 27, 1987, DeSantis Collection.
209. "Tuscaloosa is a small city": Interview with Odessa Warrick conducted by Alan DeSantis on July 6, 1987, DeSantis Collection.
209. "Well, you can ask yourself the same question": Interview with LaPelzia Rogers conducted by Alan DeSantis on June 28, 1987, DeSantis Collection.
209. "petty jealousy": Interview with Joe Mallisham conducted by Alan DeSantis on July 22, 1987, DeSantis Collection.
210. "My image of the city": The Reminiscences of T. Y. Rogers (1964), on page 57 in the CUCOHC.
210. "Regarding the whites": Ibid., 57–58.
210. "So now we have a small group": Ibid., 59.
210. "Negroes in Tuscaloosa": Ibid., 60.

Chapter 24

211. "must have the most unique": Dan Williamson, "Tuscaloosa Rights Figures Speak Out on Selma, Luizzo, Klan Investigation," *Crimson White,* May 13, 1965, 5, 8, 10, 11.
212. "To summarize," Williamson reported: Ibid.
212. "On the whole it's been quite": Billie Blair, "On the Whole It's Been Quite a Happy Year for Me," *Crimson White,* June 17, 1965, 1.
212. "Human garbage . . . a dirty little man who needs a haircut": Richard M. Miles, "RFK Hated, Respected," *Crimson White,* March 17, 1966, 1.
212. "I'm here because I was invited": Ibid.
212. "That which unites us": Dan Williamson, "RFK Makes Appeal for Unity," *Crimson White,* March 22, 1966, 1, 5.
212. "I was wondering why they sneaked me": Dan Williamson, "That Kennedy Knack Wows Screaming, Scrambling Fans," *Crimson White,* March 24, 1966, 1.
212. "wit and charm won the audience": Williamson, "RFK Makes Appeal for Unity," 1, 5.
213. "that Negroes must be as free": Ibid.
213. "And it is far easier to accept": Ibid.
213. A rain delay had stranded: Eason Dobbs, "RFK Draws 10,000." *Crimson White,* March 25, 1968, 1.
213. "I received some bad news": "Emphasis (1968: The University of Alabama), Robert F. Kennedy Who Discusses America at the Crossroads." March 22, 1968. The W. S. Hoole Special Collections Library, The University of Alabama.
213. Years prior, Kennedy had urged Bryant: McWhorter, *Carry Me Home,* 460.
214. "prepared to shock people in Alabama": Barra, *Last Coach,* 282.
214. "pleased to have a chance to meet Frank Rose again": "Emphasis (1968: The

University of Alabama), Robert F. Kennedy Who Discusses America at the Cross-roads."

214. "For when a Negro leaves his home": Ibid.

214. "The enthusiasm for Bobby Kennedy": Howell Raines, "So Small, So Vulnerable—But So Full of Life," *Tuscaloosa News,* June 6, 1968, 1, 2.

215. "hordes of handshakers": Ibid.

215. "there was that haunting awareness": Ibid.

215. "Do they know about Martin Luther King?": "Robert F. Kennedy's Statement on Dr. King's Death—Montage," YouTube.com, November 20, 2006, http://www .youtube.com/watch?v=gigsZH5HlJA.

215. "I have some very sad news for all of you": Ibid.

215. "expressed regret over King's death": "Death Triggers Strife, Marches," *Tuscaloosa News,* April 5, 1968, 1, 2.

215. "This points up vividly": Ibid.

216. "barring nonstudents": Ibid.

216. "all citizens who believe in brotherhood": "March Planned in City Today," *Tuscaloosa News,* April 7, 1968, 1.

216. "Speak now, you don't have much time": Dick Looser, "2000 March Quietly Here," *Tuscaloosa News,* April 8, 1968, 1, 3.

216. "If Dixie had a heart": Ibid.

217. "We have the power to put a man on the moon": Mary Crowe, "T. Y. Tells about His 'Black Power,'" *Crimson White,* April 25, 1968, 1, 2.

217. "really aren't treated as human beings": Ibid.

217. "I wouldn't necessarily say": Interview with William Marable II conducted February 23, 2011.

217. "And his political views": Ibid.

218. "re-emphasize service": Ann Nelson, "Police Chief Will Retire on April 30," *Tuscaloosa News,* April 5, 1976, 1.

218. "The stress he went through": Interview with William Marable II conducted February 23, 2011.

218. "truly an evil man": "Robert Shelton, 73, Leader of Big Klan Faction," *New York Times,* March 20, 2003.

218. "ashamed of his role in violence": Ibid.

218. "To me, he was always": Ibid.

218. As time pressed on, the University of Alabama's: Joe Holley, "Vivian Malone Jones Dies; Integrated U-Ala," *Washington Post,* October 14, 2005.

218. "She had very strong beliefs": Ibid.

219. After graduating from Wayne State University: Stephan Lesher, *George Wallace: American Populist* (Reading, MA: Addison-Wesley, 1994), 233.

219. "where the need is": "A New Beginning: A Tribute to Courage and Progress," http://malonehoodplaza.ua.edu/players/james-hood-2/.

219. Upon her 1956 expulsion from the University of Alabama: "Autherine Lucy," *Encyclopedia of Alabama,* http://www.encyclopediaofalabama.org/face/Article .jsp?id=h-2489.

219. "If the Negro doesn't have the right to vote in Alabama": Tuscaloosa Sheriff's Department Historical Records.

220. "In a regular war people leave home": Ibid.

220. "So this spring": Ibid.

220. "massive assault upon the laws": Ibid.

220. "Rogers asked the crowd": Ibid.

Bibliography

Books

Barra, Allen. *The Last Coach: A Life of Paul "Bear" Bryant.* New York: W. W. Norton, 2005.

Boomerhower, Ray E. *Robert F. Kennedy and the 1968 Indiana Primary.* Bloomington: Indiana University Press, 2008.

Borstelmann, Thomas. *The Cold War and the Color Line: American Race Relations in the Global Arena.* Cambridge, MA: Harvard University Press, 2001.

Branch, Taylor. *At Canaan's Edge: America in the King Years, 1965–68.* New York: Simon and Schuster Paperbacks, 2006.

———. *Pillar of Fire: America in the King Years, 1963–65.* New York: Simon and Schuster Paperbacks, 1998.

Carmer, Carl. *Stars Fell on Alabama.* Tuscaloosa: The University of Alabama Press, 1990.

Carson, Clayborne. *The Papers of Martin Luther King Jr.: Symbol of the Movement: January 1957–December 1958.* Berkeley: University of California Press, 2005.

———. *The Papers of Martin Luther King Jr.: Threshold of a New Decade: January 1959–December 1960.* Berkeley: University of California Press, 1992.

Carter, Dan T. *The Politics of Rage: George Wallace, the Origins of the New Conservatism, and the Transformation of American Politics.* New York: Simon and Schuster, 1995.

Clark, E. Culpepper. *The Schoolhouse Door: Segregation's Last Stand at The University of Alabama.* Tuscaloosa: The University of Alabama Press, 1995.

Dahmer, Claude L., Jr. "An Analysis of Student Opinion at The University of Alabama toward Current Racial Issues." Thesis, The University of Alabama, Tuscaloosa, 1949.

Dallek, Robert. *John F. Kennedy.* Oxford: Oxford University Press, 2003.

Glynn, Robert L. *How Firm a Foundation.* Friends of the Hunter's Chapel African Methodist Episcopal Zion Church and the City of Tuscaloosa, Alabama Bicentennial Committee. Tuscaloosa: 1976.

Gould, Lewis. *The Documentary History of the John F. Kennedy Presidency.* Vol. 7: *JFK and the Cuban Missile Crisis: Showdown, September–November 1962.* Lex-isNexis, 2007.

———. *The Documentary History of the John F. Kennedy Presidency.* Vol. 9: *JFK, George Wallace, and the Desegregation of the University of Alabama, 1963.* LexisNexis, 2007.

———. *The Documentary History of the John F. Kennedy Presidency.* Vol. 14: *John F. Kennedy, Martin Luther King Jr., and the Struggle for Civil Rights.* LexisNexis, 2007.

Greenhaw, Wayne. *Fighting the Devil in Dixie: How Civil Rights Activists Took On the Ku Klux Klan in Alabama.* Chicago: Lawrence Hill Books, 2011.

Halberstam, David. *The Unfinished Odyssey of Robert Kennedy.* New York: Random House, 1968.

Heymann, C. David. *RFK: A Candid Biography of Robert F. Kennedy.* New York: Dutton, 1998.

Hodges, Luther H., and Richard M. Scammon. *County and City Data Book, 1962.* Bureau of Census, Department of Commerce, 1962.

Jacobs, Seth. *Cold War Mandarin: Ngo Dinh Diem and the Origins of America's War in Vietnam, 1950–1963.* Lanham, MD: Rowman and Littlefield, 2006.

Kempton, Murray. "When the Riots Came." In *Reporting Civil Rights: Part One, American Journalism, 1941–1963,* edited by Library of America, 241–48. New York: Library of America, 2003.

Kriegel, Mark. *Namath: A Biography.* New York: Viking, 2004.

Kryn, Randy. "Movement Revision Research Summary Regarding James Bevel." In *We Shall Overcome Volume II,* edited by David Garrow. New York: Carlson Publishing, 1989.

Lesher, Stephan. *George Wallace: American Populist.* Reading, MA: Addison-Wesley, 1994.

Lord, Walter. *The Past That Would Not Die.* New York: Harper and Row, 1965.

May, Gary. *The Informant: The FBI, the Ku Klux Klan, and the Murder of Viola Liuzzo.* New Haven, CT: Yale University Press, 2005.

McWhorter, Diane. *Carry Me Home: The Climactic Battle of the Civil Rights Revolution.* New York: Touchstone, 2001.

Mitchell, Ann. "Keep 'Bama White." Thesis, Georgia Southern College, Statesboro, 1971.

Pruitt, Samory. "A Reflection of Student Desegregation at The University of Alabama as Seen through the Eyes of Some Pioneering African American Students: 1956–1976." Diss., The University of Alabama, 2003.

Raines, Howell. *My Soul Is Rested: Movement Days in the Deep South.* New York: Penguin, 1983.

Record, Wilson. *The Negro and the Communist Party.* Chapel Hill: University of North Carolina Press, 1951.

Remnick, David. *The Bridge: The Life and Rise of Barack Obama.* New York: Alfred A. Knopf, 2010.

Roberts, Gene, and Hank Klibanoff. *The Race Beat: The Press, the Civil Rights Struggle, and the Awakening of a Nation.* New York: Vintage Books, 2006.

Shattuck, Gardiner H., Jr. *Episcopalians and Race: Civil War to Civil Rights.* Lexington: University Press of Kentucky, 2000.

Sides, Hampton. *Hellhound on His Trail: The Stalking of Martin Luther King Jr. and the International Hunt for His Assassin.* New York: Doubleday, 2010.

Silver, James W. *Mississippi: The Closed Society.* New York: Harcourt, Brace and World, 1963.

Sims, Patsy. *The Klan.* Lexington: University Press of Kentucky, 1996.

Sitton, Claude. "Alabama Admits Negro Students; Wallace Bows to Federal Force." In *Reporting Civil Rights: Part One, American Journalism, 1941–1963,* edited by Library of America, 824–30. New York: Library of America, 2003.

Sorensen, Ted. *Counselor: A Life at the Edge of History.* New York: Harper Perennial, 2008.

Talbot, David. *Brothers: The Hidden History of the Kennedy Years.* New York: Free Press, 2007.

The University of Alabama Fact Book, 1986. Tuscaloosa: The Office of Institutional Research, 1986.

Ward, Gladys. "Life of Ryland Randolph." Thesis, The University of Alabama, Tuscaloosa, 1932.

Washington, Booker T. "The Atlanta Exposition Address." In *The Norton Anthology of African American Literature,* edited by Henry Louis Gates Jr. and Nellie Y. McKay. New York: W. W. Norton, 2004.

Wendt, Simon. "The Roots of Black Power? Armed Resistance and the Radicalization of the Civil Rights Movement." In *The Black Power Movement: Rethinking the Civil Rights Black Power Era,* edited by Peniel E. Joseph, 145–66. New York: Routledge, 2006.

———. *The Spirit and the Shotgun: Armed Resistance and the Struggle for Civil Rights.* Gainesville: University Press of Florida, 2007.

White, Theodore. *The Making of the President: 1960.* New York: Harper Perennial, 2009.

———. *The Making of the President: 1964.* New York: Harper Perennial, 2010.

Articles

"2 Crosses Burn at Same Time." *The Tuscaloosa News,* January 29, 1956.

"2 More Negroes Enroll in UA Summer School." *The Tuscaloosa News,* June 9, 1964, 1.

"2 Negroes Arrested Here after Student Is Beaten." *The Tuscaloosa News,* February 15, 1956, 1.

"3 Crosses Burned; Two Men Nabbed at University." *The Tuscaloosa News,* February 2, 1956, 1.

"3 Men Fined, Appeal Cases in Riot Here." *The Tuscaloosa News,* July 21, 1964, 1.

"4 Eating Places Integrated Here." *The Tuscaloosa News,* July 7, 1964, 1.

"5 Negroes Plan UA Mixing Effort: No Forms Filed Yet, Says UA." *The Tuscaloosa News,* October 20, 1962, 1.

"6 Men Arrested with Weapons." *The Tuscaloosa News,* June 9, 1963, 1.

"6 Men Seized with Weapons Free on Bond." *The Tuscaloosa News,* June 10, 1963, 1.

"6 Spots Turn Mixers Away." *The Tuscaloosa News,* July 10, 1964, 1.

"10 Spots Here Refuse Service to Negroes." *The Tuscaloosa News,* July 8, 1964, 1–2.

"15 Eating Places Here Face Civil Rights Suit." *The Tuscaloosa News,* July 30, 1964, 1, 2.

"15 Will Attend Freedom Forum." *The Tuscaloosa News,* June 9, 1963, 3.

"66 Arrested for Violating Curfew." *The Tuscaloosa News,* July 14, 1964, 1.

"100 State Troopers Remain In Tuscaloosa." *The Tuscaloosa News,* June 17, 1963, 1.

"293 to Receive Degrees at University Tomorrow." *The Tuscaloosa News,* January 27, 1956, 1, 2.

"Abernathy Urges Others to Carry On for Rogers." *The Tuscaloosa News,* March 30, 1971.

"Air of Calmness Covers Campus." *The Tuscaloosa News,* June 10, 1963, 1.

"All in One Trap—Together." *The Tuscaloosa News,* June 10, 1964, 1.

"All Is Quiet on Racial Scene Here." *The Tuscaloosa News,* July 13, 1964, 2.

"All of Us Must Listen." *The Tuscaloosa News,* June 7, 1963, 4.

"Apathy Biggest Foe, Chief Marable Says." *The Tuscaloosa News,* August 12, 1964, 1.

Armstrong, Dr. Robert G. "Letter to the Editor: Students Blind?" *The Crimson White,* February 14, 1956, 5.

"Arrest of Leaders Foils March Here." *The Tuscaloosa News,* June 11, 1964, 1.

Associated Press. "Appalled by Slaying, Says JFK." *The Tuscaloosa News,* June 12, 1963, 14.

———. "Bama Segregation Case Appealed to High Court: Folsom Said NAACP Hurt Peace Efforts." *The Tuscaloosa News,* February 14, 1956, 1.

———. "Cabinet Members Hand Wallace Confidence Vote." *The Tuscaloosa News,* June 8, 1963, 1.

———. "Citizen Army Vanishes in 'Truce' at Ole Miss." *The Tuscaloosa News,* September 28, 1962, 1.

———. "Citizens Councils Begin Organizing." *The Tuscaloosa News,* February 18, 1956, 1.

———. "Civil Rights Legislation in for Battle." *The Tuscaloosa News,* June 12, 1963, 2.

———. "Connor Meets with Wallace." *The Tuscaloosa News,* June 7, 1963, 2.

———. "Dean Says Autherine Lucy Not Looking for Education." *The Tuscaloosa News,* February 23, 1956, 1.

———. "Decision on Guard JFK's, Says Wallace." *The Tuscaloosa News,* June 18, 1963, 2.

———. "Different Wallace Stood in UA Doorway, Says Allen." *The Tuscaloosa News,* June 18, 1963, 1.

———. "Dixie Rally Charts JFK Defeat In '64." *The Tuscaloosa News,* June 18, 1963, 1, 2.

———. "Don't Block Negro, Barnett Is Ordered." *The Tuscaloosa News,* September 25, 1962, 1.

———. "Editors Differ on Question of South Ending Segregation." *The Tuscaloosa News,* February 21, 1956, 2.

———. "Feared for Life, Palance Says on New York Arrival." *The Tuscaloosa News,* July 11, 1964, 1, 3.

———. "Few Incidents Mar Mixing Tests: Most Accepting Change Quietly." *The Tuscaloosa News,* July 4, 1964, 1.

———. "Follow Order, Lawyers Ask Gov. Wallace." *The Tuscaloosa News,* June 10, 1963.

———. "Folsom Says U-A Trouble 'Overplayed.'" *The Tuscaloosa News,* February 22, 1956, 1.

———. "Folsom Takes Stand against 'Mob Rule.'" *The Tuscaloosa News,* February 11, 1956, 1.

———. "Governor Says He's Not Upset over University." *The Tuscaloosa News,* February 7, 1956, 2.

———. "Governor's Stand at UA Labeled a Political Blunder." *The Tuscaloosa News,* June 12, 1963, 3.

———. "Group Here Urges Racial Reasoning." *The Tuscaloosa News,* October 23, 1962, 1.

———. "Integration of UA Eyed." *The Tuscaloosa News,* September 26, 1962, 1.

———. "Jackson on 'Powderkeg.'" *The Tuscaloosa News,* June 13, 1963, 1, 2.

———. "King Joins Gadsden Drive." *The Tuscaloosa News,* June 17, 1963, 1.

———. "King Planning 'Army' to Push Mixing in State." *The Tuscaloosa News,* October 21, 1962, 1.

———. "King Reports Attempt Due in Few Days." *The Tuscaloosa News,* October 20, 1962, 1.

———. "King Workers Plan Tests Here, Selma." *The Tuscaloosa News,* July 7, 1964, 1.

———. "Legislature Offers Prayer for Wallace." *The Tuscaloosa News,* June 7, 1963, 1.

———. "Louisiana, Alabama Centers of Race Tension in South." *The Tuscaloosa News,* February 16, 1956, 25.

———. "Mail Pouring In to Gov. Wallace." *The Tuscaloosa News,* June 10, 1963, 9.

———. "Mayors Urged to Help Erase Racial Tension." *The Tuscaloosa News,* June 10, 1963, 1.

———. "Mississippi Chief of NAACP Killed." *The Tuscaloosa News,* June 6, 1963, 1.

———. "Mississippi Guard Placed under U.S." *The Tuscaloosa News,* September 30, 1962, 1.

———. "Negro Comedian Released on Bond after Conviction." *The Tuscaloosa News,* June 18, 1963, 2.

———. "Negro Foiled Again at Ole Miss: Federal Troops May Receive Call." *The Tuscaloosa News,* September 26, 1962, 1.

———. "Negro School Is Integrated." *The Tuscaloosa News,* June 12, 1963, 1.

———. "Negroes Here Lose Appeal." *The Tuscaloosa News,* July 21, 1964, 2.

———. "No Ill Feeling toward Negro, Says Wallace." *The Tuscaloosa News,* June 7, 1963, 2.

———. "Ole Miss Guard Bolstered: Sheriffs, Police Move on Oxford." *The Tuscaloosa News,* September 27, 1962, 1.

———. "Ole Miss Ordered to Admit Negro." *The Tuscaloosa News,* June 10, 1964, 1.

———. "People's Power Taken by Court, Wallace Says." *The Tuscaloosa News,* June 4, 1964, 2.

———. "Praise, Criticism Sound for JFK." *The Tuscaloosa News,* June 12, 1963, 2.

———. "President Outlines Rights Proposals." *The Tuscaloosa News,* June 12, 1963, 1.

———. "Racial Cases Sent Back to City Court." *The Tuscaloosa News,* June 25, 1964, 1.

———. "Racial Round-Up across the Nation." *The Tuscaloosa News,* June 15, 1963, 8.

———. "Release of Guard up to Wallace, Kennedy." *The Tuscaloosa News,* June 16, 1963, 1.

———. "Remove Signs, County Ordered." *The Tuscaloosa News,* June 26, 1964, 1.

———. "Rights Bill Goes to President: Signing Slated Tonight." *The Tuscaloosa News,* July 2, 1964, 1.

———. "Rights Law Tested." *The Tuscaloosa News,* July 3, 1964, 1–2.

———. "Rights Program Sent Congress." *The Tuscaloosa News,* June 19, 1963, 1, 2.

———. "Some Progress Reported in Erasing Racial Barriers." *The Tuscaloosa News,* June 16, 1963, 5.

———. "South's Race Cauldron Boils, Stirred by Alabama Bomb Blast." *The Tuscaloosa News,* February 2, 1956, 13.

———. "South's Racial Trouble Own Fault, Says McGill." *The Tuscaloosa News,* June 10, 1963, 10.

———. "State Solons Keeping Track of UA Crisis." *The Tuscaloosa News,* June 11, 1963, 1.

———. "Suicidal Monk's Death Mourned." *The Tuscaloosa News,* June 12, 1963, 7.

———. "To Risk Arrest, He Says." *The Tuscaloosa News,* June 6, 1963, 1, 2.

———. "Troops Alerted in Ole Miss Crisis; Kennedy Schedules Radio-TV Talk." *The Tuscaloosa News,* September 30, 1962, 1.

———. "Troops Near If JFK Calls." *The Tuscaloosa News,* June 7, 1963, 1, 2.

———. "UA, Huntsville Peaceful; Army Freeing Guard." *The Tuscaloosa News,* June 14, 1963, 1, 2.

———. "U-A Officials, Autherine Lucy Needn't Talk." *The Tuscaloosa News,* February 20, 1956, 1.

———. "U-A Officials Seek Separate Court Hearings." *The Tuscaloosa News,* February 28, 1956, 1.

———. "U-Miss Mixing Is Quiet." *The Tuscaloosa News,* June 6, 1963, 1.

———. "Wallace Renews 'Stay Away' Plea." *The Tuscaloosa News,* June 10, 1963, 1.

———. "Won't Enforce Law, Will Fight It, Wallace Says." *The Tuscaloosa News,* July 3, 1964, 1.

"Ban Defied, Marching Negroes, Police Clash." *The Tuscaloosa News,* June 9, 1964, 1.

Bassett, Norman. "Tide Roars over Ga. Tech, 96–60: Bama Effort Tops, Dee Says; Harper Leads Score with 23." *The Tuscaloosa News,* February 5, 1956, 8.

"'Bias' Is Charged at New Courthouse." *The Tuscaloosa News,* April 16, 1964, 1, 2.

"Bid to Admit Second: Carmichael Expects Negro to Return to UA Campus." *The Tuscaloosa News,* February 9, 1956, 1.

"Bi-Racial Council Urges Calmness, Courtesy Here." *The Tuscaloosa News,* February 17, 1956, 1.

Blair, Billie. "On The Whole It's Been Quite a Happy Year for Me." *The Crimson White,* June 17, 1965, 1.

Black, Hank. "Riot Rumors Cause Needless Alarm at Foster Pep Rally Last Night." *The Crimson White,* October 11, 1962, 1.

"Blackburn Discusses Oxford, Evaluation, at Palmer Meet." *The Crimson White,* November 1, 1962.

"Board Cites Police Rights to Bar Negro." *The Tuscaloosa News,* February 7, 1956, 1.

Boone, Buford. "A Message from the South." *The Tuscaloosa News,* February 12, 1956, 4.

———. "Request for Guard Aid in Monday Mob Action Made from Carmichael's Office." *The Tuscaloosa News,* February 9, 1956, 1.

"Boycott Causes Cut in City Bus Service." *The Tuscaloosa News,* August 11, 1964, 1.

"'Burning Cross' Brings Firemen out to Broom." *The Tuscaloosa News,* February 20, 1956.

"Bus Line Halting All Service Here." *The Tuscaloosa News,* August 13, 1964, 1.

"Bus Owner Eyes Complete Pullout." *The Tuscaloosa News,* August 24, 1964, 1.

"Buses Sit Idle at Garage." *The Tuscaloosa News,* August 14, 1964, 1.

"Calmness Measures Intelligence." *The Tuscaloosa News,* February 15, 1956, 1.

Capell, Arthur. "Lucy's Parents Says She Breaks Rearing." *The Tuscaloosa News,* February 26, 1956, 1, 2.

"Capstone Officials Silent on Reported Board Talks." *The Tuscaloosa News,* January 30, 1956, 1.

"Capstone's Legal Battles Center on Lucy Petitions: Officials Get Breathing Spell until Feb 29." *The Tuscaloosa News,* February 10, 1956, 1.

"Carmichael Blames 'Outside' Elements in UA Demonstrations." *The Tuscaloosa News,* February 3, 1956, 1.

"Carmichael Denies Board Succumbed to Mob Rule: President Tells Students Law, Order Must Prevail." *The Tuscaloosa News,* February 16, 1956, 1.

"Carmichael's Masterful Job." *The Tuscaloosa News,* February 16, 1956, 1.

Carter, Hodding. "Racial Crisis in the Deep South." *Saturday Evening Post,* December 17, 1955.

Case, C. Duke. "Letter to the Editor: Support Stands." *The Tuscaloosa News,* July 12, 1964, 4.

"Changing Attitudes in the White South." *Newsweek,* June 17, 1963, 23–25.

Chapin, Don. "Group to Examine, Evaluate the Lone Negro Application." *The Crimson White,* October 25, 1962, 1.

Christenson, Walter J. "Letter to the Editor: Nauseous State." *The Tuscaloosa News,* February 15, 1956, 4.

"Citizens Council Is Started Here." *The Tuscaloosa News,* February 16, 1956, 1.

"Citizens Council Meeting Is Tonight." *The Tuscaloosa News,* February 17, 1956, 1.

"The Citizens Council Starts Here." *The Tuscaloosa News,* February 22, 1956, 4.

"City Board Gets Back to Matters of Progress." *The Tuscaloosa News,* July 28, 1964, 1.

"City Police Take Arrests in Stride." *The Tuscaloosa News,* June 9, 1964, 1.

"City Quiet, Police Get Breathing Spell." *The Tuscaloosa News,* July 11, 1964, 1.

"City Streets Quiet with Curfew On." *The Tuscaloosa News,* July 12, 1964, 1.

"Civil Rights: With George and Sam on Capitol Hill." *Time Magazine,* July 26, 1963.

"Classes Started, UA Quiet." *The Tuscaloosa News,* June 12, 1963, 1.

"Coed Faints, Hood's First Class Short." *The Tuscaloosa News,* June 12, 1963, 14.

"The Congress: The Fateful Vote to Impeach." *Time Magazine,* August 5, 1974.

Conley, John. "Letter to the Editor: World Watching." *The Crimson White,* February 14, 1956, 5.

Cornett, Buddy. "Kennedy Last One to Want Another Oxford—Says Wallace." *The Crimson White,* November 15, 1963, 1.

"Council's Intent, Spirit Discussed." *The Tuscaloosa News,* February 27, 1956, 4.

"County Courthouse Box Filled Up and Sealed." *The Tuscaloosa News,* June 6, 1963, 1, 2.

"County's Officers Praised." *The Tuscaloosa News,* August 12, 1964, 1.

"Court Refuses UA Rehearing; Adams Called." *The Tuscaloosa News,* February 3, 1956, 1.

"A Crisis Passes Peacefully." *The Tuscaloosa News,* June 12, 1963, 4.

"Cross Burns at Home of Dean Adams." *The Tuscaloosa News,* February 3, 1956, 1.

Crowe, Mary. "T. Y. Tells about His 'Black Power.'" *The Crimson White,* April 25, 1968, 1, 2.

"Curfew Lifted Except Downtown: City Board Warns Move Conditional." *The Tuscaloosa News,* July 16, 1964, 1.

"Curious Asked to Keep Away." *The Tuscaloosa News,* April 23, 1964, 1.

Davis, Madison. "First Negro's Entrance Sets Off Chain Reaction; Adams Called into Court." *The Crimson White,* February 7, 1956, 1.

———. "Negro Coed's Return to Campus Said to Hinge on Court Decision." *The Crimson White,* February 14, 1956, 3.

Davis, Paul. "2 Negroes Begin Capstone Classes." *The Tuscaloosa News,* June 12, 1963, 1.

———. "Boycott Leaders Given Hard Facts by Bus Officials." *The Tuscaloosa News,* August 16, 1964, 1.

———. "City Returns to 'Normal' after Mixing." *The Tuscaloosa News,* June 12, 1963, 2.

———. "Klansmen Meet Here for Rights." *The Tuscaloosa News,* September 30, 1962, 1.

"The Day Started Quietly and Then Came 'Explosion.'" *The Tuscaloosa News,* June 9, 1964, 1.

"Day Started Quietly and Then 'Explosion.'" *The Tuscaloosa News,* June 10, 1964, 3.

"Dean's Car Hauled Lucy to Graves; Bennett Was Driver." *The Tuscaloosa News,* February 6, 1956, 1.

"Death Triggers Strife, Marches." *The Tuscaloosa News,* April 5, 1968, 1, 2.

"Demonstrators Hit with Mustard Oil." *The Tuscaloosa News,* June 5, 1964, 1.

"Demonstrators March in Downtown Section." *The Tuscaloosa News,* June 6, 1964, 1–2.

DePree, D. "Letter to the Editor: Blame the Party." *The Tuscaloosa News,* February 14, 1956, 4.

Dobbs, Eason. "RFK Draws 10,000." *The Crimson White,* March 25, 1968, 1.

"Downtown Curfew Lifted." *The Tuscaloosa News,* July 23, 1964, 1.

"Drop Rights Suit, 15 Here Ask Court." *The Tuscaloosa News,* August 18, 1964, 1.

"Druid Transit School Bus Service Halted—Too Costly." *The Tuscaloosa News,* September 12, 1964, 1.

"Education: Goodbye to 'Bama." *Time Magazine,* November 19, 1956.

"Eggs Splatter UA Minister; 3 Men Arrested." *The Tuscaloosa News,* February 7, 1956, 1.

"Entire City Bus Service in Doubt: Outlook Termed Gloomy." *The Tuscaloosa News,* August 12, 1964, 1.

"Ex-Alumni Head Asks Move to 'Keep UA White.'" *The Tuscaloosa News,* February 21, 1956, 1.

"Exercise in Responsibility." *The Tuscaloosa News,* June 10, 1963, 4.

"Faculty Group Calls Students for Questioning." *The Tuscaloosa News,* February 23, 1956, 1.

"Faculty Probe of Mob Violence Continues Today." *The Tuscaloosa News,* February 25, 1956, 1.

"Faculty Probe of UA Riots Nearing End: Return-Lucy Petitions Turned In." *The Tuscaloosa News,* February 24, 1956, 1.

Falk, Lonnie. "All-Out Peace Effort Sees Campus Guarded." *The Crimson White,* June 9, 1963, 1.

Faulkner, William. "A Faulkner Letter." *The Crimson White,* June 9, 1963, 1–3.

"Few Clashes Occur Here." *The Tuscaloosa News,* July 6, 1964, 1.

"Fight Lawless Elements, Merchants Challenge." *The Tuscaloosa News,* July 25, 1964, 1.

"Five UA Officials Subpoenaed for Statements in Lucy Case." *The Tuscaloosa News,* February 17, 1956, 1.

Flowers, Walter. "Letter to the Student Body." *The Crimson White,* February 7, 1956, 1.

"Folsom Calls Editors to Capital Meeting." *The Tuscaloosa News,* February 22, 1956, 1.

"Folsom Likes Way Things Ended at UA." *The Tuscaloosa News,* June 12, 1963, 15.

"Folsom Pledges Order to Be Kept at UA: Governor Flies Here, Talks with Carmichael." *The Tuscaloosa News,* February 27, 1956, 1.

"Foster Auditorium Looks Like Stadium after Game." *The Tuscaloosa News,* June 12, 1963, 2.

"Four Crosses Are Burned on UA Campus." *The Tuscaloosa News,* February 1, 1956, 1.

"Full Text Is Given on Carmichael Talk." *The Tuscaloosa News,* February 16, 1956, 13.

"Further Tests of Rights Act Planned Here." *The Tuscaloosa News,* July 8, 1964, 1.

"Gas Used on Mob; City Orders Curfew." *The Tuscaloosa News,* July 10, 1964, 1–2.

Gibb, Bill. "Cross Burns, UA Students Shout, Then Go Home: 'Rally' Ends Quietly." *The Tuscaloosa News,* February 5, 1956, 1.

———. "Legal Fight Is Urged to Save Segregation: Dallas Senator Sparks Council Formation Here." *The Tuscaloosa News,* February 18, 1956, 1, 3.

———. "Lucy Parries Answers with Capstone Lawyer: Lawyer Says NAACP Pays Her Money." *The Tuscaloosa News,* February 29, 1956, 1.

———. "Negro Vows Court Fight to Get Dormitory Room: Trustees Order No-Room Action." *The Tuscaloosa News,* February 1, 1956, 1.

———. "Proposed Citizens Group Constitution Vows Maintenance of Segregation." *The Tuscaloosa News,* February 26, 1956, 1.

———. "UA's Future up to Court Carmichael Tells Newsmen." *The Tuscaloosa News,* February 11, 1956, 1.

———. "Walking Steps to History." *The Tuscaloosa News,* February 5, 1956, 4.

Gibb, Bill, and Stroube Smith. "Patrol Slips Lucy away from Mob: Apparent Ruse Thwarts Crowd." *The Tuscaloosa News,* February 6, 1956, 1.

"Girl 'Quiet'; Boy 'Congenial' Students Say of Negroes." *The Crimson White,* June 9, 1963, 2.

Gould, Geoffrey. "Hate Mail Still Flows." *The Tuscaloosa News,* June 13, 1963, 39.

"Graham 'Hopes' Troops to Leave UA by June 23." *The Tuscaloosa News,* June 15, 1963, 1.

Grayson, Wayne. "State SCLC Rally Recalls 'Bloody Tuesday.'" *The Tuscaloosa News,* February 27, 2010.

"Greene County White Council Is Organized." *The Tuscaloosa News,* February 28, 1956, 2.

"Gunplay Here Leaves Three with Wounds." *The Tuscaloosa News,* July 10, 1964, 1.

"Halt Called on Marchers." *The Tuscaloosa News,* June 12, 1964, 1.

Hamner, John. "Faculty Revolters Plan No New Action." *The Tuscaloosa News,* February 8, 1956, 1.

———. "President May Move to Take Stronger Role in UA Action." *The Tuscaloosa News,* February 10, 1956, 1.

Hoffman, Fred S. "'War Room' Tuned In on Alabama." *The Tuscaloosa News,* June 12, 1963, 3.

Holley, Joe. "Vivian Malone Jones Dies; Integrated U-Ala." *Washington Post,* October 14, 2005.

Hood, James. "Needed: More Students, Less Pickets." *The Crimson White,* June 27, 1963, 4.

"Hope Lies with Students." *The Tuscaloosa News,* February 8, 1956, 1.

"Hoping, Praying, Thinking." *The Tuscaloosa News,* June 9, 1963, 4.

Huttlinger, Frank D. "Letter to the Editor: Fears Unfounded." *The Tuscaloosa News,* August 21, 1964, 4.

"In Human Probability." *The Crimson White,* June 13, 1963, 4.

"In Our Interest." *The Crimson White,* June 9, 1963, 3.

"International Press Corps on Duty at Capstone." *The Tuscaloosa News,* February 8, 1956, 9.

"The Irresponsible 'Leaders.'" *The Crimson White,* February 7, 1956, 4.

"It Was Quiet Trip into Tuscaloosa." *The Tuscaloosa News,* June 11, 1963, 2.

"JFK Federalizes State Guard after Governor Blocks: Will Be Enrolled Says U.S. Officials." *The Tuscaloosa News,* June 11, 1963, 1.

"JFK Guard Action Called 'Bitter Pill.'" *The Tuscaloosa News,* June 11, 1963, 1, 2.

"JFK Watchful . . . Bobby, Too." *New York Journal-American,* June 11, 1963.

Johnson, Kathryn. "UA Atmosphere Friendlier, Report 2 Negro Students." *The Tuscaloosa News,* June 13, 1963, 9.

"Judge Holds Off on March Ruling." *The Tuscaloosa News,* July 7, 1964, 1.

"Judge Puts Off March Ruling Affecting City." *The Tuscaloosa News,* July 7, 1964, 1.

"Keep on Marching, Negro Comedian Urges Group Here." *The Tuscaloosa News,* June 2, 1964, 2.

"King Talks Here, Calls for End of Segregation." *The Tuscaloosa News,* March 9, 1964, 2.

"Klan Chief Says Racial Appeals to Bring Strife." *The Tuscaloosa News,* November 2, 1962, 7.

"Klan Growing, Its Leaders Claim." *The Tuscaloosa News,* July 17, 1964, 3.

"Klansman Says Crosses Were Burned Here by KKK." *The Tuscaloosa News,* January 30, 1956, 1.

Kyle, Bob. "1,200 Students Stage Midnight Demonstration." *The Tuscaloosa News,* February 4, 1956, 1.

———. "City Promises UA 'All Possible' Aid in Riots: Tompkins Vows Full Effort in UA Crisis." *The Tuscaloosa News,* February 8, 1956, 1.

———. "Cross Burns in Center of University Ave." *The Tuscaloosa News,* February 4, 1956, 1.

———. "No Guns Fired, No Rocks Thrown, But Old Flavor to Federal Victory at UA." *The Tuscaloosa News,* June 12, 1963, 2.

———. "Rain Christens Courthouse for Throng at Dedication." *The Tuscaloosa News,* April 13, 1964, 1, 2.

Lanier, Al. "NAACP Leader's Home Hit by Bomb, Second in Days: Official's Home Blasted in Montgomery Dispute." *The Tuscaloosa News,* February 2, 1956, 1.

Laxson, Jim. "Violence, Judge's Threat Mark Race Tension Rise." *The Tuscaloosa News,* February 12, 1956, 1.

"Let City Police Handle Situation, Board Urges." *The Tuscaloosa News,* July 7, 1964, 1.

Linton, Thomas. "'Bloody Tuesday' a Public Crime Unacknowledged." *The Tuscaloosa News,* March 1, 2009.

Lippman, Walter. "The Point of No Return." *The Tuscaloosa News,* June 13, 1963, 4.

———. "Setback to Law and Good Sense." *The Tuscaloosa News,* February 12, 1956, 4.

———. "Stop, Think on Integration Is Plea." *The Tuscaloosa News,* February 16, 1956, 4.

Looser, Dick, "2000 March Quietly Here." *The Tuscaloosa News,* April 8, 1968, 1, 3.

———. "Hearing Recessed on Marches Here." *The Tuscaloosa News,* June 23, 1964, 1.

———. "Letter to the Editor: Civil Rights March Misinformation Abounds." *The Tuscaloosa News,* May 1, 2011.

———. "No Troop Control At UA—Guthman." *The Tuscaloosa News,* June 12, 1963, 1.

———. "Tightly Sealed UA Awaiting Governor." *The Tuscaloosa News,* June 10, 1963, 1.

———. "University Showdown at Hand: Wallace Prepares to Stand in Door." *The Tuscaloosa News,* June 11, 1963, 1, 2.

———. "Wallace Flies Here for Capstone Stand." *The Tuscaloosa News,* June 10, 1963, 1.

"A Lot of Loose Ends Tied by UA in Year." *The Crimson White,* June 9, 1963, 3.

"Lullaby and Goodnight." *The Tuscaloosa News,* July 8, 1964, 1.

"Man Arrested during March Freed on Bonds of $4,000." *The Tuscaloosa News,* April 24, 1964, 1, 2.

"March, Boycott, Planned in City." *The Tuscaloosa News,* April 22, 1964, 1, 2.

"March in Protest to Negro Girl's Admission: Photographer Catches Scenes of Bama's 'Involved' Week." *The Crimson White,* February 7, 1956, 3.

"Marchers Turned Back Here." *The Tuscaloosa News,* June 8, 1964, 2.

"A Mature Movement." *The Crimson White,* November 15, 1963.

"May We Pray—And Listen." *The Tuscaloosa News,* July 12, 1964, 1.

"McCall to Testify Negro's Return to Result in Violence." *The Tuscaloosa News,* February 28, 1956, 1.

McCusker, Ed. "Patrol Is Waiting." *The Tuscaloosa News,* June 19, 1964, 1–2.

McEachern, Bill. "Campus Curious, Calm as Negro Starts Class." *The Tuscaloosa News,* February 3, 1956, 3.

———. "City's Church Leaders Take Stand for Law and Order Here." *The Tuscaloosa News,* February 13, 1956, 1.

———. "Integration in Other Colleges Less Violent Than UA." *The Tuscaloosa News,* February 12, 1956, 1.

———. "Student Response to Negro Seems Mostly Resignation." *The Tuscaloosa News,* February 1, 1956, 1.

———. "'UA on Brink of Disgrace,' Carmichael Tells Faculty." *The Tuscaloosa News,* February 7, 1956, 1.

McKee, Don. "Trooper's Chief Sees No Trouble at UA." *The Tuscaloosa News,* June 7, 1963, 8.

"'Mean' Image Dispelled." *The Crimson White,* June 13, 1963, 4.

Merrill, Hugh D., III. "Tuesday Will See Result of Many Resolutions, Lawsuits." *The Crimson White,* June 9, 1963, 1.

"Middleman in Alabama: Frank Anthony Rose." *The New York Times,* June 11, 1963, 20.

"Ministerial Groups Urges Calmness, Wisdom, Prayer." *The Tuscaloosa News,* February 13, 1956, 1.

"Mississippi and Meredith Remember." CNN.com, September 30, 2002. http://articles.cnn.com/2002-09–30/us/meredith_1_james-meredith-federal-prison-guards-mississippi?_s=PM:US.

"Mixing Leaders Ready to Stage Protest March." *The Tuscaloosa News,* April 23, 1964, 1, 2.

Mizell, James. "Stay Clear of Campus Connor Urges Council: Says Boycotts, Votes Can Defeat Integration." *The Tuscaloosa News,* June 8, 1963, 1.

Mob Pressure Political Cartoon. *The Tuscaloosa News,* July 10, 1964, 1.

"Mob Rule at Tuscaloosa." *The New York Times,* reprinted in *The Tuscaloosa News,* February 17, 1956, 4.

"More Sit-Ins Are Tried Here; Pickets March." *The Tuscaloosa News,* June 3, 1964, 1.

Morin, Relman. "The Big Question: What Next?" *The Tuscaloosa News,* October 2, 1962, 1.

———. "Birmingham—What a Difference a Year Makes." *The Tuscaloosa News,* June 12, 1964, 1.

———. "NAACP Leader's Slaying Blow to the Moderates." *The Tuscaloosa News,* June 14, 1963, 16.

———. "Negroes Riot after Funeral." *The Tuscaloosa News,* June 16, 1963, 1, 2.

———. "Violence Absent from UA Scene." *The Tuscaloosa News,* June 12, 1963, 3.

"National Spotlight Falls on Capstone." *The Tuscaloosa News,* June 9, 1963, 1.

"Nations' Crisis Crowds in on One Man." *Life Magazine,* June 14, 1963, 77–80.

"Nations: Where the Stars Fall." *Time Magazine,* September 27, 1963.

"Need to Assure Calmness." *The Tuscaloosa News,* June 17, 1963, 4.

"Negro Applications Top New Items of Old Year." *The Crimson White,* January 10, 1963.

"Negro Coed to Seek Entry This Spring." *The Crimson White,* November 29, 1962, 1, 2.

"Negro Group Here Calls Off Boycott." *The Tuscaloosa News,* July 14, 1964, 1.

"Negro Indicted in Deputy Murder." *The Tuscaloosa News,* June 23, 1964, 1.

"Negro Mails In Application to University." *The Tuscaloosa News,* October 24, 1962, 1.

"Negroes Call Off Boycott in City." *The Tuscaloosa News,* July 14, 1964, 1.

"Negroes Delay Filing Suit." *The Tuscaloosa News,* July 15, 1964, 1.

"Negroes Described as 'Stoic,' Congenial." *The Tuscaloosa News,* June 11, 1963, 2.

"Negroes Join In on Talks." *The Tuscaloosa News,* June 6, 1963, 1, 2.

"Negroes Never Asked for Talk, Officials Say." *The Tuscaloosa News,* June 12, 1964, 1–2.

"Negroes Resume Non-Buying Drive." *The Tuscaloosa News,* July 16, 1964, 1.

"Negroes to Chart Strategy." *The Tuscaloosa News,* June 10, 1964, 1–2.

"Negroes Vow They'll March." *The Tuscaloosa News,* June 11, 1964, 1.

"Negroes Waiting on Court." *The Tuscaloosa News,* June 13, 1964, 1–2.

Nelson, Ann. "Police Chief Will Retire on April 30." *The Tuscaloosa News,* April 5, 1976, 1.

"No Charges Filed in Picture-Taking Action in Foster." *The Tuscaloosa News,* February 17, 1956, 1.

"No Legal Leg to Stand on, Wallace Told." *The Tuscaloosa News,* June 11, 1963, 1.

"'No Thought' of Closing UA Dr. Rose Says." *The Crimson White,* November 1, 1962, 1, 3.

"Other Papers View UA Integration." *The Tuscaloosa News,* June 17, 1963, 2.

"Our Continuing Hope and Goal." *The Tuscaloosa News,* June 15, 1963, 4.

"Our Danger Is Fear." *The Tuscaloosa News,* June 8, 1963, 1.

"Our Own Back." *The Crimson White,* June 9, 1963, 3.

"Ours Is Not Only Story." *The Tuscaloosa News,* June 11, 1963, 4.

"Pair Taking Early Classes." *The Tuscaloosa News,* June 12, 1963, 2.

"Parents Brief on Capstone Life." *The Tuscaloosa News,* June 7, 1963, 2.

"Past Won't Conquer Race Problem—Stewart." *The Crimson White,* May 9, 1963.

"Patrol Had Orders to Lay Off Students." *The Tuscaloosa News,* February 8, 1956, 2.

Pearson, Drew. "Bull Connor Tells His Side." *The Tuscaloosa News,* August 30, 1964, 5.

———. "Factors behind New Measures on Civil Rights." *The Tuscaloosa News,* June 10, 1963, 4.

———. "JFK's Speech Spelled Out Need for Peace." *The Tuscaloosa News,* June 15, 1963, 4.

———. "Senators Met with Kennedy on Race Issue." *The Tuscaloosa News,* June 14, 1963, 4.

———. "Violence Loses Friends along with Victory." *The Tuscaloosa News,* June 16, 1963, 4.

"Petitions Asking Lucy's Return Date at Capstone Today." *The Tuscaloosa News,* February 23, 1956, 1.

Phillips, Wayne. "Tuscaloosa: A Tense Drama Unfolds." *The New York Times,* February 26, 1956.

"Police, Firemen Lauded for Work." *The Tuscaloosa News,* July 14, 1964, 1.

"Police Here Alert for Race Trouble." *The Tuscaloosa News,* June 9, 1964, 1.

"Praise Due City's Police and Others." *The Tuscaloosa News,* June 14, 1963, 4.

"Prayer or Peril Is City's Choice Minister Warns." *The Tuscaloosa News,* February 8, 1956, 1.

"The Price of Our Silence." *The Tuscaloosa News,* July 9, 1964, 1.

"Protest March Free of Violence." *The Tuscaloosa News,* April 23, 1964, 1, 2.

"Putting On the Squeeze." *The Tuscaloosa News,* July 10, 1964, 1.

"Quiet Holiday Weekend Expected in City Area." *The Tuscaloosa News,* July 2, 1964, 1.

"R. Kennedy Praises City in UA Case." *The Tuscaloosa News,* June 14, 1963, 6.

"Races: The Long March." *Time Magazine,* June 21, 1963.

"Races: The Revolution." *Time Magazine,* June 7, 1963.

"Racial Trouble 'Drains' City Treasury." *The Tuscaloosa News,* July 14, 1964, 1.

Raines, Howell. "So Small, So Vulnerable—But So Full of Life." *The Tuscaloosa News,* June 6, 1968, 1, 2.

Randle, Frank. "Letter to the Editor: Protect Dignity." *The Crimson White,* February 14, 1956, 4.

"Ready for Mob Control?" *The Tuscaloosa News,* July 7, 1964, 1.

"Reasons Given for Rejecting Second Negro." *The Tuscaloosa News,* February 14, 1956, 1.

"Registration Takes Only 15 Minutes." *The Tuscaloosa News,* June 11, 1963, 1.

"Resolution." *The Crimson White,* February 14, 1956, 1.

"Rev. T. Y. Rogers Killed in Atlanta Auto Accident." *The Tuscaloosa News,* March 26, 1971, 1, 2.

"Rise in Tension Brings Halt to Demonstrations." *The Tuscaloosa News,* June 9, 1964, 2.

Risen, Clay. "How the South Was Won." *The Boston Globe,* March 5, 2006.

"Roadblocks Gone from UA Campus." *The Tuscaloosa News,* June 13, 1963, 1, 2.

"Roadblocks Will Ring UA." *The Tuscaloosa News,* June 6, 1963, 1.

"Robert Shelton, 73, Leader of Big Klan Faction." *The New York Times,* March 20, 2003.

"Robert Shelton Replies." *The Tuscaloosa News,* July 10, 1964, 1–2.

"Rogers Family Requests Fund Contributions." *The Tuscaloosa News,* March 28, 1971, 1.

"Rubber Workers Blast UA Dean's 'Blame Shifting.'" *The Tuscaloosa News,* February 10, 1956, 1.

Ryan, William L. "Reds Fully Exploiting Racial Violence." *The Tuscaloosa News,* June 17, 1963, 10.

Samuels, Gertrude. "Alabama U: A Story of 2 among 4,000." *The New York Times,* July 28, 1963.

Sanders, Rex. "Actor's Visit to City Cut Short by Violence." *The Tuscaloosa News,* July 10, 1964, 1.

———. "Governor Brings His Crusade to UA." *The Tuscaloosa News,* April 16, 1964, 1, 2.

Sayre, Nora. "Barred at the Schoolhouse Door." *The Progressive,* July 1984.

"Scattered Violence Reported." *The Tuscaloosa News,* June 10, 1964, 1.

"School Bells Ring Out." *The Tuscaloosa News,* September 8, 1964, 1.

"School Buses to Run Here." *The Tuscaloosa News,* September 5, 1964, 1, 2.

Schutte, Hugh. "Huntsville Negro Quiet on UA Developments." *The Tuscaloosa News,* June 12, 1963, 3.

Selden, Armistead. "Entire Nation Hit by Racial Crisis." *The Tuscaloosa News,* June 12, 1963, 8.

"Several Seized with Weapons Here Released." *The Tuscaloosa News,* June 16, 1963, 32.

"SGA Blasts Mob Rule at UA; Uneasy Peace Rules on Campus." *The Tuscaloosa News,* February 3, 1956, 1.

Shamblin, Bill, Jr. "No Easy Life for Troopers on UA Campus." *The Crimson White,* June 13, 1963, 1.

"Shelton Predicts Economic Boycott." *The Tuscaloosa News,* June 9, 1963, 1.

"Shelton Says Klan to Fight Mixing on Economic Front." *The Tuscaloosa News,* June 13, 1963.

"Shots from Car Wounds Negro." *The Tuscaloosa News,* July 10, 1964, 1.

"Signs Removed on Restrooms at Courthouse." *The Tuscaloosa News,* July 1, 1964, 1.

Simms, Leroy. "World Will Watch as Negro Tries Again to Enter UA." *The Tuscaloosa News,* February 27, 1956, 12.

Smith, Hedrick. "Courtesy and Curiosity Mark Campus Reception." *The New York Times,* June 12, 1963, 1, 21.

Smith, Stroube. "Lucy Vows Legal Fight to Return to Campus: 48-Hour Deadline Put on Reinstatement Bid." *The Tuscaloosa News,* February 7, 1956, 1.

Smithey, Waylon. "Memorial Service Held Here for T. Y. Rogers." *The Tuscaloosa News,* March 29, 1971, 1.

"Some Officers Leaving Duty at UA Campus." *The Tuscaloosa News,* June 12, 1963, 2.

"Speaker Assails News, Publisher." *The Tuscaloosa News,* July 10, 1964, 1–2.

"Stations Here Join for UA Coverage." *The Tuscaloosa News,* June 9, 1963, 1.

Stevenson, Tommy. "Tuscaloosa's Bloody Tuesday." *The Tuscaloosa News,* February 22, 2009.

"Stillman Head Praises Calm of Student Body." *The Tuscaloosa News,* April 6, 1968, 1.

Stillman, Jack. "Capstone Story Well Covered by Media." *The Tuscaloosa News,* June 12, 1963, 3.

———. "College Integration Quiet This Summer." *The Tuscaloosa News,* June 14, 1964, 3.

———. "Price of Peace Major Concern for Businessmen." *The Tuscaloosa News,* June 11, 1963, 1.

———. "USIA Observer Here to Report on UA Story." *The Tuscaloosa News,* June 10, 1963, 1.

"Stones and Bottles Hurled at Negroes." *The Tuscaloosa News,* July 9, 1964, 1–2.

"Stones, Bottles Greet Negroes at City Theater." *The Tuscaloosa News,* July 9, 1964, 1.

"Student Leaders Generally Back Trustees' Action." *The Tuscaloosa News,* February 12, 1956, 7.

"Students Mildly Surprised by Gov. Wallace's Action." *The Tuscaloosa News,* June 11, 1963, 1.

"Students Who Met Crisis." *The New York Times,* June 12, 1963, 21.

"Terribly Dangerous." *Newsweek,* June 10, 1963, 27–30.

"Theater Mixed Here; No Trouble." *The Tuscaloosa News,* July 5, 1964, 1.

"This Pushing, Pushing Is No Good." *The Tuscaloosa News,* February 3, 1956, 4.

Thomas, Rex. "Roadblocks Seal Campus." *The Tuscaloosa News,* June 8, 1963, 1.

———. "Tempers Cool in Face of More Integration." *The Tuscaloosa News,* August 20, 1964, 3.

———. "Too Early to Tell about Mixing, Say University Student Leaders." *The Tuscaloosa News,* June 16, 1963, 29.

———. "UA Mixing May Cost JFK Support in 1964." *The Tuscaloosa News,* June 17, 1963, 10.

———. "Wallace's Stand Not Likely to Bring Prosecution by U.S." *The Tuscaloosa News,* June 12, 1963, 3.

———. "Whatever Wallace Wants, Wallace Gets." *The Tuscaloosa News,* June 7, 1964, 19.

Thomas, Rex, and Al Lanier. "Senator Asks Continued Fight on Integration." *The Tuscaloosa News,* February 11, 1956, 1.

"Thumbnail Sketches of Three Students." *The Huntsville Times,* June 11, 1963.

Tillotson, Ann. "Curfew a Pain, But Needed, Students Say about Restriction." *The Crimson White,* June 13, 1963, 1.

"To Dr. and Mrs. O. C. Carmichael." *The Crimson White,* February 14, 1956, 1.

"Troublemakers Handed Warning." *The Tuscaloosa News,* June 10, 1964, 1.

"Trustees Feared Murder in Barring Negro Co-Ed." *The Tuscaloosa News,* February 8, 1956, 1.

"Tuesday Is Set for Enrollment of Two Negroes." *The Tuscaloosa News,* June 7, 1963, 1, 2.

"Tuscaloosa Mix Target, King Reports." *The Tuscaloosa News,* July 1, 1964, 1.

"*Tuscaloosa News* Sued by Shelton." *The Tuscaloosa News,* July 25, 1964, 1.

"Tuscaloosans Keeping Quiet about Situation." *The Tuscaloosa News,* June 12, 1963, 5.

"Two Men Arrested in Racial Incident." *The Tuscaloosa News,* June 5, 1964, 1–2.

"Two Photographers Held for Taking UA Pictures Freed." *The Tuscaloosa News,* February 15, 1956, 1.

"T. Y. Rogers Services Set Monday." *The Tuscaloosa News,* March 27, 1971, 1, 2.

"UA Can Be Model for Nation Hood Says after Peaceful Entry." *The Crimson White,* June 13, 1963, 1.

"UA Fears 'Climate' Will Affect Faculty." *The Tuscaloosa News,* July 14, 1964, 1.

"U-A Investigators Question Wilson." *The Tuscaloosa News,* February 29, 1956, 1.

"UA Religious Group Moves to Prevent Further Mob Acts." *The Tuscaloosa News,* February 7, 1956, 2.

"Union Turns Down Negro Bus Demand." *The Tuscaloosa News,* August 18, 1964, 1, 2.

"University Seeks to Halt Depositions in Lucy Case." *The Tuscaloosa News,* February 19, 1956, 1.

"University Writes Negro She Can Enroll for Classes: No Word Yet of Ruling for Other Woman." *The Tuscaloosa News,* January 31, 1956, 1.

"Wallace Again Urges Citizens to Keep Clear Of UA." *The Tuscaloosa News,* June 9, 1963, 1.

"Wallace Orders 500 Guardsmen into Tuscaloosa." *The Tuscaloosa News,* June 9, 1963, 1.

"Wallace's Statement at Foster." *The Tuscaloosa News,* June 11, 1963, 1.

Watkins, Ed. "'March against Repression' Starts in Eutaw." *The Tuscaloosa News,* March 31, 1971, 1, 2.

"What a Price for Peace." *The Tuscaloosa News,* February 7, 1956.

"White Citizens Call for Action." *The Tuscaloosa News,* July 1, 1964, 1.

White, Sarah. "School Buses Revving Up." *The Tuscaloosa News,* August 27, 1964, 6.

Williamson, Dan. "George Hits Papers at Courthouse Rally." *The Crimson White,* March 22, 1966, 1, 5.

———. "RFK Makes Appeal for Unity." *The Crimson White,* March 22, 1966, 1, 5.

———. "That Kennedy Knack Wows Screaming, Scrambling Fans." *The Crimson White,* March 24, 1966, 1.

———. "Tuscaloosa Rights Figures Speak Out on Selma, Liuzzo, Klan Investigation." *The Crimson White,* May 13, 1965, 5, 8, 10, 11.

"World Turned Eyes on UA This Week." *The Tuscaloosa News,* February 3, 1956, 1.

"Writer Says Integration Problem in North, Too." *The Tuscaloosa News,* June 14, 1963, 2.

"Year Ago Today, UA in Spotlight." *The Tuscaloosa News,* June 11, 1964, 1.

Transcripts

"Integrating the University of Alabama." Nicholas Katzenbach, Vivian Malone Jones. Moderated by Juan Williams. Transcript. John F. Kennedy Library and Foundation. September 30, 2002. November 17, 2003.

Interview with David J. Vann, conducted by Blackside, Inc., on November 1, 1985. *Eyes on the Prize: America's Civil Rights Years (1954–1965).* Transcript. Washington University Libraries, Film and Media Archive, Henry Hampton Collection.

Interview with Sheriff James Clark, conducted by Blackside, Inc. for *Eyes on the Prize: America's Civil Rights Years (1954-1965).* American Experience. August 19, 2011. http://www.pbs.org/wgbh/amex/eyesontheprize/about/pt_106.html

Nicholas D. Katzenbach Oral History Interview I, 11/12/68, by Paige E. Mulhollan. Transcript. Internet Copy, LBJ Library. http://www.lbjlib.utexas.edu/johnson /archives.hom/oralhistory.hom/katzenbach/katzenb1.pdf. November 5, 2010.

Nicholas D. Katzenbach Oral History Interview II, 11/23/68, by Paige Mulhollan. Transcript. Internet Copy, LBJ Library. http://www.lbjlib.utexas.edu/johnson /archives.hom/oralhistory.hom/katzenbach/katzenb2.pdf. November 5, 2010.

Nicholas D. Katzenbach Oral History Interview III, 12/11/68, by Paige E. Mulhollan. Transcript. Internet Copy, LBJ Library. http://www.lbjlib.utexas.edu/johnson /archives.hom/oralhistory.hom/katzenbach/katzenb3.pdf. November 5, 2010.

Web Sources/Electronic Texts

"Autherine Lucy." *Encyclopedia of Alabama.* http://www.encyclopediaofalabama.org /face/Article.jsp?id=h-2489.

"Buford Boone." *Encyclopedia of Alabama.* http://encyclopediaofalabama.org/face /Article.jsp?id=h-1783.

King Jr., Martin Luther. "Letter from a Birmingham Jail." African Studies Center, University of Pennsylvania. July 22, 2010. http://www.africa.upenn.edu.

"A New Beginning: A Tribute to Courage and Progress." http://malonehoodplaza .ua.edu/players/james-hood-2/.

"Report to the American People on Civil Rights, 11 June 1963." John F. Kennedy Presidential Library and Museum. http://www.jfklibrary.org/Asset-Viewer/LH8F _0Mzv0e6Ro1yEm74Ng.aspx.

"Theopholius [*sic*] Yelverton Rogers Jr." *King Encyclopedia*. http://mlk-kpp01.stanford .edu/kingweb/about_king/encyclopedia/rogers_theopholius.html.

Audio

"Emphasis (1968: The University of Alabama), Robert F. Kennedy Who Discusses America at the Crossroads." March 22, 1968. http://acumen.lib.ua.edu/a/u0008 _0000001_0000013_0002. W. S. Hoole Special Collections Library, The University of Alabama.

Films

Crisis: Behind a Presidential Commitment. Dir. Robert Drew. 1963.

"Robert F. Kennedy's Statement on Dr. King's Death-Montage." YouTube.com. November 20, 2006. *http://www.youtube.com/watch?v=gigsZH5HlJA.*

"A Voice of Justice and Reason: Buford Boone's *Tuscaloosa News.*" *The Alabama Experience.* University of Alabama Center for Public Television and Radio, 1994.

Journal Articles

Nelson, Harold A. "The Defenders: A Case Study of an Informal Police Organization." *Social Problems* 15, no. 2 (1967): 127–47.

Southern Commission on the Study of Lynching. *The Plight of Tuscaloosa: Mob Murders, Community Hysteria, Official Incompetence.* Atlanta: 1933.

Wendt, Simon. "God, Gandhi, and Guns: The African American Freedom Struggle in Tuscaloosa, Alabama, 1964–1965." *Journal of African American History* 89, no. 1 (2004): 36–56.

Index

Page numbers in italics refer to figures.